YEARBOOK IN EARLY CHILDHOOD EDUCATION

Bernard Spodek • Olivia N. Saracho
EDITORS

VOLUME 1
Early Childhood Teacher Preparation
Bernard Spodek and Olivia N. Saracho, Editors

VOLUME 2
Issues in Early Childhood Curriculum
Bernard Spodek and Olivia N. Saracho, Editors

VOLUME 3
Issues in Child Care
Bernard Spodek and Olivia N. Saracho, Editors

VOLUME 4
Language and Literacy in Early Childhood Education
Bernard Spodek and Olivia N. Saracho, Editors

VOLUME 5
Early Childhood Special Education
*Philip L. Safford, editor, with Bernard Spodek
and Olivia N. Saracho*

The *Yearbook in Early Childhood Education* is a series of annual publications. Each volume addresses a timely topic of major significance in the field of early childhood education, and contains chapters that present and interpret current knowledge on aspects of that topic, written by experts in the field. Key issues—including concerns about educational equity, multiculturalism, the needs of diverse populations of children and families, and the ethical dimensions of the field—are woven into the organization of each of the volumes.

YEARBOOK
IN
EARLY CHILDHOOD EDUCATION
VOLUME 4

LANGUAGE AND LITERACY
IN
EARLY CHILDHOOD EDUCATION

Bernard Spodek   •   Olivia N. Saracho
EDITORS

TEACHERS
COLLEGE
PRESS

Teachers College, Columbia University
New York • London

Published by Teachers College Press, 1234 Amsterdam Avenue
New York, NY 10027

Library of Congress Cataloging-in-Publication Data
Language and literacy in early childhood education / Bernard Spodek,
  Olivia N. Saracho, editors.
    p.   cm. — (Yearbook in early childhood education ; v. 4)
  Includes bibliographical references and index.
  ISBN 0-8077-3280-X. — ISBN 0-8077-3279-6 (pbk.)
    1. Early childhood education — United States.   2. Language arts
(Preschool) — United States.   3. Language experience approach in
education — United States.   4. Child development — United States.
I. Spodek, Bernard.   II. Saracho, Olivia N.   III. Series.
LB1139.25.L36   1993
372.6 — dc20   93-5818

Printed on acid-free paper

Manufactured in the United States of America

99 98 97 96 95 94 93   8 7 6 5 4 3 2 1

Contents

Introduction—Language and Literacy in Early Childhood Education

Olivia N. Saracho
Bernard Spodek

This volume reflects a significant revolution that has taken place in the fields of early childhood education and language arts and reading education. When we started our careers as early childhood educators, the conventional wisdom of the field was that children at the prekindergarten and kindergarten levels should not be introduced to reading in any way. Today, as reflected in this volume, research and theory suggest that teachers of young children, from the beginning, need to be actively engaged in providing experiences that will build children's language and eventually lead these children to become competent readers. Rather than wait for young children to mature before providing instruction, appropriate instruction should be provided to children from the beginning—instruction that is matched to the child's level of language development and that builds new competence in both oral and written language.

CHANGES INFLUENCING LITERACY EDUCATION

The changes that have occurred in the field reflect changes in the sources of early childhood practice. They include changes in developmental theories related to language and cognition, changes in the populations currently enrolled in our schools, and changes in the nature of reading instruction. Each of these is briefly reviewed here to place the contents of this volume into perspective.

Changes in Developmental Theory

In the past, kindergarten and prekindergarten teachers were often admonished not to provide any print material in the classroom. Making such material available would only force children to begin reading prematurely or create frustrations in children who were not yet "ready" to read. The conventional wisdom of that time was that children would become ready to read when they reached the mental age of 6½ years. This reflected a classic study of the 1930s by Morphett and Washburne (1931) as well as a maturationist view of development based on the theories of Arnold Gesell. Gesell (1940) spent his career seeking developmental norms for children that would describe the flow of children's development. The theory suggested that development was based on maturation. Education, in order to be effective, should follow this flow of development. To introduce any kind of learning prematurely was to create failure and frustration. One needed to determine a child's readiness for learning before providing instruction. Various reading readiness tests were available for teachers to use to determine this, or they could observe children directly for signs of readiness before beginning to teach them to read.

In the 1960s and 1970s we saw a change in the developmental theories underlying early childhood programs. The work of Jean Piaget was used increasingly to justify these programs. Children were seen as constructing their knowledge, including knowledge of language, from their experiences. However, the way in which they constructed knowledge and the kinds of knowledge they could construct were determined by their developmental levels. These levels were heavily influenced by maturational factors. Rather than provide experiences that would move children to higher levels of development, teachers were exhorted to match experiences to the child's current levels of development. Educational practices should be "developmentally appropriate" (Bredekamp, 1987); children should not be "hurried" (Elkind, 1981). Thus, while the methods of instruction suggested for early childhood education might differ, Piagetian theory still suggested that education follow development. Interestingly, while Piagetian theory significantly influenced early childhood methods in mathematics and science, it had relatively little influence on methods in language and literacy. Thus the "reading readiness" approach of the previous era continued to be prevalent.

More recently, the work of L. S. Vygotsky (1962, 1978) has been rediscovered by Western educators and especially applied to early childhood education in the area of language and literacy. Vygotsky differentiates between "natural" and "cultural" development. Cultural development allows people to master forms of cultural behavior, including methods of reasoning. Language and literacy development is a form of cultural development. This development takes place in a sociohistoric framework, so that what the child comes to know is influenced by the forms of knowledge created within the culture. These forms of knowledge are passed on from the more sophisticated to the less sophisticated in a culture—from adults and older children to younger children, for example.

One of the key concepts in this theory is the notion of the "zone of proximal development (ZPD)." This represents the area beyond which a child is capable of doing things alone; it is an area in which a child can do things with some help. Providing this form of help has been characterized as providing "scaffolding," or supporting children to move them ahead. It is this learning just beyond children's levels of development that extends development. Thus, in Vygotsky's theory, education should enhance and lead development rather than follow it.

This conception of development has heavily influenced modern views of language and literacy education, as noted in the chapters that follow. Literacy is seen as emerging over a long period of time from early in children's lives. What prekindergarten and kindergarten teachers do in their classrooms, long before children can actually read, significantly influences their reading competence.

Changes in the Populations Currently Enrolled in Our Schools

The population of our schools has undergone an ethnic upheaval. Increasing numbers of cultural and linguistic minority children are being enrolled today. Often these children are labeled as "at risk." The risk comes not so much from the children's inability to master linguistic forms but from difficulties in functional language competency. Traditional approaches to language and literacy education continue to place these children at risk of later school failure.

Some young children, when they first enter school, may find that their home language and culture differ from the one found in school and in books and used by teachers. When this occurs, children may respond to the instructional circumstance at a variety of levels. Saracho (1986) identified four levels of responses (beginning with the lowest):

1. Students may become confused as a result of the drastic difference they experience between the two languages and cultures.
2. Students may pretend that their language and culture are the same as the school's, denying their own language and culture.
3. Students adapt to the customs of the more advanced culture. Therefore, children adapt to the best patterns or customs to make them their own.
4. Students become comfortable in both languages and cultures and are able to make the transition between them.

Children who are culturally and linguistically different have language problems, but these are not so much phonological or grammatical ones as functional language ones, including the use of language for numerous communication purposes. The need for new approaches to language and literacy education that consider these children's language competency and help them become biliterate as well as bilingual has also been a driving force to create changes in language and literacy education for young children.

Changes in the Nature of Reading Instruction

Almost from the beginning of formal schooling in America, there has been controversy about how reading should be taught. At different times, different approaches have been in ascendance. Sometimes educators recommended a whole-word methodology, with children learning the verbal equivalents of complete words. At other times, phonics approaches to reading were recommended, with children learning to sound out individual letters that are later put together into words. Each approach had its advocates, and each had its proportion of successes and failures. Because of the continual failure of some children to learn to read, educators and critics continue to ask "Why Johnny can't read" (Flesch, 1955, 1988).

The concern for improving the success of schoolchildren in learning to read has led increasingly, in the last decade, to suggestions that formal reading instruction should begin earlier, moving that instruction down into the kindergarten. It was this movement of the primary curriculum downward that led to the need for position papers such at that related to "developmentally appropriate practices" promulgated by the National Association for the Education of Young Children (Bredekamp, 1987).

With the use of newer theories of learning and language development, as noted above, a change has taken place in the way in which reading is being taught. The separation between reading readiness and reading was replaced by a concept of emergent literacy. Emergent literacy suggests that young children are engaged in language learning that is preparatory to learning to read much sooner than when they are introduced to formal reading instruction. This literacy learning is closely tied to the children's understanding of oral language and is supported by a range of activities, many of which do not look anything like reading or writing. The understanding that all language learning is interrelated has led to the use of the Whole Language approach to language and literacy. Proponents of this approach take issue with the task analysis view of initial reading instruction. They suggest that reading is a highly complex intellectual process and that a deep understanding of the nature of both oral and written language and the relationship between the two are necessary for children to become competent in reading and writing. Thus they prepare children for the intellectual task of reading rather than the mechanical task of "code cracking." They also argue that the intellectual skills needed result from a broad range of experiences with language and with other symbolic activity, including discourse with others, play, and the arts.

All early childhood teachers, at every level, must now be considered teachers of reading, even if they do not offer formal reading instruction. Rather than push formal reading instruction down into the preprimary grades, the new methods make use of the evolving language abilities of young children to provide activities that will create more competent readers later.

Teachers of young children need to become more sensitive to this role in support of literacy and language development. They need to become more aware of how they offer a range of symbolic activity, from story reading to dramatic play to art. They need to be more sensitive to the consequences of the physical and social arrangements of their class. They need to acquire a professional knowledge base that is quite different from what was expected of early childhood teachers just a few years ago.

OVERVIEW OF THE VOLUME

The first two chapters of this volume address the issue of the early childhood curriculum and language learning. Catherine E. Snow and Patton O. Tabors, in Chapter 1, describe the pattern of language learning in the early childhood years. They also look at the contributions of various early childhood activities to this language learning. In Chapter 2 Anne Haas Dyson helps us see the importance of all forms of symbol making to language learning. Art production and dramatic play, along with gesture and speech, are the precursors to writing. The variety of early writing forms that are developed by children are important to their formal use of the written language.

Chapter 3 presents a view of the Whole Language approach to language and literacy teaching in early childhood education. Olivia N. Saracho describes the philosophy of that approach, along with the way it is implemented and evaluated in classes. In Chapter 4 Celia Genishi's discussion of ways of assessing young children's language and literacy are consistent with the Whole Language approach. Genishi criticizes the indiscriminate use of standardized tests, advocating instead the use of a broad range of assessment techniques to judge children's understanding and application of language in a variety of settings and for a variety of purposes. The use of portfolio assessment provides a broad form of assessment of children's language and literacy.

Kris D. Gutierrez makes us aware, in Chapter 5, of the needs of language minority children in our schools. She helps us see that these children need to become biliterate as well as bilingual. Her study suggests that the same theory that is used to support language and literacy for monolingual children can be used to generate approaches to biliteracy education as well. Gay Su Pinnell makes the point, in Chapter 6, that children are labeled "at risk" because we place them in "risky situations" in the schools, in programs that are unresponsive to their educational needs. Pinnell presents Reading Recovery, a beginning reading program for such children that was developed in New Zealand and is presently being used successfully by a number of school systems. The process of preparing teachers is described, along with the program itself.

A concern for language and literacy must go beyond teaching reading skills; we must be as concerned with *what* children read. In Chapter 7 Violet Harris describes the state of children's literature today. She asserts that the literature we provide children should reflect the multicultural society in which they are growing up. She discusses the availability of good literature for children written from African American, Asian American, Hispanic American, and Native American perspectives.

The newer approaches to teaching language and literacy to young children require new understandings of what the early childhood teacher must do. Judith A. Schickedanz, in Chapter 8, describes research on the effects of classroom environments on young children's language and literacy development. She suggests designs for the physical and social dimensions of the classroom. In Chapter 9 Elizabeth Sulzby and Patricia A. Edwards discuss the role of the parent in supporting language and literacy. Teachers need to work with parents to enhance this role. Lesley Mandel Morrow and Muriel K. Rand present strategies in Chapter 10 for preparing teachers to support language and literacy development of young children. We need to become increasingly aware of the knowledge base teachers must have in this new role. We also need to design preservice and inservice programs of teacher education to achieve that goal.

The final chapter is devoted to a look to the future of the language and literacy area of early childhood education. Over the years, as noted in Volume 2 of this Yearbook series, early childhood education has undergone repeated curriculum changes. Significant changes that have taken place in the area of language and literacy are described in this volume. Early childhood educators must become increasingly aware of these changes. They must develop the knowledge and skills needed to support an early childhood education that is responsive to the needs of young children in contemporary society.

REFERENCES

Bredekamp, S. (Ed.). (1987). *Developmentally appropriate practices in early childhood programs serving children from birth through age eight.* Washington, DC: National Association for the Education of Young Children.

Elkind, D. (1981). *The hurried child.* Reading, MA: Addison-Wesley.

Flesch, R. (1955). *Why Johnny can't read.* New York: Harper.

Flesch, R. (1988). *Why Johnny still can't read.* New York: Harper & Row.

Gesell, A. (1940). *The first five years of life.* New York: Harper & Brothers.

Morphett, M. V., & Washburne, C. (1931). When should children begin to read? *Elementary School Journal, 31,* 496–503.

Saracho, O. N. (1986). Teaching second language literacy with computers. In D. Hainline (Ed.), *New developments in language CAI* (pp. 53–68). Kent, England: Croom Helm.

Vygotsky, L. S. (1962). *Thought and language.* Cambridge, MA: MIT Press.

Vygotsky, L. S. (1978). *Mind in society: The development of higher psychological processes.* Cambridge, MA: Harvard University Press.

CHAPTER 1

Language Skills That Relate to Literacy Development

Catherine E. Snow and Patton O. Tabors

If a naive observer spent a morning in a model early childhood education classroom to inventory the aspects of the classroom that related to literacy, the resulting list might be quite short. The observer might come up with such items as the use of labels on various objects, the presence of story-books in a reading corner, information dictated by children and written by teachers on artwork, and children's names written on projects they have completed. During the time in the classroom, the visitor might also observe children singing the alphabet song during circle time, discussing the sound made by the letter of the day, and listening to a story read aloud by the teacher—all activities that would be easily identified as related to literacy.

However, the observer would also see a variety of other activities during the day that might seem unrelated to literacy, such as a group of children doing sociodramatic play in the house corner, the teacher explaining to a small group of children how a science experiment works, a child telling the class at group time about a trip to the zoo with his family, and children developing a recipe for play dough pudding. In fact, the visitor would be incorrect in assuming these activities were irrelevant to literacy. Like the more obviously literacy-based activities mentioned above (reviewed in Teale & Sulzby, 1986), many of the purely oral language activities that go on in early childhood classrooms have also been shown to relate to later literacy development. In this chapter, we discuss connections between oral language skills and literacy development as well as exemplary practice in early childhood education classrooms in light of the need to promote language as well as print skills.

1

THE NATURE OF LANGUAGE

In order to understand how language development relates to literacy development, we must first lay out what we mean by language. Learning a language may be the most impressive accomplishment of the young child. Language is a complex set of systems, each of which has its own rules. As children learn a language, they master these various rule systems without knowing it, although their growing control over the rules means that their capacity to communicate effectively and about matters of ever-greater urgency and complexity is expanding. For purposes of analyzing precursors to literacy in language, however, we must discuss these various rule systems as separate abstractions.

Each of the various rule systems we will discuss is acquired relatively unconsciously in the course of use; each, however, may at some point emerge into consciousness and become a topic of conversation for children or a target for play and problem solving. We will argue that the emergence of the various domains of language into conscious awareness is one of the important achievements of the early childhood years. This emergence of "metalinguistic awareness" is, we argue, one major conduit between oral language and literacy. Thus, in addition to discussing each of the domains of language development that young children master, we will present information about how metalinguistic awareness in each of those domains emerges. In a subsequent section we will consider how the language skills themselves, as well as metalinguistic awareness of them, relate to literacy.

Phonology

First and foremost, knowing a language involves speaking and understanding words. Those words are made up of syllables, which are the basic units for language production. When infants are 5 to 8 months old, they start producing such syllables (*ba*, *ma*, *ga*, etc.) in the course of their babbling. Open syllables such as *ba* and *ma* are relatively easy to pronounce and thus form the basis for many "babytalk" words (e.g., *mama*, *booboo*, *peepee*). Words that contain closed syllables (those with a consonant at the end) are harder to pronounce, especially if quite different consonants need to be articulated within one syllable. Thus young children often say "goggie" for *doggie* or "guck" for *truck* because they simply cannot yet put two such different sounds as /g/ and /d/ or /t/ into one syllable.

Children's pronunciation of words comes increasingly to resemble adults' during the early childhood years; however, very young children still do not think of the sounds they are producing in the same ways that adults do. Adults' representations of words are, for one thing, heavily influenced by having learned to spell them. Ask an adult to list as many words as possible that begin with the sound /s/; chances are the list will include *sugar* or *sure*, although these do not begin with an /s/ sound at all. Young children would never make this error. Young children, on the other hand, find it hard to do things such as produce rhymes or segment particular sounds (e.g., if asked to say *meat* without the /m/ sound or without the /t/ sound). The reason for this is that, in producing words, we do not in fact produce separate segments; rather, we produce syllables in which the articulation of each sound overlaps the articulation of those before and after it. Thus recognizing those abstract segments as separate requires considerable sophistication in the ability to analyze phonological patterns, also called metaphonological awareness. As we discuss in the next section, those abstract segments are precisely what letters in alphabetic writing systems represent.

Metaphonological awareness develops during the early childhood years, at least for some children. Clark (1978) has described spontaneous comments and self-repairs in the speech of 2- and 3-year-olds. Three-year-olds can be taught to identify the initial phonemes in words with a fair degree of consistency (Zhurova, 1973), although segmenting final phonemes or understanding the internal structure of words with consonant clusters comes much later (Bruck & Treiman, 1990; Treiman, 1985, 1988). Four-year-olds can judge whether words rhyme with very high accuracy (Lenel & Cantor, 1981; Smith & Tager-Flusberg, 1982), and many can produce rhymes as well.

Vocabulary

After a rather slow start, vocabulary knowledge grows very rapidly during this period. Children typically acquire their first word at about 1 year of age. The first fifty words may take several months. Thereafter the process of word acquisition goes so fast that it is impossible to keep accurate records, but it has been estimated that children acquire six to ten new words a day between the ages of 2 and 6. Such rapid vocabulary acquisition relies on very powerful strategies for guessing what words mean, considerable willingness to take chances in using new words, and lots of help from adults in providing information about words and their meanings.

It is important to recognize that the words a child acquires fall into various categories. Early words tend to be names for important people (*mommy, daddy, gramma*) or concrete objects (*socks, spoon, bed, teddy, cookie, bottle*), as well as words used to express important social functions (greetings such as *hi* or *bye-bye*; request forms such as *wanna, mommy,* or *mine*; and ways of directing attention such as *there, that,* or *what that?*). Starting a bit later, verbs that refer to various actions are acquired (*eat, sleep, read, sing*). As they get older, though, children increasingly come to use verbs that refer to private, complex, cognitive, or communicative activities (*think, wonder, dream, tell, disagree with, deny*); nouns that refer to abstract, superordinate, or affective entities (*thought, argument, animal, furniture, sadness, glee*); and other words that have roles in structuring discourse (*because, but, however*) or representing one's perspective on matters (*hopefully, doubtfully, despairingly*). For avid readers, the process of word acquisition can continue well into adulthood.

It is crucial in talking about vocabulary to acknowledge that children not only acquire new words as they get older but also expand their understandings of old words. Thus a word such as *deep* might first be learned and understood in a relatively restricted context, such as the bathtub: It could take a child several years to learn exactly how *deep* relates to *shallow* and to *tall*, precisely what sorts of things can be called *deep* (deep water in a swimming pool, but not deep soup in a bowl; ditches and canyons can be deep, but mountains and buildings are tall or steep or high), and ultimately that *deep* can be used of persons, of knowledge, and of thinking as well as of liquids and terrain. Standard multiple-choice assessments of vocabulary knowledge do not typically plumb the full depths of children's knowledge. When children are asked to use words they get correct on such multiple-choice tests productively in sentences, they often reveal how limited is their understanding of the proper extension of word meanings, producing sentences such as "I took the *chaste* dishes out of the dishwasher," "If you do that, there will be nothing but *consequences*," or "I *antagonize* your point of view."

At some point during the early childhood years, words and their meanings come to be a topic children think, wonder, and talk about (Papandropoulou & Sinclair, 1974). We call this the development of metalexical awareness. For example, children start to use words such as *word* or *sentence*. They come to be able correctly to count the number of words in a sentence — although this ability emerges remarkably late. Three- and four-year-olds typically count meaningful phrases ("The fearsome cat lay on the sofa" would have two: *the fearsome cat* and *lay on the sofa*), syllables (nine), or stressed syllables (four) (Holden & MacGinitie, 1972; Tunmer, Bowey, & Grieve, 1983). Older children count words but tend to ignore function words such as *the* and *on*, so would count only *fearsome, cat, lay,* and *sofa* in our example sentence. Children at this point may be able correctly, when asked, to think of a long word (*caterpillar*) rather than only a word referring to a long thing (*train*). They have come to understand that words are arbitrary symbols whose forms have no intrinsic connection to their meanings. This sort of understanding is clearly relevant to seeing written forms as arbitrary representations of meaning.

Grammar

Grammar refers to the system of rules that children acquire, on the basis of which utterances make sense and are correct. Grammar here does not mean prescriptive grammar ("Don't say, 'he don't' or 'I ain't'"). Rather it refers to the system of rules by virtue of which we know whether words are nouns or verbs ("the hit" versus "he hit") and we can interpret which word specifies the subject, object, or indirect object of a sentence ("John served Jim ragout").

As soon as children put two words together to express simple meanings such as rejection ("no tickle"), recurrence ("more juice"), object and location ("daddy kitchen"), actor and agent ("mommy help"), and so on, they begin to demonstrate what they are learning about the rules of grammar in their native language. Children learning English, for instance, show awareness of word order as an important feature of the grammatical system. In English, the sentence pattern subject–verb–object is so common that developing the ability to comprehend and use constructions that deviate from this pattern (passives such as "The lion was bitten by the flea," complement constructions such as "Promise Mary you will go," and relative clauses such as "The dog bit the cat that chased the rat") can last well into the early childhood years.

Children typically acquire the rules of grammar in their native language with little difficulty from normal communicative interactions with adults. Some children also develop a metagrammatical capacity, displayed when they comment spontaneously on grammatical correctness or easily respond to questions about sentences being right or wrong. Nonetheless, it is hard even for school-aged children to attend more seriously to grammatical correctness than to meaning; they are likely to accept as correct sentences such as "The boys is jumping in the lake," while rejecting perfectly grammatical but anomalous sentences such as "Ice cream tastes yucky."

Pragmatics and Discourse Rules

Knowing words, how to pronounce them, what they mean, and how to put them into sentences is only a small part of learning a language. One must also learn how to use language appropriately — how to be communicatively effective and responsive to the needs of one's listeners. Pragmatics refers to an enormous array of phenomena, which have in common only that they all relate to appropriateness and communicative effectiveness in the use of language. Thus rules such as "Don't talk with your mouth full" fall under pragmatics, as do rules for politeness—ranging from saying "please" to avoiding discussion of delicate topics—and the many discourse rules designed to make language interpretable. Further examples of pragmatics include rules controlling the use of tense and aspect in storytelling, which make it possible for the listener to understand the order and relative importance of events, and rules about antecedents for pronouns, designed so that listeners know who "he" or "they" refers to.

Metapragmatic awareness tends to emerge first in areas of politeness, perhaps because parents initiate many explicitly metapragmatic discussions with children ("What's the magic word?" and "Don't interrupt; I'm talking on the phone."). Young children often violate pragmatic rules concerned with giving their listeners enough information, but by the age of 4 or so they do understand clearly that strange adults are likely to need some explanation if names of classmates and friends or brand names of toys are introduced (Sachs, Anselmi, & McCollam, 1990). Unlike grammar, though, which is pretty much acquired by the time children get to school, pragmatic skills, particularly those associated with understanding how to adjust one's language for different audiences, continue to grow at least throughout the school years.

THE NATURE OF LITERACY

We have presented information suggesting the size and complexity of the language system young children acquire during the early childhood period. The purpose of this chapter, though, is to discuss how these various language skills relate to literacy. Obviously, oral language and written language to a large extent are the same system—the words and the grammar are much the same. On the other hand, one can easily be misled if one thinks that written language is just oral language written down. There are many ways in which writing is a system of its own; thus many aspects of literacy build on, but also go beyond, what children know about oral language use.

Oral forms of language are in some sense prior to literacy forms. Children learn to speak before they learn to read, and all languages existed as oral languages before they were written. In fact, many languages spoken today still have no written form. Thus oral language skills are the basis for the development of written language skills by children. But we should not ignore the differences that exist between oral and written language forms, despite their high degree of overlap. We will argue that many of the difficulties children can have in acquiring literacy skills derive from these areas of difference between oral and literate usage. On the other hand, children who have developed considerable metalinguistic skill in each of the language areas may be in a better position to analyze and learn about the oral/literate differences than children who have not.

Consider the child who writes "Your not aloud to come along," "There dog was very big," or "I wish I could of gone." This child is failing to make distinctions in writing that need not be made (in the first two cases, cannot be made) in oral language. Consider the following quotation from an essay written by a high school graduate taking an extension course in writing: "I think the state of the blacks in the U.S. is a easly debated subject. I think this becaus their is evidance if you want to look at it" (Rose, 1989, p. 151). The deficiencies of this essay as a piece of writing are obvious even from this fragment; but if read aloud, the basic logic of the argument and clarity of the ideas come through. This is a perfectly sensible piece of oral language, written down without taking into account the kinds of adaptations to literacy many writers make automatically. In the following pages, we will discuss how oral language skills provide the basis for literacy but also can fall short of full or automatic transferability to literacy.

How Phonology Relates to Orthography

An early problem children face in learning to read is figuring out how letters relate to the sounds in words. In English, these relationships are less regular than in some other languages (e.g., Spanish), but the predictability of the relationship is not the real problem. The real problem is figuring out that one must try to relate letters not to pronounceable sounds but to abstract segments that no one can pronounce. The kindergarten teacher who says, "*B* makes a 'buh' sound," is obviously oversimplifying, in a way that many children understand but some do not. *B* does not make a "buh" sound — it makes the sound that *boo*, *bay*, *bye*, *bee*, and *bow* have in common, but that is an intrinsically unpronounceable bit of each of those words. (If *B* really made a "buh" sound, then we could spell *bubble* "bbl," of course.)

Children think of syllables quite naturally as the units of language production. Thus learning to read syllabic systems (such as the one taught to young Japanese speakers) is relatively easy — the only problem is to remember which symbol goes with which syllable. Children learning alphabetic systems must stop thinking of syllables as the relevant unit to relate to orthographic symbols. One route for children to understanding that words must be analyzed into abstract rather than pronounceable segments is their metaphonological awareness. Children who practice rhyming words (*sat, fat, rat, pat*) have figured out that there is a distinction between the initial phonemes and the rest of those words. Children who practice thinking of lists of words that all start with "puh" are, in effect, giving themselves a chance to notice what initial-*p* words do and do not have in common. Such metaphonological awareness is a direct route into the sound–symbol correspondences crucial to reading. And there is a great deal of evidence that the ability to raise to consciousness information about the abstract phonemic structure of words relates to ease of reading acquisition (e.g., Blachman, 1984; Bradley & Bryant, 1983; Fox & Routh, 1980; Goldstein, 1976; Helfgott, 1976; Treiman & Baron, 1981; Vellutino & Scanlon, 1987).

There is considerable controversy, though, about whether children who develop metaphonological awareness early turn into better readers, or whether children develop such skills early because they have been trained in literacy. Evidence that phonological awareness in kindergarten predicts reading ability later comes from several studies (Blachman, 1983; Bradley & Bryant, 1985; Mann, 1991; Mann & Brady, 1988; Mann & Liberman, 1984; Stanovich, Cunningham, & Cramer, 1984; Wagner & Torgesen, 1987). On the other hand, findings that illiterate adults have trouble with phoneme-segmentation tasks suggest that learning to read rather than simple maturation contributes to metaphonological analysis (Liberman, Rubin, Duques, & Carlisle, 1985). Further support for this direction of effect comes from findings that Japanese first graders (who have learned to read a syllabic, not an alphabetic, system) perform worse than American agemates in phoneme-segmentation ability (Mann, 1986). Clearly, one way to be alerted to the presence of abstract phonological segments is to discover that words, when written down, consist of letters whose sounds have to be blended together to make the word. The conclusion seems to be that metaphonological skills promote reading acquisition, and learning to read promotes metaphonology as well.

Another source of opportunity for discoveries about sound–symbol correspondences comes from children's attempts to write. If children have not been trained in sound–symbol relationships, but just try to guess based on knowledge of letter names what letters stand for what sounds, their resultant spellings show remarkable sophistication in phonological analysis (Read, 1975). Glenda Bissex (1980) wrote a book about her son's invented spellings, calling it, appropriately enough, *Gnys at wrk*. Paul Bissex and other young children reveal their theories about segments, symbols, words, and literacy when they spell; they tend to focus on consonants, not vowels (FR is *fur*, but also *fire*); ignore word boundaries (THQ is *thank you*); and represent phonetics quite accurately (the very brief nasal segment in *bent* is ignored in the spelling BT; the highly affricated beginning of *train* is represented by *H* in the spelling HAN). These and many other examples of invented spelling demonstrate that young children are analyzing the sounds they themselves produce, although not always in ways that exactly match adult analyses (Read, 1986). Furthermore, the sophistication of invented spellings by kindergarten-aged children seems to relate closely to their phonological awareness (Liberman et al., 1985), which in turn we know predicts early reading skills.

There are many studies of early reading development suggesting that the major obstacle children face in learning to read is in achieving awareness of phonemes as units. As complex as the sound–symbol relationship is, it is, however, only a small part of how oral language skills need to be reconfigured, supplemented, and brought to conscious awareness in order to serve as a basis for literacy skills. Developments in the area of vocabulary, grammar, and pragmatics are equally crucial.

Vocabulary and Word Recognition

A few thousand words account for 90% of the spoken vocabulary anyone uses or hears, and a list of 10,000 words essentially exhausts the vocabulary anyone—even a highly educated adult—uses in speaking (Hayes & Ahrens, 1988). For reading and writing, on the other hand, educated English speakers may know as many as 100,000 words. Clearly, the gap between the spoken vocabulary and the written vocabulary constitutes a challenge to children. This challenge is not, however, typically a major problem for beginning readers. The reading texts considered appropriate for the primary grades are limited in vocabulary to words that most children know and use orally. Of course, if 6- or 7-year-olds have very large vocabularies, they may well be able to read books that are much more interesting and lively than their classmates with poor vocabularies. On the other hand, if a first grader has a very poor vocabulary (which is not unlikely if, for example, the child is being taught to read in a language he or she does not speak at home), then the task of word recognition even in those simple books is rather daunting.

Oral word knowledge helps children in reading words for two reasons:

1. Sounding out a word is much easier if one knows what the target sounds like; for example, there is no way of knowing just from reading them that *broccoli* should be pronounced with the accent on the first syllable and *spaghetti* with the accent on the second

syllable. Having these words in one's oral vocabulary, though, will help.

2. Knowing what words mean can often help a child predict where they might occur in a text. Thus the word *carburetor* might be hard to read, but in the context "He opened the hood and checked the . . . " a child who knows what a carburetor is might be able to use a combination of semantic and orthographic cues to read the word correctly.

Recognizing words is, of course, crucial to reading with comprehension. Just as young children learn most words incidentally, without direct teaching, school-aged children can learn vocabulary words from reading them in context (Jenkins & Wysocki, 1985; McKeown, 1985; Nagy, Herman, & Anderson, 1985a, 1985b; Shefelbine, 1983), but only if the unknown words are well-enough spaced that their presence does not interfere with comprehension of the text. Furthermore, of course, the chance of learning a word on a single exposure in context is relatively small; repeated exposures are necessary to ensure acquisition.

Vocabulary size is one of the most robust correlates of scores on tests of reading comprehension (Davis, 1944, 1968; Thurstone, 1946). We can relate this fact to the "benign circle" linking oral vocabulary and reading — a larger vocabulary makes reading easier, and more reading builds a larger vocabulary by virtue of the ability to learn words from exposure in context.

An aspect of vocabulary knowledge that has particular relevance to literacy in English is understanding morphological relationships among words. These morphological relationships are reflected in English spelling, and they explain a good deal of what may seem illogical in our spelling system. It certainly appears counterintuitive that one should spell *sign* with a *g*, but if we adopted a more phonetic spelling this word's morphological relationship to *signature* and to *signal* would be obscured. Similarly, we could eliminate the letter *c* and replace it with *s* or *k* depending on its pronunciation, but then we would make less accessible the connections between *elektrik* and *elektrisity* or between *ransid* and *rankor*. Vowels in unstressed syllables in English are all pronounced pretty much the same — as a schwa or /uh/ sound. But we would not want to spell words so as to reflect this fact of spoken language, because then we would lose completely the graphic connections between different forms of the same word:

grammur	*grummatucul*
uconumi	*ekunomucs*
demucrat	*dumocrusi*

This is a spelling system that is closer to oral language, but one that fails to reward the reader who understands morphological relationships between nouns and adjectives and one that prevents less sophisticated readers from ever discovering those relationships. Again, with reference to the relation between reading and the growth of morphological sophistication, we can speak of a benign circle: Reading reveals morphological relations that may not be obvious in the spoken language, and knowing about morphological relations helps one in reading and in spelling.

Grammar in Speaking and Writing

There is general agreement that poor readers also show deficits in grammatical processing (see Mann, 1991, for a review), although the explanations for these effects are several. Gough, in his "simple view" of reading (Gough, 1991; Hoover & Gough, 1990), suggests that decoding or word-recognition ability and listening comprehension together explain reading comprehension. Listening comprehension is, of course, dependent on processing the grammatical and the discourse structures of the language. Shankweiler (1989) suggests, though, that the basic deficit shown by poor readers is one of phonological processing and that problems with sentence comprehension are secondary to memory and processing deficits associated with the phonological system. In addition to processing problems, though, reading presents a rather more difficult grammar than does oral language.

Although the grammatical rules for spoken and written English are in fact the same, the use of the options the grammar offers turns out to be quite different in speaking and in writing. The syntax in written language is more complex than in spoken language, and a wider variety of sentence forms are used. Spoken utterances tend to have pronominal subjects, tend to avoid passives and very complex sentence structures, and especially tend to avoid constructions that interrupt subject-verb or verb-object sequences. Consider the following oral and written versions of the same anecdote:

When I was in college, I had this boyfriend. I never knew what happened to him. He just disappeared. Well the other day he called me up. He said he'd seen my name in the company directory. Turns out he works right here, almost next door to me.

The boyfriend I had in college disappeared suddenly, without saying goodbye, so I never knew what happened to him. The other day he called me at work. He had taken a job at the same place I work, a big advertising agency, and had seen my name in the company directory.

Subject relatives ("The boyfriend *I had in college*"), for example, are found almost exclusively in writing, as are appositives ("the same place I work, *a big advertising agency*"). Connections that are made across sentences in speaking are often compressed into sentences in writing by using conjunctions and participial constructions. The density of information in written texts is much higher than in oral language, and this can cause a problem for young readers who do not have the skills to process so much information. The need to be concise, exact, and complete in writing leads to the use of grammatical structures quite different from those common in oral language (De Temple, Wu, & Snow, 1991).

Pragmatics of Oral Versus Written Language

The prototypical purposes for which language is used orally involve face-to-face conversation with familiars. Young children talk with their mothers about their own and their mothers' ongoing activities—building towers, baking cookies, getting bathed and dressed. They talk about the books they are looking at or the experiences they have just shared. As they get older, they increasingly come to talk about unshared events (what happened at daycare), but even then their mothers are fairly well informed about the general topic and likely to be able to fill in the missing information, or else willing to work by questioning and interpreting to co-construct missing information.

Literate uses of language can differ from oral uses in their purposes as well as on dimensions such as the type of audience, the relation of speaker/ writer to audience, and the distribution of responsibility for effective communication over writer and audience. Literate pragmatics might find its prototype in essayist literacy—that displayed in editorials in the better newspapers, which are meant to make a point clearly and completely, in the process providing any background information necessary to understand the point so as to be accessible to everyone in the audience on first reading.

Obviously, many oral language uses approach the pragmatics of essayist literacy—public lectures, for example, or telephone conversations with strangers. And some literate forms of expression are appropriately private, personal, ambiguous, even inaccessible to many potential readers—diaries or journals, for example, or poetry. Nonetheless, it is clear that the pragmatic rules governing effective conversational exchange of the type most young children have mastered are not a sufficient basis for understanding the pragmatics of literacy, nor even of much oral classroom discourse (see Cazden, 1988). We would argue that young children can best be exposed first in oral contexts to the pragmatic considerations that govern sophisticated literate uses of language.

One dimension distinguishing the different pragmatic demands is audience collaboration. Can one expect one's listeners to participate actively, asking clarification questions, chiming in with agreements or supportive statements, proposing interpretations and conclusions? If so, one need not preplan so carefully to assure comprehensibility, nor make all the implications of one's message so clear. Note that this dimension of expected audience participation is one that differs across cultures both for oral and for written forms; Hawaiian and Athabaskan children have been described as active participants when listening to stories (Scollon & Scollon, 1981; Watson-Gegeo & Boggs, 1977), in contrast to mainstream American models in which the storyteller has full responsibility for plot development and performance and the audience is supposed to be silent until the end. Japanese novelists clearly demand considerably more work from their readers than do Western novelists, never providing the tidily wrapped-up conclusion to the plot that is required in the West. American working-class, teenage girls participating in discussions of serious topics share turns with one another, the audience audibly echoing or even anticipating the speakers' points, whereas middle-class girls tend to take long and uninterrupted turns producing, in effect, brief oral editorials (Hemphill, 1986). It is equally challenging to participate effectively in discourse forms where the responsibility is shared with the audience and in those where it rests almost exclusively on the speaker; practice with the latter, however, transfers more effectively to the kinds of writing American children are expected to do in school.

A second dimension governing the pragmatics of different discourse forms is the degree to which background knowledge can be assumed to be shared with the audience. Consider the difference between recounting a harrowing experience to a friend who was not there at the time and reminiscing about the harrowing experience with the person with whom it was shared. The first account requires considerably more attention to clarity about who participated, the order of events, and exactly what happened—demands that are played out linguistically in reduced use of pronouns, more elaborated use of tense and aspect marking, and more explicit backgrounding and foregrounding of events. This is the dimension Bernstein captured with his terms "elaborated" versus "restricted" codes (1962, 1972); the more information about a topic one shares with one's interlocutors, the more adequate a restricted code is in discussing that topic.

An additional dimension of pragmatic complexity is added when the genre being used requires that the speaker or writer act *as if* background knowledge is not shared, when in fact it is. This situation emerges in the classroom discourse when teachers ask test questions (questions to which they already know the answer) or when, at sharing time, children are expected to describe objects they are holding that the whole class can clearly see. A task that taps this dimension, performed with the understanding that shared knowledge and context must be ignored, involves giving definitions for common words. When asked, "What is a clock?" it should be perfectly appropriate to point to one or to say something such as, "They are like watches, but larger." Children who are sophisticated in the pragmatics of school discourse, on the other hand, tend to avoid responses such as these that presume shared knowledge, and to respond instead with something like "A clock is a machine that tells time" (Snow, 1990; Snow, Cancino, Gonzalez, & Shriberg, 1989).

Essential prerequisites to pragmatic effectiveness are understanding the listener's perspective and knowing the range of expectations the listener might hold. As members of a culture, all of us have acquired culture-specific expectations about how interpersonal relationships should be marked linguistically and how information should be packaged for easy communication. All children have to expand those expectations as they learn to interact in new settings and with different people. Exposure in early childhood education settings to a wide variety of pragmatic demands can help children prepare themselves for the peculiar pragmatics of classroom discourse and of literacy.

LANGUAGE, LITERACY, AND
THE EARLY CHILDHOOD CLASSROOM

As the above discussion has indicated, not only is helping children develop a wide variety of oral language capabilities a crucial precursor to literacy development, but making children aware of these connections is equally as important. The ways in which these connections can be made, and be made explicit, in the early childhood classroom is the topic of this concluding section.

Reading books aloud to children in a group setting has long been a common activity in early childhood classrooms. Based on the previous discussion, it is now possible to outline the ways in which book reading might contribute to children's literacy development beyond the obvious "developing familiarity with books and print."

Book reading is an opportune time for teachers to help children build vocabulary, extend phonological awareness, and develop familiarity with literate forms. Selecting books from a wide spectrum of topics and engaging children in a discussion of the meanings of words in context can promote the acquisition of new vocabulary, which is then available for children when they begin to meet these words in written texts. Emphasizing rhyming characteristics and other phonological phenomena in the context of reading aloud will also help children begin to segment sounds even before they make the connections with letters. Reading books aloud to children exposes them to grammatical forms of written language and displays literate discourse rules for them in ways that conversation cannot. Making these differences explicit — for instance, by discussing how a written story and a spoken story may "sound" different — will be particularly helpful for children whose families do not include these literate discourse forms in their spoken repertoires.

Further, engaging children in discussions that encourage them to analyze the text of the book being read aloud extends the experience in beneficial ways. In one-on-one contexts, a shared picture book reading intervention in which the child took an active role in talking about the book resulted in substantial gains on a variety of language measures for low-income Mexican children (Valdez-Menchaca & Whitehurst, 1992). In a group experience, children's exposure to analytical talk during book reading was found to have a strong effect on vocabulary scores and a moderate effect on story understanding scores a year later (Dickinson & Smith, 1992). These findings would indicate that book reading and discussion can have a powerful effect on the development of complex oral language, vocabulary, and story understanding, all critical abilities that young children will need when faced with later literacy tasks.

Group times in early childhood classrooms are also used for a variety of other activities besides book reading. In many classrooms there is a specific sharing time when children are asked to talk about an experience before the entire group. This activity is frequently structured by the teacher so that children must fulfill the requirements for a highly literate production (unfamiliar audience, tightly developed narrative form), even though the event could be, and often is, construed by the children to be merely an oral storytelling activity. Children from nonmainstream communities may find the requirements of this "oral preparation for literacy" confusing (Michaels, 1981, 1986; Michaels & Cazden, 1986), but teachers who let children in on the secret of the how and why of this form of story construction, and help children move back and forth between various cultural expressions of narration (see Delpit, 1992), will be helping children make the transition to the literacy requirements that they will meet later on in school.

Sociodramatic play is another area of activity in early childhood class-rooms with implications for connections between oral language and literacy development. In sociodramatic play children must use language explicitly in order to develop the necessary transformation of objects, ideas, and roles, and they must use extended language to play out a variety of scripts or narrative-based actions. Multiple correlations have been found between various aspects of children's play and the use of past, future, and cognitive verbs, noun phrases, and cohesion markers (Pellegrini, 1985), all aspects of language connected to literate forms. Further, children who have a variety of play scripts come to school with a better developed sense of narrative than those who do not (Heath, 1982). These findings indicate that teachers who promote and monitor sociodramatic play opportunities that call on a rich variety of scripts and ideas will be helping children develop extended language and narrative abilities.

Finally, small group times and one-on-one interactions are also times when teachers can have an impact on the oral language development of children in early childhood classrooms. Many small-group activities involve developing a project around a topic of interest. When teachers talk about what they are doing, explain why particular results occur, and let children ask questions about procedures and results, children will have more exposure to and experience with extended forms of discourse. The use of open-ended and "wh-" questions to get children thinking and talking about the activity they are involved in will help them to structure and comprehend similar arguments when they come across them later in a written context. In small-group or one-on-one interaction, teachers have more opportunities to help children move from co-constructing literate forms to producing them independently. Again, as in the above discussions, it is critical for teachers to make their own assumptions about what they are doing explicit to the children, so that all the children will be able to understand what is required.

Just as it was not possible to discuss language without breaking it down into a number of different but interconnected domains, it has not been possible to discuss the activities in an early childhood classroom related to language without breaking them down into a number of categories. Of course, this does not mean that these activities are not connected, nor that they can occur only in the domains mentioned. Teachers who wish to promote language development that will help children in literacy activities later in school will certainly find a multiplicity of opportunities to do so within a variety of contexts in their classrooms.

Acknowledgments. The authors would like to express their appreciation to the Ford Foundation and the Spencer Foundation, which have supported our work on the acquisition of language and literacy skills as well as the writing of this paper; and to David Dickinson, Petra Nicholson, Miriam Smith, and Jeanne De Temple, whose collaboration on the project and knowledge of early childhood classrooms has greatly enriched our thinking.

REFERENCES

Bernstein, B. (1962). Social class, linguistic codes and grammatical elements. *Language and Speech, 5,* 31–46.

Bernstein, B. (1972). Social class, language, and socialization. In P. Giglioli (Ed.), *Language and social context* (pp. 157–178). Harmondsworth, England: Viking Penguin.

Bissex, G. (1980). *Gnys at wrk.* Cambridge, MA: Harvard University Press.

Blachman, B. (1983). Are we assessing the linguistic factors critical in early reading? *Annals of Dyslexia, 33,* 91–109.

Blachman, B. (1984). The relationships of rapid naming ability and language analysis skills to kindergarten and first grade reading achievement. *Journal of Educational Psychology, 76,* 10–22.

Bradley, L., & Bryant, P. (1983). Categorizing sounds and learning to read — A causal connection. *Nature, 301,* 419–421.

Bradley, L., & Bryant, P. (1985). *Rhyme and reason in reading and spelling.* Ann Arbor: University of Michigan Press.

Bruck, M., & Treiman, R. (1990). Phonological awareness and spelling in normal children and dyslexics: The case of initial consonant clusters. *Journal of Experimental Child Psychology, 50,* 156–178.

Cazden, C. (1988). *Classroom discourse: The language of teaching and learning.* Portsmouth, NH: Heinemann.

Clark, E. (1978). Awareness of language: Some evidence from what children say and do. In A. Sinclair, R. Jarvella, & W. Levelt (Eds.), *The child's conception of language* (pp. 17–43). Berlin: Springer-Verlag.

Davis, F. (1944). Fundamental factors in reading comprehension. *Psychometrika, 9,* 185–197.

Davis, F. (1968). Research in comprehension in reading. *Reading Research Quarterly, 3,* 499–545.

Delpit, L. (1992). Interview. *Harvard Educational Letter, 8*(6), 3–5.

De Temple, J., Wu, H.-F., & Snow, C. (1991). Papa pig just left for pigtown: Children's oral and written picture descriptions under varying instructions. *Discourse Processes, 14,* 469–495.

Dickinson, D., & Smith, M. (1992). *Long-term effects of preschool teachers' book readings on low-income children's vocabulary, story comprehension, and print skills.* Manuscript submitted for publication.

Fox, B., & Routh, D. (1980). Phonetic analysis and severe reading disability in children. *Journal of Psycholinguistic Research, 9,* 115–119.

Goldstein, D. (1976). Cognitive-linguistic functioning and learning to read in preschoolers. *Journal of Educational Psychology, 68,* 680–688.

Gough, P. (1991). The complexity of reading. In R. Hoffman & D. Palermo (Eds.), *Cognition and the symbolic processes* (pp. 141–149). Hillsdale, NJ: Erlbaum.

Hayes, D., & Ahrens, M. (1988). Vocabulary simplification for children. *Journal of Child Language, 15,* 457–472.

Heath, S. (1982). What no bedtime story means: Narrative skills at home and school. *Language in Society, 11,* 49–76.

Helfgott, J. (1976). Phoneme segmentation and blending skills of kindergarten children: Implications for beginning reading acquisition. *Contemporary Education Psychology, 1,* 157–169.

Hemphill, L. (1986). *Context and conversational style: A reappraisal of social class differences in group discussion.* Unpublished dissertation, Harvard Graduate School of Education, Cambridge, MA.

Holden, W., & MacGinitie, W. (1972). Children's conception of word boundaries in speech and print. *Journal of Educational Psychology, 63,* 551–557.

Hoover, W., & Gough, P. (1990). The simple view of reading. *Reading and Writing, 2,* 127–160.

Jenkins, J., & Wysocki, K. (1985). *Deriving word meanings from context.* Unpublished manuscript.

Lenel, J., & Cantor, J. (1981). Rhyme recognition and phoneme perception in young children. *Journal of Psycholinguistic Research, 10,* 57–67.

Liberman, I., Rubin, H., Duques, S., & Carlisle, J. (1985). Linguistic abilities and spelling proficiency in kindergartners and adult poor spellers. In J. Kavanaugh & D. Gray (Eds.), *Behavioral measures of dyslexia* (pp. 163–175). Parkton, MD: York.

Mann, V. (1986). Distinguishing universal and language-dependent levels of speech perception: Evidence from Japanese listeners' perception of English "l" and "r." *Cognition, 24,* 169–196.

Mann, V. (1991). Language problems: A key to early reading problems. In B. Wong (Ed.), *Learning about learning disabilities* (pp. 129–162). New York: Academic Press.

Mann, V., & Brady, S. (1988). Reading disability: The role of language deficiencies. *Journal of Consulting and Clinical Psychology, 56,* 811–816.

Mann, V., & Liberman, I. (1984). Phonological awareness and verbal short-term memory. *Journal of Learning Disabilities, 17,* 592–598.

McKeown, M. (1985). The acquisition of word meaning from context by children of high and low ability. *Reading Research Quarterly, 20,* 482–496.

Michaels, S. (1981). "Sharing time": Children's narrative styles and differential access to literacy. *Language in Society, 10,* 423–442.

Michaels, S. (1986). Narrative presentations: An oral preparation for literacy with first graders. In J. Cook-Gumperz (Ed.), *The social construction of literacy* (pp. 94–116). Cambridge, England: Cambridge University Press.

Michaels, S., & Cazden, C. (1986). Teacher/child collaboration as oral preparation for literacy. In B. Schieffelin & P. Gillmore (Eds.), *The acquisition of literacy: Ethnographic perspectives* (pp. 132–154). Norwood, NJ: Ablex.

Nagy, W., Herman, P., & Anderson, R. (1985a). Learning words from context. *Reading Research Quarterly, 20*, 233–253.

Nagy, W., Herman, P., & Anderson, R. (1985b). *Learning word meanings from context: How broadly generalizable?* Unpublished manuscript, University of Illinois, Center for the Study of Reading, Champaign-Urbana.

Papandropoulou, I., & Sinclair, H. (1974). What is a word? *Human Development, 17*, 241–258.

Pellegrini, A. (1985). Relations between preschool children's symbolic play and literate behavior. In L. Galda & A. Pellegrini (Eds.), *Play, language, and stories: The development of children's literate behavior* (pp. 79–98). Norwood, NJ: Ablex.

Read, C. (1975). *Children's categorization of speech sounds in English* (Research Report No. 17). Urbana, IL: National Council of Teachers of English.

Read, C. (1986). *Children's creative spelling.* London: Routledge & Kegan Paul.

Rose, M. (1989). *Lives on the boundary.* New York: Penguin.

Sachs, J., Anselmi, D., & McCollam, K. (1990, July). *Young children's awareness of presupposition based on community awareness.* Paper presented at the International Association for the Study of Child Language, Budapest.

Scollon, R., & Scollon, S. (1981). *Narrative, literacy and face in interethnic communication.* Norwood, NJ: Ablex.

Shankweiler, D. (1989). How problems of comprehension are related to difficulties in decoding. In D. Shankweiler & I. Liberman (Eds.), *Phonology and reading disability: Solving the reading puzzle* (pp. 35–68). Ann Arbor: University of Michigan Press.

Shefelbine, J. (1983, April). *Learning word meanings from context.* Paper presented at the annual meeting of the American Educational Research Association, Montreal.

Smith, C., & Tager-Flusberg, H. (1982). Metalinguistic awareness and language development. *Journal of Experimental Child Psychology, 34*, 449–468.

Snow, C. (1990). The development of definitional skill. *Journal of Child Language, 17*, 697–710.

Snow, C., Cancino, H., Gonzalez, P., & Shriberg, E. (1989). Giving formal definitions: An oral language correlate of school literacy. In D. Bloome (Ed.), *Classrooms and literacy* (pp. 233–249). Norwood, NJ: Ablex.

Stanovich, K., Cunningham, A., & Cramer, B. (1984). Assessing phonological awareness in kindergarten children: Issues of task comparability. *Journal of Experimental Child Psychology, 38*, 175–190.

Teale, W., & Sulzby, E. (Eds.). (1986). *Emergent literacy: Writing and reading.* Norwood, NJ: Ablex.

Thurstone, L. (1946). A note on a reanalysis of Davis' reading tests. *Psychometrika, 11*, 185–188.

Treiman, R. (1985). Onsets and rimes as units of spoken syllables: Evidence from children. *Journal of Experimental Child Psychology, 39*, 161–181.

Treiman, R. (1988). The internal structure of the syllable. In G. Carlson & M. Tanenhaus (Eds.), *Linguistic structure in language processing* (pp. 27–52). Norwell, MA: Kluwer Academic.

Treiman, R., & Baron, J. (1981). Segmental analysis ability: Development and relation to reading ability. In G. MacKinnon & T. Walker (Eds.), *Reading research: Advances in theory and practice* (Vol. 3, pp. 159–198). New York: Academic Press.

Tunmer, W., Bowey, J., & Grieve, R. (1983). The development of young children's awareness of the word as a unit of spoken language. *Journal of Psycholinguistic Research, 12,* 567–593.

Valdez-Menchaca, M. C., & Whitehurst, G. J. (1992). Accelerating language development through picture book reading: A systematic extension to Mexican daycare. *Developmental Psychology, 28,* 1106–1114.

Vellutino, F. R., & Scanlon, D. M. (1987). Phonological coding, phonological awareness, and reading ability: Evidence from longitudinal and experimental study. *Merrill-Palmer Quarterly, 33,* 321–363.

Wagner, R., & Torgesen, J. (1987). The nature of phonological processing and its causal role in the acquisition of reading skills. *Psychological Bulletin, 101,* 192–212.

Watson-Gegeo, K., & Boggs, S. (1977). From verbal play to talk-story: The role of routines in speech events among Hawaiian children. In S. Ervin-Tripp & C. Mitchell-Kernan (Eds.), *Child discourse* (pp. 67–90). New York: Academic Press.

Zhurova, L. (1973). The development of analysis of words into their sounds by preschool children. In C. Ferguson & D. Slobin (Eds.), *Studies of child language development* (pp. 141–154). New York: Holt, Rinehart & Winston.

CHAPTER 2

From Prop to Mediator: The Changing Role of Written Language in Children's Symbolic Repertoires

Anne Haas Dyson

Lamar and James are nearing the end of their kindergarten year. Whether reading books or playing cops and robbers, doing puzzles or sharing lunch, they have been steadfast companions. One of their favorite activities has been verbal one-upmanship. This game can accompany and structure even their daily drawing and writing. In the following example, the two boys are drawing themselves swimming; this is part of an activity in which class members are making their own versions of an "I am a _____" pattern book:

James: I'm swimming in the lake, I'm swimming in the lake. I won't come in and eat my cake. *(chanting and drawing)* This gonna be the waves. *(drawing waves)*

Lamar: Do you know what these lines are? *(pointing to his own drawing)* They're the waves . . . And then the water gets higher. *(drawing his waves higher)*

James: Mine's gonna get higher too. My water's higher than you.

Lamar: Shoot. Mine is higher than yours. Look at this . . . Mine is over my head . . . Mine got deeper. And then a shark was coming. Then a shark was coming. *(drawing a shark)*

James: If they had a shark in the water, we'd get ready to get out of the water.

Lamar: I'm getting ready to get out of the water 'cause the shark . . . *(chanting)* I'm deep in the water. The shark's gonna kill me.

James: But ooh! There's a shark in the water. *(Now James puts a shark in his own picture.)*

21

At the end of this long and complex episode, Lamar writes: "I am a swimmer."

Considering this book's focus on early literacy development, what in Lamar's and James's activity is particularly relevant? Should we attend most closely to how Lamar goes about writing, "I am a swimmer"? Lamar's caption, though, seems a mere supplement to his playful talking and drawing. It is not through print but through words and pictures that Lamar represents his ideas, reflects on them, and interacts with James about them. Lamar has a long and complex way to go before the written forms themselves will be able to mediate in substantive ways Lamar's intellectual and social activities.

To understand the development of written language, therefore, we must examine most closely not the written forms themselves but the changing role of those forms in children's symbolic activity. The purpose of this chapter is to examine how children's use of written language changes during the early childhood years. By *written language*, I do not mean simply children's handwriting and spelling; I mean children's use of letter forms as symbols that help them to represent and to reflect on their ideas and to interact with other people about them. The major change of interest is from children's use of print as a kind of prop, an interesting object to be used *in* varied kinds of social, often playful, activity, to the use of print as a mediator *through* which new kinds of social activity, including new kinds of play, can happen.

The ultimate aim of this chapter is to illustrate that the development of written language is intertwined with children's experiences with diverse symbolic media. The symbolic tool of writing is, or should be, a remarkably accessible one to young schoolchildren from diverse cultural backgrounds, for it is a tool that takes root amidst more comfortable symbolic media and much interaction with appreciative others. I also aim, however, to make clear the limits of written language as an expressive and learning tool in the early years and, thus, the importance of the arts in their own right.

To these ends, throughout the chapter I will turn to Lamar and his classmates, children from an ongoing study of literacy development among African American children in an urban school (Dyson, 1992). They will provide clear illustrations of how children's abilities as drawers, talkers, and social players are linked in dynamic ways to their emerging skills as writers.

To set the stage for this exploration of written language, I first discuss the nature of symbol making and, then, turn to drawing, a graphic medium whose developmental history may help pave the way for writing. Undergirding this chapter is a social constructivist vision of development;

that is, I assume that children construct their own understandings of the world, including their understandings of how symbolic media work, and that they do so as they engage in social activities with other people (Vygotsky, 1978).

THE NATURE OF SYMBOL MAKING

A symbol—a word, a picture, a dance—exists because of a human intention to infuse some tangible form—a sound, a mark, a movement—with meaning and, thereby, to comment on or take action in the social world. Imagine, for example, Lamar as he draws a flowing graphic mark across his paper. That mark has an identity of its own—it is a line. At the same time, however, Lamar links the dynamic and sensual quality of the line—its fluidity—to that of a wave. Lamar's line thus becomes a "vehicle"; it carries meaning beyond itself (Werner & Kaplan, 1963). That vehicle not only allows Lamar to play with waves as he sits in his classroom, but it also allows James to join the play. Such symbol making is the essence of what it means to be human. We as humans use symbols to liberate us from the here-and-now, to enter worlds of possibility, and, at the same time, to join with others who share the same "imaginative universe." People who share a culture share similar ways of infusing meaning into sounds (language), movement (dance), and lines (drawings), among other media (Geertz, 1983).

And yet, despite its universality—that is, despite the biological predisposition of human beings to infuse meaning into objects (Winner, 1989)—Lamar's control of his wavy line should not be taken for granted. Its developmental evolution is linked not simply to biology but also to cultural activity. Taking a closer look at the evolution of drawing, and the critical role of talk and gesture in that evolution, will help clarify the evolution of the more complex graphic medium of written language.

GRAPHIC SYMBOLISM BEGINS:
THE EMERGENCE OF DRAWING

During the early childhood years, children acquire the basic symbolic tools or repertoire of their culture (Piaget & Inhelder, 1969; Vygotsky, 1978; Werner & Kaplan, 1963). Children initially explore each available medium without any intention to symbolize. Rather, they manipulate the sounds of language, the movement of their own body, the graphic marks of drawing and painting implements, the structural possibilities of blocks and other constructive media. Each medium offers children distinctive physical and visual properties to explore. And so, in Nancy Smith's words (1979), the child "does what he does, it [the medium] does what it does. . . . One discovery leads to the next as he responds to the material and as the material responds to him" (p. 21).

During the second year of life, children begin to use gestures and words to symbolize—to represent—significant actions in their world (Gardner & Wolf, 1987). Moreover, they also begin to use these symbolic tools to invest meaning in drawn marks. The child runs across the page making marks with a pencil, and thus the child has drawn someone running. The child jumps with a marker and thus draws a rabbit jumping. Symbolic meaning comes from the *gestures*, not the marks. The marks are thus a kind of prop—a critically important prop, but nonetheless a prop—for children's dramatic play (Mathews, 1984; Vygotsky, 1978; Wolf & Perry, 1989).

Around age 3, children begin to notice similarities between salient physical features of the world and their own graphic constructions. However, these discoveries come *after* their drawing, when they attempt to "read" the meaning of what they have made and, just as importantly, to communicate its potential meaning to other people. Through *talk* with others, children invest their marks with meaning. Golomb's (1974, 1988) extensive studies reveal how the interest of other people prompts children to talk about their drawings, read their marks, and discover hidden meanings.

As children gain experience, they begin to accompany their drawing with talk about their evolving intentions. Those intentions often prove too ambitious, and so children reinterpret their original intentions, making them more suited to their products (Golomb, 1974; see also Brittain, 1979). "This gonna be the waves," said James. But when his scribbly waves did not look like Lamar's controlled ones, he changed: "This is a storm."

As Vygotsky (1978) argued, talk eventually serves not only to represent meanings and to interact with others about those meanings but also to *regulate* drawing itself. That is, talk helps the child to plan a particular drawing and to monitor his or her shaping of lines and curves. Indeed, even for adult artists, talk may be a way of articulating plans and evaluating progress. In a sense, such talk helps drawing become a mediator, a way of giving graphic voice to an intention; because of this, Vygotsky described drawing as a kind of "graphic speech" that paves the way for writing (see also Dyson, 1982).

Speech also serves a regulatory function in children's play. Initially objects gain their meaning from the child's gestures. A block of wood might be a baby if it can be held; a broom can be a horse if it can be ridden. Eventually, however, speech allows children to represent meaning, to share their ideas with other people, and *to engage in increasingly more deliberate, more planful activity* (Vygotsky, 1978; see also Garvey, 1990, for related research). With the support of talk, then, play becomes a kind of "canvas" on which young children can collaboratively symbolize ideas and feelings (Fein, 1987). Guided by talk, children use sound, motion, and tempo to create dramas in which people scream or soothe, rush or relax, worry or reassure.

In fact, collaborative, playful talk can support the evolution of drawing itself, a more literal canvas, as Lamar and James illustrated. Lamar had originally used drawing as a prop, a graphic mark within an elaborate and told story; the story was in no way bound by the drawing but, given an interested other, evolved far away from the page. When Lamar's drawing became a way of engaging in social play with James, he attended more carefully to the meaning of each line, trying to outdo James. Listen to Lamar again as he adds wavy line after wavy line to his picture; his drawing is deliberate, controlled, as he seeks to make his waves "higher than yours":

Shoot. Mine [my water] is higher than yours. Look at this . . . Mine is over my head . . . Mine go deeper. Deeper. Draw over the top. My head's under the water. Everything's under water!

Taking a long view — comparing his current drawing efforts to earlier ones — Lamar was beginning to differentiate the symbolic potential of drawing from that of talk and gesture. That is, he was figuring out how to accomplish his representational and social goals *through* the graphic medium. Drawing was thus becoming a mediator: Lamar was using drawing to convey his intentions and, at the same time, the possibilities of the medium shaped his intentions. Lamar's social play with James helped transform his drawing, and drawing itself led to a new kind of social play.

In sum, the evolution of drawing is linked in complex ways to dramatic gesture and speech, sometimes combined in social play. As in all areas of symbol development (Gardner & Wolf, 1987), children approach the new symbolic medium of drawing through old, comfortable procedures (e.g., dramatic gesture). Gradually, there are functional shifts, as the visual symbols of drawing become more capable of mediating — shaping and being shaped by — the child's social and representational intentions (Dyson, 1991; for a seminal discussion of symbolic differentiation, see Werner & Kaplan, 1963).

I now turn to writing development, where similar phenomena occur:

the initial exploratory behavior; the shaping of children's symbolic behavior by social activity; the emergence of written forms as kinds of props or supplements to other symbolic tools, among them, gesture and talk; and functional shifts, as children begin to use writing as a mediator — that is, as writing assumes some of the representational and social work earlier accomplished by other media.

THE EMERGENCE OF WRITING:
EARLY EXPLORATORY PLAY

Initially, young children's use of writing is very idiosyncratic; they explore the system's nature, gaining some familiarity with its functions (what written language can socially accomplish), rhetorical content (how it sounds in particular situations), and graphic marks (what it looks like), but they do not control the system as a whole. That is, they do not understand precisely how letters or words are manipulated in order to represent and reflect on experiences and to interact with other people. As in their first drawing, the writing act itself — the gesture and any accompanying talk — makes their letters and letterlike marks meaningful (Dyson, 1983; Luria, 1983).

Much of young children's writing is a kind of exploratory play, common in the developmental beginnings of all symbolic media. After a careful study of the products of such play, Clay (1975) provided a seminal analysis of the kinds of discovery and practice it furthers. Children explore, for example, the nature of letter forms, their directional layout on the paper, and the spatial arrangement of text itself. And, as with drawing, when questioned by an adult, children may invent a meaning for their marks. A child manipulating lines, though, may discover a shape that looks like a wave, but the potential meaning of a child's own manipulated letters does not so readily reveal itself. Thus a great deal of questioning accompanies the early exploration of writing (Durkin, 1966). Indeed, Clay entitled her book *What Did I Write?*, a question more likely to occur than "What did I draw?"

Another kind of early play with print may happen in the context of dramatic play, when, given the opportunity, children explore the functions of written language. For example, in the "home" center, children may make grocery lists and take phone messages (Schickedanz, 1978); in the "doctor's office," they may read in the waiting room, write out prescriptions, and make appointments (Morrow & Rand, 1991). In this play, which, like exploratory play with letter forms, continues throughout the early childhood period, children do not typically focus on precisely encoding meaning. Rather, as with exploratory play, the accompanying gestures and talk make the child's intentions clear.

Exploratory play with print and the use of print as a prop within dramatic play are valuable supports for young children's entry into written language. But neither kind of play in and of itself leads the child to an understanding of the inner workings of the system — to the ability to manipulate letters and thereby words to interact with others. In a discussion of Vygotsky's ideas, Wertsch (1989) explained that symbolic tools are not "props that simply facilitate" (p. 18) human activities; rather, they are mediators that reshape the nature of activities themselves.

To gain insight into how written language becomes a mediator of social activity, we must focus not simply on children's knowledge of the kinds of functions writing serves in the adult world or on their knowledge of graphic marks such as letters. Rather, we must examine how children begin to orchestrate their functional and graphic knowledge into systematic use — that is, how they begin to precisely match meanings and graphics to carry out important activities in particular situations. Within social activities deemed by the child's culture "literacy activities" and given the social assistance of others, children begin to use written symbols to carry some of the functional load earlier handled by speech, gesture, and drawing. This developmental process is discussed in the two sections that follow.

ORCHESTRATING THE WRITTEN SYSTEM

As in all other areas of symbol development, children first attempt to orchestrate the system during familiar, manageable activities. Children may continue to "just write" letters or to use "curspid" (wavy-line) writing (e.g., when writing stories or extended texts in dramatic play) but attempt more precise encoding when writing smaller units, especially names. While such labeling can occur as part of dramatic play, naming is in and of itself an activity of great interest to many young children and one in which they will invest considerable intellectual energy, especially if they are in the company of interested adults and peers (e.g., Durkin, 1966; Ferreiro & Teberosky, 1982).

Initially children's written names do not represent "oral language"; they are letters that belong to certain people or things. That is, rather than trying to encode speech into graphics, children typically made meaningful graphics about which they can talk (e.g., "This is my Mama's name") (Dyson, 1983). Just as speech helps to organize and elaborate on the meaning of early drawn objects, so too it aids early written names. For children, in fact, names are kinds of objects; they belong to people and things (Ferreiro & Teberosky, 1982; Papandropolou & Sinclair, 1974).

Figure 2.1 presents a drawn and written piece from Lamar's daily journal, completed early in the school year. The piece illustrates both early exploration of letterlike forms and the representational use of drawing and writing to name important people and things in a child's world. Lamar drew a sun, a rainbow, and flying insects and wrote letterlike forms and his name (not discernible).

Later in the year, Lamar made more extensive use of labeling in the context of a social activity that accentuated the value of names. The children had been to visit the aquarium, a very exciting trip for Lamar. After the experience, he drew and talked with his friends about the fish they had seen (see Figure 2.2). The children's drawing and talking supported each other, as they drew visual details and verbally discussed and, indeed, argued about the characteristics and names of different fish. Moreover, Lamar used a classroom "ocean animal" chart as a resource for the spelling of each creature's name; writing labels was a way to mark graphically his

Figure 2.1. Lamar's early writing: exploring and naming.

Figure 2.2. Lamar's naming of known ocean creatures through draw-ing and writing.

verbal claims about the kinds of fish he and his friends had seen and, therefore, drawn. Labeling was a common functional use of writing in his classroom, and one he could, by the spring of his kindergarten year, man-age himself with the support of teacher help and graphic aids.

While Lamar was clearly matching particular letters to particular names, children's engagement in such labeling activities does not require understanding that writing represents speech. For writing to become graphic discourse — written language — children must become aware that it is language itself that is written (Vygotsky, 1978). To illustrate how this discovery may happen, I turn to studies of young children's encoding of names.

Ferreiro (1980; Ferreiro & Teberosky, 1982), who conducted her work in Latin America, used Piagetian clinical interview techniques as children engaged in a range of literacy tasks. Within the context of these tasks, children seem to progress from simply making letters to hypothesizing a direct and concrete relationship between features of those letters and their intended meaning. Children seem particularly sensitive to the size and age of the referent. For example, one 4-year-old, Marianna, asked the experimenter to write a small number of letters for her own name and "as much as a thousand" for her father's name (which has only two syllables).

Such hypotheses introduce many puzzling circumstances for children. For example, Marianna will learn that her own name has, in fact, more letters than her father's. Eventually, children begin to search for some sort of reliable one-to-one correspondence between the letters of a name and the name itself. This search will lead some children to begin to use characteristics of the *sound* of the name to invent spellings, evidence that children are beginning to use written language as a second-order symbol system. Participating in language activities involving rhymes (found in plentiful supply in Mother Goose verses, poetry, and picture books built on language patterns) may help children become more conscious of the sounds in words and in this way contribute to early spelling (Bryant, Bradley, Maclean, & Crossland, 1989).

Read (1971, 1986) provided the seminal studies of the evolution of children's alphabetic spellings and the rule system underlying how they relate sounds to letters. Their spellings, like a 5-year-old's BS for "basghetti," can be as captivating as their pictures and, like all children's symbolic efforts, will evolve over time as their understandings become more sophisticated.

WRITTEN LANGUAGE: FROM PROP TO MEDIATOR IN STORY WRITING

While writing labels can mediate some functional activities, such as listing names of people and objects, it may also support more extended efforts, such as composing stories. When children "write" stories, they may engage in "symbol weaving": Written words are intertwined with talk and drawing, as children call upon all their symbolic powers (Dyson, 1986). Typically, any written words are indeed words in, rather than the essential stuff of, their world. That is, the words are the names of objects or figures or, perhaps, the sound of an event (e.g., *BOOM*). The bulk of the meaning may be in drawing or talk—or perhaps remain unarticulated in their own memories and imaginations. Writing is more prop than mediator.

Beginning to Manipulate Written Words

Lamar provides a good illustration of how early writing is shaped by social activity and how, within an activity, writing can begin to assume greater functional importance. Late in the spring of his kindergarten year, Lamar first displayed an attempt to manipulate written words to help compose a story. Lamar's teacher had suggested that he write a story about his visit to the aquarium. Such a suggestion was usually followed by drawing and dictation. However, Lamar had made an important discovery when he was labeling his ocean animals (see Figure 2.2). In writing the label *catfish*, Lamar recognized *C-A-T* ("*C-A-T* spells *cat*" was a common chant among the kindergartners). The conscious realization that the spoken and written names of two animals could together create the name of an entirely different animal intrigued him. He played with that discovery, manipulating the written words as he told a story, just as earlier he had manipulated the drawn waves as he told a story.

On a new sheet of paper, Lamar wrote *catfish*. "No," he said. He turned the paper over and wrote *cat* and, underneath, *fish*. (See Figure 2.3.) Next, he drew a cat and a fish. He "read" his story: "The cat wants to eat the fish." Lamar's written graphics were beginning to mediate his stories. He wrote them in a deliberate way, thinking about the placement of the names and how different placements would represent different stories. His wanted a story about a *cat* and a *fish*, not a *catfish*.

Lamar's story was quite simple. He was using written names to represent only part of his told story; moreover, he was not attempting to manipulate readers' emotions or their evolving understandings of his tale. Still, Lamar was attempting to control the slow, deliberate process of using graphic symbols to mediate linguistic meaning.

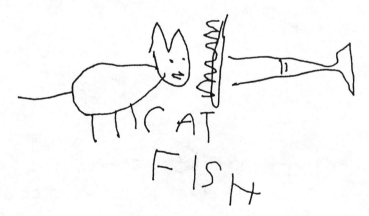

Figure 2.3. Lamar's drawing and labeling for his story about a cat and a fish.

Discovering Literacy's Social Power

Soon after this event, in fact, Lamar received a vivid example of the social power literacy can potentially exert, for good or ill. Lamar had drawn and told a story in which two boys are by the ocean; they fall in, and a shark eats them. After he drew, with his teacher's encouragement, he attempted to write his story. Lamar wrote a much reduced version of his story, one without the compelling dialogue he dramatized and the dramatic images he drew. (See Figure 2.4.)

> TO BYS WT
> N TE WD
> A SRK

Translation: Two boys went in the water. A shark.

James was intrigued by Lamar's efforts. Because he was less knowledgeable about print—and more dependent than Lamar on an oral investment

Figure 2.4. Lamar's written story: Two boys went in the water. A shark.

of the print's meaning—James asked Lamar how to write, "Once there was a boy and Jaws come." Lamar responded:

Lamar: Man, you should write this. *(pointing to his own text)*
James: Why?
Lamar: 'Cause *(reading)* "boys go in the water."

James asks again and Lamar reiterates that he should write what he has written. He knows that what he has written is not what James has asked for, but he also knows that James has no way of knowing that and he would find it very difficult to write James's request. So Lamar tells James to copy his letters, "So the boy can go in the water." And when James asks him about writing that Jaws came, Lamar tells him to copy SRK and then grins sheepishly at me:

Lamar: I tricked him. I can read. I didn't know I could do that. I
   didn't know I could do nothing but sit here all day.

In the midst of interacting with James, Lamar discovered his own literacy and its potential social power.

Still, Lamar at this point is using writing only as a supplement to represent a small part of his story. The adventure is played out in all its drama in the drawing and playing. And it is the drawing and dramatic play that make his work accessible to others — that elicited James's attention — and that also provide him with the most satisfying "canvas" for replaying the emotional quality of experiences.

Interacting Through Written Words

How do children's written words themselves become sites for dramatic, vivid adventures? This was the question I investigated during a 3-year study in an urban magnet school that placed particular value on the expressive arts (Dyson, 1989). I focused on the changing role of writing in 4- to 8-year-olds' symbol making and social interactions during a daily composing period.

The observed children initially relied on drawing and talking to carry much of their story meaning and, also, to engage their peers' attention. Their writing and dictating was primarily a descriptive supplement to their pictures. In time, though, the children began to attend to each other's reading and planning of their texts, evidencing the curiosity children have about what their peers are doing. Their playful and critical talk thus engulfed their writing and helped it become a legitimate object of attention, separate from their pictures.

Children began to consider critically the relationship between their pictures and their texts, as they assumed more deliberate control over the kind of information they would include in each medium. Gradually their written stories contained more narrative action, their pictures more illustrations of key ideas. Moreover, they began to use writing playfully to engage their peers. They made their friends characters in their stories, and they also began to plan deliberately to include certain words or actions to amuse or tease them.

Thus the children came to understand that story writers and their readers interact through — play within — the words, and, as authors, they were in charge of the interaction. Through manipulating the elements (and thereby the words) of written language, they could manipulate as well the social responses of others, that is, the way their audience visualized, emotionally responded to, and reasoned about their efforts. Indeed, as Edelsky's (1986) work has suggested, young bilingual writers may manipulate not only words but also languages themselves in order to convey emphasis, to show concern for the audience (who may know only one language or the other), or simply to capture a memory or feeling that is metaphorically more vivid in one language rather than another.

To illustrate the artistic and social potential of young writers, I turn to William, a third grader in Lamar's school. As a story writer, William had a strong sense of writing as interactive play, a sense that seemed supported by his sociocultural traditions. Playful storytelling is an important part of African American culture, and, indeed, William was a fine storyteller. It was not until the latter half of the third grade, however, that the written medium effectively mediated his artful tales.

In the following story, William played with his audience, anticipating his peers' curiosity and giggles, their reflective evaluations of his uncle (whom he displays as not too smart) and of himself (a disparaged but eventually respected character in his own story). William spent quite a bit of time with his uncle, who cared for him when his mother's work schedule kept her away long hours. His uncle, he felt, could be awfully bossy, and William took no small delight in stories of the teasing uncle who, in the end, was always put in his place:

My Uncle and the Cussing Bird

OK this how it started. My uncle wanted a bird so bad, he tried to get one out of the sky. Now that's dumb. So one day he was hoping that he can get a bird free. And I said to my Uncle Glen, "How are you going to do that?" And he said, "I don't know." So two months later a box came, and it said bird. And my uncle started screaming and teasing me. He was saying, "Oh yes. I have a bird. Ha, ha, ha ha, ha. I have a bird. Ha, ha, ha ha, ha." And he opened it, and the bird was dead. And he started to cry. The whole couch was wet with tears. I tried onions but he started to cry more. Then, he started to cry more. The next week, more and more boxes, and he kept saying, "Ha, ha, ha ha, ha." And one day a box came—Yes yes yes! The bird said "I'm polly-want-a cracker." [And] he said, "F_____ you big mouth." And my uncle never wanted a bird again. Do you know what he wanted? A fish. [Story given conventional spelling and punctuation for ease of reading]

William was most anxious to share his story with his classmates, and, indeed, the tale *was* exceedingly well-received by his peers. They asked him to read it again and again, giggling at his humorous images—the uncle trying to get a bird out of the sky, the boxes that came and came—and laughing loudly at his expressive dialogue. It is, in fact, pictures, dramatic action, and dialogue—drawing, playing, and talking—that provide the developmental link between William's "Cussing Bird" and Lamar's "Cat Fish." Unlike Lamar, William drew his pictures with words and conveyed his drama through voices on paper. But both children orchestrated images and talk to compose, and, in so doing, they participated in an involving classroom social life in which both they and their texts mattered.

Although story writing has been stressed in this chapter, the foundation for reading and writing is built across the curriculum through talk-filled activities in which children have access to many symbolic tools. Those tools may allow children to give form to their understandings and more easily share those understandings with others. There is a need, in other words, for putting child literacy in its place.

PUTTING CHILD LITERACY IN ITS (SYMBOLIC) PLACE: IMPLICATIONS FOR EARLY CHILDHOOD EDUCATION

In many publications for early childhood teachers, readers are told of "developmental stages of writing," progressing from child scribbles to invented spelling (a more accurate statement might be the stages of "spelling"). In this chapter, I have hoped to make clear that such statements are based on attention to the surface manifestations of writing (the marks on the page), not to the complex underlying reality. *There is no linear progression in written language development.* Rather its development is linked in complex ways to the whole of children's symbolic repertoires; its evolution involves shifts of function and symbolic form, social give-and-take, as children explore and gradually control new ways to organize and represent their world and to interact with other people about that world.

Figuring out how to make word pictures and visible rhythms and sounds, how to make a string of black-and-white squiggles an enacted and dialogic world is a basic developmental challenge. Thus the roots of William's story — and the ones Lamar has yet to write — are not in squiggles but in drawn pictures, told stories, dramatic play, and in much talk with people interested in what the children have to "say" in many media.

Putting writing in its symbolic place — seeing its emergence within the child's total symbolic repertoire — suggests, first, that *children in the early childhood years need many opportunities to use the arts* — to draw, play, dance, and sing. For young children, the most accessible media are those that most directly capture the movements of their own bodies, the sounds of their own voices, and the images made by their own hands, as lines, curves, and colors take form on paper.

First-grade teacher Karen Gallas (1991) describes a unit on insects and their life cycles and, in the process, beautifully details how drawing, painting, music, movement, drama, poetry, and storytelling, "each domain separately and together, became part of [the children's] total repertoire as learners" (p. 40). In a classroom in which cultural, social, and language barriers might have kept children apart, use of the arts allowed individuals many avenues for learning, expression, and communication. Some children sketched insects, focusing on visual details, while others dramatized the life cycle of an insect, their bodies capturing the changing shapes of life, and still others drew grass as seen from the perspective of an insect. New intelligences, in Gardner's (1985) sense, were visible as children forged new understandings through colorful images and felt movements, understandings that will surely inform their writing and reading of static, black-and-white squiggles on a page.

The curious world and the children themselves should be the center of the curriculum, not writing or reading. Indeed the point of this article has been that making literacy the center of the curriculum in early childhood may keep those black-and-white squiggles from becoming dynamic, colorful intellectual and social tools. This point leads to a second recommendation — that *teachers help connect print with the liveliness of children's use of other symbolic forms.* Paley and Soderbergh provide child-rich examples of how this can be done.

In a series of books on her own classroom life with children, Paley (e.g., 1981, 1986) has illustrated how 3-, 4-, and 5-year-olds can collaboratively transform themes of their dramatic play into dictated texts and back again to play. For many children, dictated words "did not sufficiently represent the action, which needed to be shared" through the media of their own voices and actions (1981, p. 12). Transforming their own texts into dramas allows children and teachers opportunities to find words for unarticulated ideas.

Soderbergh (1990) studied a 5½-year-old's spontaneous illustrations of stories she had read. She suggests how drawing may help some children reveal the "inner pictures" that underlay their efforts to make sense of text (p. 189). In one especially vivid example, the child illustrated a Bible story about the Israelites' trip to Canaan "with their children, cows and sheep and all the precious things they had received [i.e., from the Egyptians]" (p. 178); she drew a procession of people, all carrying parcels wrapped up in paper and bound with ribbons.

Third, *children should be allowed the artistic and social space they need to infuse meaning into their own writing through drawing, social talk, and dramatic play.* Children's first explorations of writing's forms and functions may give rise to more focused attempts to match precisely meanings and forms inside familiar activities, such as composing letters, making names, or, as Lamar illustrated, drawing and telling stories.

Lamar made good progress in literacy learning during his kindergarten year, but he did not make progress in his first-grade year. One difficulty was that his teacher viewed talk during writing as useful *only* for getting or giving "help" — all other talk was just "playing around." Drawing was also discouraged during daily "journal" time. But it was playful and social talk during drawing that, in fact, helped Lamar shape his ideas and that provided the social energy for his writing. Without such support, he maintained only minimal involvement in writing.

Children's interweaving of media does pose developmental challenges as, eventually, children must differentiate and gain control over the unique powers of each medium. So a fourth implication is to *talk to children about their efforts and, in that way, to help them reflect upon their processes.* Indeed, many early childhood educators consider reflecting with young children about their ways of drawing (Schirrmacher, 1988; Thompson, 1990), playing (Christie, 1991), and writing to be major ways of supporting young children's development. What aspects of their imagined world are in the pictures? The print? In dramatized action? Or still unarticulated, waiting for an interested other to help give them shape. At the same time, children must be allowed to stay in charge of their own intentions (Genishi & Dyson, 1984). Young children feel no compulsion to put into written words the meanings they express through drawing and talk. The differentiation and control of these varied media is a gradual developmental process, one we nurture but cannot force.

All of the preceding implications lead to a fifth: *As early childhood educators we should be cautious about uncritically applying "writing-process" curricula developed for older children.* Many educators, elementary through college level, make use of writing-process pedagogy (e.g., Graves, 1983). This pedagogy has made critical contributions to language arts curricula, as it has very sensibly called attention to the process, rather than the product, of writing — the brainstorming of ideas, the drafting of first efforts for feedback during "conferences," revising, and finally publishing. But some applications of these pedagogical ideas may be too structured and too focused on writing per se for very young children.

Process pedagogy emphasizes individual children's production of "meaningful" text, but young children sometimes freely explore writing's forms in ways that may be, for an adult, very "meaningless." In addition, early attempts to write may happen in socially playful ways, as in Lamar's case; serious talk during a writing "conference" with their teacher may be less important than playful and reflective talk during an activity involving writing. Most importantly, young children do not seem to "revise" in the same ways older children do. As discussed, children often freely reinterpret their products when their initial goals do not work out. For example, if their drawings do not match their intentions, they do not necessarily revise their drawings — they revise their intentions. In their *next* efforts, they may try a new approach.

In similar ways, children persist in exploring a theme in composition after composition, in playful drama after drama, much as Lamar did with his ocean scenes. Unfulfilled intentions spur next efforts. This is quite different from "revising," in which children redo the same product. Such revisions might happen first in joint efforts between teachers and children, such as in class-dictated texts.

Finally, the complexity of written language development and its complex links to the whole of children's symbolic repertoire suggest a need for *caution in applying simple functional models of oral language in research on written language growth.* In early childhood, a number of researchers have studied children's dramatic play for evidence of oral language functions as applied to writing, assuming that written language is an extension only of oral language. The observation of children's awareness of literacy functions is a helpful tool for teachers, allowing them insight into children's awareness of literacy's uses. But functional awareness does not ensure development (Vygotsky, 1932–1934/1987), the complex social and cognitive processes that underlie change.

Unlike oral language, written language involves the use of a deliberately controlled symbolic system to mediate activity. A child, for example, who says she is pretending to write a letter may not be using written language to mediate her activity. To use Halliday's (1973) terms, the child perhaps is showing an awareness of the interactional function of literacy, but the letter is fulfilling an imaginary as much as an interactional function. It is more prop than mediator. To understand how development occurs, it would be necessary to study how the child attempts to write a letter, the role of that letter writing in the child's social activity (including inside dramatic social play), the role of other media (e.g., drawing, talking, and dramatic gestures) in the accomplishment of the letter writing, and how the child's interaction with other people and with other media changes over time, as writing is transformed from primarily a prop to a mediator.

In closing, to understand and foster written language development, we must view that development within the particularities of children's social and artistic lives. Indeed, we as adult writers may turn to media that seem to fit most comfortably the initial contours of our ideas before struggling to craft those ideas within the linear confines of print: we may draw, map, make gestures in the air, or even sprawl conversational language across a page. It was in the midst of dramatic happenings at sea that Lamar's writing took hold in the kindergarten — and, without such support, he seemed adrift in the first grade. In brief, written language emerges most strongly when firmly embedded within the supportive symbolic sea of playful gestures, pictures, and talk.

Acknowledgments. I thank my research assistant, Paula Crivello. The work reported herein was supported under the Educational Research and Development Center Program (R117G10036) as administered by the Office of Educational Research and Improvement, Department of Education. The findings and opinions expressed in this report do not reflect the position or policy of the Office of Educational Research and Improvement or the U.S. Department of Education.

REFERENCES

Brittain, W. L. (1979). *Creativity, art, and the young child*. New York: Macmillan.

Bryant, P. E., Bradley, L., Maclean, M., & Crossland, J. (1989). Nursery rhymes, phonological skills, and reading. *Journal of Child Language, 16*, 407–428.

Christie, J. F. (Ed.) (1991). *Play and early literacy development*. Albany: State University of New York Press.

Clay, M. (1975). *What did I write?*. Auckland, New Zealand: Heinemann.

Durkin, D. (1966). *Children who read early: Two longitudinal studies*. New York: Teachers College Press.

Dyson, A. H. (1982). The emergence of visible language: Interrelationships between drawing and early writing. *Visible Language, 6*, 360–381.

Dyson, A. H. (1983). The role of oral language in early writing processes. *Research in the Teaching of English, 17*, 1–30.

Dyson, A. H. (1986). Transitions and tensions: Interrelationships between the drawing, talking, and dictating of young children. *Research in the Teaching of English, 20*, 379–409.

Dyson, A. H. (1989). *Multiple worlds of child writers: Friends learning to write.* New York: Teachers College Press.

Dyson, A. H. (1991). The word and the world: Reconceptualizing written language development, or, Do rainbows mean a lot to little girls? *Research in the Teaching of English, 25*, 97–123.

Dyson, A. H. (1992). The case of the singing scientist: A performance perspective on the "stages" of school literacy. *Written Communication, 9*, 3–47.

Edelsky, C. (1986). *Writing in a bilingual program: Habia una vez.* Norwood, NJ: Ablex.

Fein, G. G. (1987). Pretend play: Creativity and consciousness. In D. Gorlitz & J. F. Wohlwill (Eds.), *Curiosity, imagination, and play: On the development of spontaneous cognitive and motivational processes* (pp. 281–304). Hillsdale, NJ: Erlbaum.

Ferreiro, E. (1980, May). *The relationship between oral and written language: The children's viewpoint.* Paper presented at the Third Impact Conference of the National Council of Teachers of English and the International Reading Association, St. Louis, MO.

Ferreiro E., & Teberosky, A. (1982). *Literacy before schooling.* Exeter, NH: Heinemann.

Gallas, K. (1991). Arts as epistemology: Enabling children to know what they know. *Harvard Educational Review, 61*, 40–50.

Gardner, H. (1985). *Frames of mind: The theory of multiple intelligences.* New York: Basic Books.

Gardner, H., & Wolf, D. (1987). The symbolic products of early childhood. In D. Gorlitz & J. F. Wohlwill (Eds.), *Curiosity, imagination, and play: On the development of spontaneous cognitive and motivational processes* (pp. 305–325). Hillsdale, NJ: Erlbaum.

Garvey, C. (1990). *Play* (enl. ed.). Cambridge, MA: Harvard University Press.

Geertz, C. (1983). *Local knowledge.* New York: Basic Books.

Genishi, C., & Dyson, A. H. (1984). *Language assessment in the early years.* Norwood, NJ: Ablex.

Golomb, C. (1974). *Young children's sculpture and drawing: A study in representational development.* Cambridge, MA: Harvard University Press.

Golomb, C. (1988). Symbolic inventions and transformations in child art. In K. Egan & D. Nadaner (Eds.), *Imagination and education* (pp. 222–236). New York: Teachers College Press.

Graves, D. (1983). *Writing: Teachers and children at work.* Exeter, NH: Heinemann.

Halliday, M. A. K. (1973). *Explorations in the functions of language.* London: Edward Arnold.

Luria, A. (1983). The development of writing in the child. In M. Martlew (Ed.), *The psychology of written language* (pp. 237–277). New York: Wiley.

Mathews, J. (1984). Children drawing: Are young children really scribbling? *Early Child Development and Care, 17*, 1–39.

Morrow, L. M., & Rand, M. (1991). Preparing the classroom environment to promote literacy during play. In J. F. Christie (Ed.), *Play and early literacy development* (pp. 141–166). Albany: State University of New York Press.

Paley, V. (1981). *Wally's stories.* Cambridge, MA: Harvard University Press.

Paley, V. (1986). *Mollie is three: Growing up in school.* Chicago: University of Chicago Press.

Papandropolou, I., & Sinclair, H. (1974). What's in a word? Experimental study of children's ideas on grammar. *Human Development, 17*, 241–258.

Piaget, J., & Inhelder, B. (1969). *The psychology of the child.* New York: Basic Books.

Read, C. (1971). Pre-school children's knowledge of English phonology. *Harvard Educational Review, 41*, 1–34.

Read, C. (1986). *Children's creative spelling.* London: Routledge & Kegan Paul.

Schickedanz, J. A. (1978). "You be the doctor and I'll be sick." *Language Arts, 55*, 713–718.

Schirrmacher, R. (1988). *Art and creative development for young children.* Albany, NY: Delmar.

Smith, N. (1979). Developmental origins of structural variation in symbol form. In N. R. Smith & M. B. Franklin (Eds.), *Symbolic functioning in childhood* (pp. 11–26). Hillsdale, NJ: Erlbaum.

Soderbergh, R. (1990). Semiotic play: A child translates text into pictures. *Working Papers* (Lund University, Department of Linguistics), *36*, 163–190.

Thompson, C. (1990). "I made a mark": The significance of talk in young children's artistic development. *Early Childhood Research Quarterly, 5*, 215–233.

Vygotsky, L. S. (1978). *Mind in society.* Cambridge, MA: Harvard University Press.

Vygotsky, L. (1987). *Collected works: Vol. 1. Problems of general psychology* (R. W. Rieber & A. S. Carton, Eds.; N. Minick, Trans.). New York: Plenum. (Original work published 1932–1934)

Werner, H., & Kaplan, B. (1963). *Symbol formation: An organismic-developmental approach to language and the expression of thought.* New York: Wiley.

Wertsch, J. (1989). A sociocultural approach to mind. In W. Damon (Ed.), *Child development today and tomorrow* (pp. 14–33). San Francisco: Jossey-Bass.

Winner, E. (1989). Development in the visual arts. In W. Damon (Ed.), *Child development today and tomorrow* (pp. 199–221). San Francisco: Jossey-Bass.

Wolf, D., & Perry, M. D. (1989). From endpoints to repertoires: Some new conclusions about drawing development. In H. Gardner & D. Perkins (Eds.), *Art, mind, and education: Research from Project Zero* (pp. 17–34). Urbana and Chicago: University of Illinois Press.

CHAPTER 3

Literacy Development: The Whole Language Approach

Olivia N. Saracho

Research in language and literacy acquisition over the past two decades has suggested that initial reading instruction should be offered in a natural context and should reflect the children's own language. Some educators (e.g., Edelsky, Altwerger, & Flores, 1991; Goodman, 1986; Harste, 1985; Newman, 1985) have used the results of this research to propose a *Whole Language* approach to language and literacy instruction.

In Whole Language the focus is the integrated practice of reading, writing, and speaking, listening, and knowing. Process, product, and content are fused, and the purposeful use of language is stressed over skill acquisition. The Whole Language approach was developed to improve the process by which children learned to read and to provide students with more time to engage in language activities, including reading, during each school day. It is believed that reading and writing, listening and speaking are reciprocal processes that should have equal time in the curriculum (Stahl & Miller, 1989).

Whole Language is seen as a liberating pedagogy (Edelsky et al., 1991). The Whole Language movement is related to previous movements for child-centered education (e.g., progressive education, language experience approach to reading, open education). While all these movements share common beliefs, there are also differences among them. Whole Language may be considered a movement concerned with reconstructing education, especially in the way that reading and writing are taught. Mac-Ginite (1991) notes that education movements last a short period of time. This time is often insufficient to determine the merit of the movement. Ideas or theories are too often transformed before being fully implemented, evaluated, or even comprehended.

UNDERSTANDING THE WHOLE LANGUAGE MOVEMENT

Psycholinguist Kenneth Goodman adapted and modified various of the principles of language learning suggested by language theorists in New Zealand, Australia, Canada, Great Britain, and the United States to initiate Whole Language. He believes that one cannot teach segments of language in isolation from one another. In fact, he asserts that language is not language if it is not whole.

The Whole Language approach is more than an activity-based language learning program. The manifestations are a core approach in which children focus on the communication of written language (Goodman, 1986; Harste, 1985; Newman, 1985). Students learn reading and writing in a meaningful context. According to Altwerger, Edelsky, and Flores (1987):

> Whole language is based on the following ideas: (a) language is for making meanings, for accomplishing purposes; (b) written language is language — thus what is true for language in general is true for written language; (c) the cuing systems of language (phonology in oral, orthography in written language, morphology, syntax, semantics, pragmatic) are always simultaneously present and interacting in any instance of language in use; (d) language used always occurs in a situation; (e) situations are critical to meaning-making. (p. 154)

While there are different definitions of Whole Language, they all share a set of beliefs that incorporates compatible practice in its richest sense (not just methods and materials). Ganopole (1988) summarized the views that characterize Whole Language as follows:

1. Learning is an active constructive process with prior knowledge, interests, and self-motivated purposes having a major role in the process.
2. Language is central to the learning process.
3. Social interactions are essential to the learning process.
4. Language is learned through using it to serve relevant purposes.
5. Reading is a process of making meaning where meaning is constructed through the associations of what is in the text and what the reader knows and believes.
6. Writing is a process of making meaning by making connections and constructing meanings.

Thus language is seen as an indivisible whole instead of a set of isolated elements, such as writing, reading, or spelling. Students' needs and interests are central to instruction. Their active involvement is vital in making instruction meaningful to them. Together students and teachers plan and implement instruction.

Whole Language advocates (e.g., Altwerger et al., 1987; Goodman, 1986; Harste, 1985; Newman, 1985) believe that Whole Language is an explicit theory in practice. Although most advocates of the approach do not provide a theoretical definition, they do describe a set of beliefs and practices, such as that language is learned in a meaningful context but not through the performance of language exercises. The basic belief in Whole Language is that students must actively engage in reading and writing experiences instead of working on exercises or developing "make-believe" language or reading skills. Students assimilate knowledge of language when they immerse themselves in meaningful language experiences. The theory of Whole Language may be based on a philosophical position similar to that found in early childhood education: that children learn through active engagement — as in play, which allows children to interact with one another and to engage in a variety of learning experiences. Because of the centrality of this set of beliefs, the Whole Language approach is often seen as an ideology rather than a theory of instruction.

In Whole Language, reading is a social act that recapitulates social–historical–cultural activities and psychological–linguistic processes (Bloome & Solsken, 1988). Whole Language challenges the validity of skill-based reading instruction (worksheet activities) and skills checkups (comprehension questions), even if such reading assignments use exercise skills with an enriching reading event (see Edelsky & Draper, 1989, for a contrast between an enriching reading event and reading exercises). In traditional initial reading instruction, students are drilled on the identification and association of letters and sounds. In Whole Language instruction, students read stories, poems, signs, and a variety of other print materials. As children write, they become aware of spelling rules, first using their knowledge of letter–sound associations to invent spelling, and then moving toward standard spelling. Meaningful stories and texts help children acquire strategies to make sense of the written word. Such procedures help children to capture phonic rules and to identify words in a variety of contexts.

Since Whole Language refers to a philosophy rather than a methodology, a wide range of instructional practices can be found in Whole Language classrooms (Altwerger et al., 1987). Generally, planning, writing, editing, and revising in peer conferences are used in the writing process. Reading activities include daily reading of trade books, newspapers, materials written by the students, and similar literacy activities that rely on the students' interests (Smith-Burke, 1987).

A radical assumption of Whole Language is the claim that children learn how to write and read, especially during the initial stages, merely by having the written language displayed in the environment (Goelman, Oberg, & Smith, 1984). Writing and reading competence is acquired without direct instruction within a supportive environment. There is insufficient research evidence, however, to support the assumption that most children learn this way (Dickinson, 1987). Exposing children to print may not necessarily teach them how to read (Calfee & Drum, 1985; Ehri, 1987; Richgels, McGee, & Slaton, 1988). One study by Ehri (1987) found that even after children had considerable experience with print in their environments, they did not acquire the ability to read. Another study showed that nonreaders paid some attention to graphic information but observed only individual letters and numbers (Richgels et al., 1988).

The professional literature on the Whole Language approach (see Jaggar & Harwood, 1989) describes what occurs in classrooms. However, because such a great variety of classrooms are labeled as "Whole Language," it is hard to generalize about all classrooms. It is possible, though, to identify the attributes that would characterize Whole Language classrooms to varying degrees.

WHOLE LANGUAGE CLASSROOMS

A Whole Language classroom provides activities in which children learn to read by reading, learn to write by writing, and engage in meaning-centered, integrated language arts activities based on specific topics or themes (Goodman, 1986; Slaughter, 1988). Ability groups are not used for instruction. Rather, groups are formed based on common interests or goals. Instruction in Whole Language classrooms usually takes place in learning centers that focus on a topic or theme for integrated study, such as "the post office." A writing center may have several learning alternatives that allow students to compose in different writing forms related to the theme. A social studies center may provide opportunities for students to learn the ways that people communicated with one another in early times. A music center may provide a variety of recorded songs about America, focusing attention on the messages that song lyrics provide. All the centers would offer opportunities for children to read, write, listen, and speak. There is a degree of noise in the classroom as students work and move among the different learning areas.

In a Whole Language classroom, teachers create a print-rich environment with children's literature, which is available in all its variety: enlarged texts (such as Big Books) for shared reading; books related to music, art, science, and social studies curriculum areas; and books in the reading, listening, and special-interest areas (Fountas & Hannigan, 1989).

Whole Language classrooms are often designed to provide a homelike environment. The room may be softened with pillows and carpeted areas for reading and discussions. Large pillows, reading lofts, round tables and chairs, beanbag chairs, and old couches may be positioned around the classroom. Children can sit or lie down while they enjoy their favorite books. Students' compositions, dictations, and any of their work related to reading and writing are displayed throughout the classroom on walls and windows. They may even be displayed on the floor or suspended from the ceiling.

A Whole Language program needs careful planning to provide a balanced and coherent language arts component. It should gradually evolve to avoid simply grafting some of the trappings of a Whole Language program onto a traditional program, for example, merely including Big Books and writing activities with invented spelling in the traditional language arts program. Teachers need to focus on how to fully implement the basic principles that guide Whole Language teaching. Fountas and Hannigan (1989) suggest these principles:

1. *Children are empowered as language users.* As students actively use language for reading and other functions, they come to understand its potential.
2. *Oral language is given greater prominence.* Whole Language focuses instruction on a variety of oral language forms as a means of communication.
3. *Reading is viewed as a thinking process.* Students learn to use semantic, syntactic, and graphic cuing systems of the language in an active, constructive process.
4. *The focus is on the text as whole.* A text must be complete to communicate its entire purpose. A whole text helps children learn important structural patterns in both fiction and nonfiction. Thus whole stories, poems, songs, and chants should be the basis of reading in Whole Language classrooms.
5. *Classic literature is revitalized.* A focus on language emphasizes literature in its variety of dialects and genres.
6. *Writing is a learning process.* Writing is an active, constructive process. Writers at all stages construct meaning.
7. *Skills are grasped within the reading and writing context.* Students must understand the context in which skills are used in their broader application.
8. *The connection between reading and writing is highlighted.* At the all levels, children are provided with opportunities to dictate group or individual stories to express their ideas. They then see them in written form.

9. *The curriculum is fused.* Skills and subject matter must be interwoven to help children experience continuity in the curriculum. Skills are developed within units of experience built on a familiar idea.
10. *The teachers assume an important role.* Teachers must provide developmentally appropriate skills in reading and writing, in children's literature, and in content areas.

Whole Language is an important movement in education. However, like other important educational movements in the past, it may just be a rising trend, soon to be ignored. To protect children enrolled in these programs, they must be provided with opportunities to learn literacy and language skills at all stages of their development. Skill development must not be left to chance alone. As a matter of fact, skill development should be considered an important part of Whole Language methodology. Pedagogy and content must be related to each other to establish meaningful contexts for learning. However, while skills should be taught in context, as needed, this can be done systematically.

Teachers

Teachers may encounter problems if they attempt to integrate a Whole Language program into their regular school curriculum. A Whole Language approach requires that teachers modify their approach to teaching throughout the curriculum. The characteristics of a Whole Language approach include time, ownership, process, conferences, and resources (Butler & Turbill, 1984; Prenn & Scanlan, 1991). Implementing a program with these characteristics challenges both teachers and students. According to Prenn and Scanlan (1991):

1. *Time* allows students to practice the reading and writing by reading aloud, engaging in whole-group instruction, providing for small-group sharing of self-selected texts and literature, creating reading/writing workshops, meeting with students in individual conferences, and providing a brief closure.
2. *Ownership* suggests that the students select activities and assume responsibility in a Whole Language class. They feel a degree of proprietorship in the program. They reflect on their work, make decisions, and gain satisfaction from functioning in a productive learning environment.
3. *Process* is essential to teaching and learning. It demands reflection, time, and personal involvement. Students learn as they manipulate and apply concepts, making and correcting mistakes.

4. *Conferences* are an integral part of a Whole Language program. They permit teachers to assist students on an individual basis and to clarify the value of ideas or strategies.
5. *Resources*, such as people or printed and visual materials, must be multiple and diverse. Students can interview, correspond with, and telephone resource people.

These elements of the Whole Language approach require teachers to develop a different classroom structure. They also encourage teachers and students to modify their roles. Teachers often have to rethink their teaching strategies and assess their habits as readers and writers. These characteristics yield an exciting and effective means of teaching (Prenn & Scanlan, 1991).

A major shift is the teacher's role. Since a Whole Language classroom is an activities-based classroom (Goodman, 1986; Slaughter, 1988), the teacher's role is modified in the process of its development. "Since in the current active approaches to writing the teacher is regarded as collaborator rather than as expert instructor, the degree to which a learner profits eventually from this collaboration must depend to some extent upon his/her success in internalizing the teacher's contribution" (Britton, 1987, p. 19).

Duffy and Roehler (1986) refer to this type of teaching as "indirect instruction."

> Instruction is indirect when the teacher intentionally orchestrates various aspects of the classroom environment in ways that lead students to specific outcomes. While it may not appear that teachers are engaged in instruction when they are sitting and reading a library book or quietly observing students interacting in pairs, they really are. Such activity is intentional, it involves work, a strategy for presenting the work, and interactions with students as they pursue it. (p. 82)

Whole Language teachers need to concentrate on the students' learning instead of on teachers' teaching. They teach language and literacy by reading stories and poetry aloud to their students to initiate interest. Students may reread favorite stories as a group on large charts or in Big Books. In preparing students for a story, Whole Language teachers often employ such strategies as brainstorming and prediction. They encourage students to share their knowledge about the story or topic and to predict the setting, plot, and conclusion of the story. As a result, reading becomes a process of prediction and confirmation.

This contrasts with the role of the teacher in traditional language and literacy programs. As Duffy and Roehler (1986) suggest, "when teachers instruct directly they assume a highly structured, active, and dominant role in which teacher talk is relied upon to ensure that students interpret the work in the intended way and achieve the desired outcome" (p. 76).

The focus in the Whole Language approach is on the learner rather than on the teacher. Goodman (1986) notes that "teaching doesn't make language learning happen; it supports its development . . . effective teaching supports and extends learning; it can never control it" (p. 361). This shift in focus requires work on the part of the teacher. Klesius, Griffith, and Zielonka (1991) examined teachers in the transition from an approach using textbooks and teachers' manuals to the Whole Language approach. They found that the Whole Language teachers benefited from inservice preparation prior to their work and coaching throughout the year. One of the investigators demonstrated the Whole Language approach for two days in one of the classes and one day in another class, with follow-up visits throughout the remainder of the year. Although the teachers initiating the Whole Language approach encountered problems at first, they had made the transition successfully by the end of the study.

A staff developer, Wollman-Bonilla (1991), introduced Whole Language to a group of teachers. Her experience with teachers during their initial contact with the Whole Language approach suggests that the teachers must have a personal sense of its purpose during the transition to that approach.

Within the Whole Language approach, teachers only teach specific reading skills as the need for them emerges during their experiences. Direct instruction is circumvented (Edelsky et al., 1991; Goodman, 1986; Rentzel & Hollingsworth, 1988). However, Slaughter (1988) insists that some direct teaching of reading skills must occur. Edelsky and colleagues (1991), in contrast, suggest that a Whole Language approach cannot be employed half-way. Teachers cannot implement Whole Language only part of the time, or for only some hours or on some days, or even exercise only some of the Whole Language concepts. Teachers must either adopt Whole Language in its entirety or reject it completely. This seems an extreme position, especially since Whole Language classrooms differ so much from one another.

Students

Whole Language builds on the students' interests to develop written language strategies (Doake, 1985). Students choose topics that interest them instead of writing on an assigned topic. They read books that interest them — literature as well as informational and reference books needed for their work. They cooperate with one another in reading and writing activities. Students may also spend long periods of time in their own silent reading and writing activities.

Students use their language activities as tools to inquire into their world and to express the new knowledge they acquire. A Whole Language environment invites students to take intellectual risks, formulating and testing hypotheses they develop, correcting their own work, and collaborating with others in a community of learners. Students explore the functions of language as they integrate their language processes with their conceptual learning. All of this requires a rich, literate environment in which children have the opportunity to read, write, listen, and speak. Materials in the environment are used in meaningful literary events that support the development of thematic units.

In a Whole Language environment, students share information, solve problems, interact with one another, independently read a wide variety of material, write for many different purposes, raise questions about what they hear and read, and observe and emulate adults who demonstrate various literacy functions in the classroom. A supportive environment helps students develop their skills within a context of meaningful reading and writing. It also offers a high level of motivation, which is supported by the students' success and active involvement in Whole Language activities (Fountas & Hannigan, 1989).

Students cooperate with each other. They may instruct one another, serve as sounding boards for each other's ideas, act as sources of knowledge, and provide different forms of support to one another in their learning tasks. Such classrooms avoid competition for grades or other rewards. They do acknowledge the importance and joy of learning, so that the language act becomes its own reward.

EFFECTIVENESS OF WHOLE LANGUAGE

Problems have been encountered in assessing the effectiveness of Whole Language programs. One problem is that the movement may be too young to assess in terms of long-term outcomes. In addition, Whole Language eludes definition (Stahl & Miller, 1989). Many describe it as an "attitude, not methods" (Rich, 1985, p. 718) and as a "philosophy rather than a methodology" (Clarke, 1987, p. 386). Goodman (1986) believes that many methods can be used within a Whole Language classroom and that many different approaches to Whole Language are acceptable. Newman (1985) confesses, "I find myself in the uncomfortable position of being unable to tell you succinctly what 'whole language' is" (p. 1). Watson (1989) concludes that "most whole-language advocates reject a diction-ary-type definition that can be looked up and memorized" (p. 131). Each teacher's definition of Whole Language is considered personal and unique. These views of Whole Language present a perplexing situation to research-ers wishing to study the approach. It is unclear what the approach is, or whether there really is a single approach. Thus one is not sure what should be evaluated, or whether one can generalize from the study of any one class or set of classes. Such a condition may have contributed to inconsis-tent outcomes of studies, since one Whole Language approach varies in important ways from the next (McKenna, Robinson, & Miller, 1990).

Klesius and colleagues (1991) compared three first-grade Whole Lan-guage classrooms with three traditional first-grade classrooms. They found no significant differences in outcomes between the two instructional treat-ments. A meta-analysis of 51 studies comparing different approaches to Whole Language/language experience methods of instruction indicated that Whole Language/language experience approaches and basal reader programs were equally effective. The more contemporary and rigorous studies support basal reader programs, especially for children with special needs. It is suggested that the Whole Language/language experience ap-proach is more effective with beginning readers but should be followed by systematic instruction in word recognition/decoding (Stahl & Miller, 1989). Children must first comprehend the practical facets of reading (e.g., concepts about print, understanding that reading is a form of com-munication) and then learn word recognition/decoding skills to a level that permits them to comprehend smoothly what they are reading (Harris & Sipay, 1990). Through Whole Language young children learn that read-ing is a form of communication. Once this is learned, they must learn the reading skills to decode written language fluently and automatically (Stahl & Miller, 1989). Thus the Whole Language approach serves an important function for initial reading instruction.

The results of studies of the effectiveness of Whole Language ap-proaches based on traditional standardized testing do not support Whole Language instruction. The Commission on Reading described its effects as "indifferent" compared to traditional instruction (Anderson, Hiebert, Scott, & Wilkerson, 1985). Such conclusions disturb Whole Language advocates, who have criticized the report (e.g., Grundin, 1985; F. Smith, 1988), protesting the selectivity of studies that were reviewed.

As mentioned above, Stahl and Miller's (1989) meta-analysis of recent studies of Whole Language programs found that the effects of Whole Language/language experience approaches were approximately equal to basal reading approaches. These results were consistent for studies that used standardized and nonstandardized measures and for those that used measures of attitudes and achievement. Outcomes were not consistent within all studies, however. Whole Language/language experience approaches appeared to be more effective with kindergarten students or as a substitute for a reading-readiness program and had greater effects on measures of word recognition than on measures of comprehension.

A number of scholars are concerned with the methods that have been used to measure the effectiveness of Whole Language programs. Whole Language advocates such as Goodman (1989) and Weaver (1989) criticize the use of the comparative designs used in this research. They believe that the manipulation of variables in these studies represents an unnatural characteristic of Whole Language. They also take issue with the use of standardized tests, a customary gauge for measuring the effectiveness of these programs (Clarke, 1987). They question whether these tests are neutral, since they are designed specifically to reflect the outcomes of traditional reading instructions. McKenna and colleagues (1990) have responded with four principal points:

1. Narrative survey tests frequently incorporate subtests of specific, decontextualized skills that do not permit students to show their true proficiency (Goodman, 1986; Weaver, 1989). Nonetheless, such measures also include comprehension subtests, and researchers employ these scores as dependent variables (Chall, 1989).
2. Standardized measures, including comprehension, lack the reflective conceptualization of the reading process. Presently, these are being adapted to assess Whole Language by including longer passages, more inferential questions (Dutcher, 1989; Peters & Wixson, 1989), and such global tasks as summary writing (Valencia & Pearson, 1987). Time limits are also being eliminated (Dutcher, 1989; Peters & Wixson, 1989). Such modifications are an attempt to deal with the criticism that the very concise passages found in standardized tests do not allow Whole Language students to implement the holistic meaning-seeking strategies they are assumed to be developing.
3. Standardized tests formats resemble worksheet formats (Harste, 1985), which is a characteristic of traditional reading instruction but not a characteristic of Whole Language instruction. New test formats include complete stories to be read without time limits.
4. Achievement tests fail to completely assess the acquisition of literacy; therefore, research using such test scores may inadequately assess what children have learned. However, Clay (1990) has noted that the effectiveness of Whole Language can be better addressed by supplementing instead of suspending the use of standardized tests. Standardized tests are only one of the many sources of information that can be used.

Information collected for assessment should include a combination of methods, including different types of observations (e.g., brief narratives, portrayals, product displays, or graphs) along with standardized and informal tests.

Edelsky (1990) has criticized much of the research on Whole Language because it does not look at the purposes of the programs. It is important to ask why such assessment is done and whose interests it serves (Gibson, 1986). Research on the effectiveness of instruction can be questioned because issues of effectiveness depend on the educational paradigm from which one is working (J. Smith & Heshusius, 1986). Studying outcomes alone is inadequate. It is also important to consider what happens within a Whole Language framework (Goodman, 1989). Whole Language advocates, as noted above, also question effectiveness studies that rely on test score data, feeling that such studies encourage test-driven curricula (Edelsky, 1990).

Questions have been raised about the validity of standardized tests, as well as the validity of using subparts of tests, including comprehension subtests, longer passages, and inferential questions as independent measures. Critics even question the use of the newer tests that conceive of reading as an interactional process (in which text and reader can be separately analyzed) as a way of evaluating reading within the Whole Language conception. They argue that these approaches are inadequate because reading is a transactional process in which print provides only text-potential and in which meaning is infused with sociohistorical particularities as it is created by readers (Edelsky, 1990; Rosenblatt, 1985).

Whole Language is also difficult to assess because of its lack of focus on specific teaching outcomes. It does, however, teach students to think critically, value themselves as readers and writers, value others as readers and writers, and value their literacy products. They read, listen, speak, and write to learn how to read; they read, listen, speak, and communicate with a model that helps them move toward expected standards (Goodman, 1986). Some believe that evaluation should focus on student interaction and cooperative learning to develop communication skills (Linek, 1991).

The Whole Language perspective needs a different type of program evaluation.

Given the problems in standardized testing, responsible educators no longer can assume that tests are valid and programs invalid. If the program implemented reflects what we know about supportive environments for language learning, educators might begin by assuming that their program is valid and the test invalid. Given this new assumption,

the task becomes one of finding measures that support what is known.
(Harste & Woodward, 1989, p. 158)

Some traditionalists feel that such reasoning begs the very question it
addresses by insisting on measures that support the preconceived notions
of program planners. However, many educators who are not Whole Language advocates have criticized the use of standardized tests in general
(e.g., Shepard, 1991) and comprehension tests in particular as a basis for
evaluating programs or children (Farr & Carey, 1986; Johnston, 1983;
McNeil, 1984; Valencia & Pearson, 1987). It has been suggested that the
evaluation processes used should be modified to reflect the Whole Language beliefs and practices.

Researchers interested in studying the outcomes of Whole Language
programs must become aware of their perceptions of language and literacy
and strive to appreciate the participants' position. Whole Language researchers should reject meaningless outcome studies and raise questions
such as

What transpires within a Whole Language program?
What activities and interactions are to be found?
What are the consequences of such activities and interactions?

Researchers need to be aware that research in Whole Language is never
neutral. It intentionally sanctions a definite metanarrative concerning education, language, and literacy.

Advocates of Whole Language programs and advocates of traditional
reading and language arts programs differ in their views of what constitutes acceptable research. Goodman (1989), for example, does not accept
the validity of effectiveness studies that compare children on comprehension skills. It is felt that research on Whole Language must accept its
ideology and design studies that are consistent with that ideology. Research that is consistent with the Whole Language ideology would have
to be qualitative (Edelsky, 1990). Whole Language advocates reject the
traditional quantitative research methods used in psychology and education. They prefer ethnographic or descriptive investigations to test the
Whole Language ideology (Rentzel & Hollingsworth, 1988).

EVALUATION IN WHOLE LANGUAGE PROGRAMS

Teachers need to assess what children learn in any program. Documentation of learning validates Whole Language instruction and provides
evidence to administrators, parents, students, and skeptics. This documen-

tation should be an ongoing process. Observations, anecdotal records, tally lists, checklists, and video- or audiotaping can be selectively and intermittently used throughout the year to record children's learning focus and to identify student needs. Students can keep dialogue journals, to which teachers or peers can respond based on the purpose and content of the journals. Before recording their entries, students must know in advance who will be responding to their journal.

Linek (1991) suggests that individuals be compared to themselves, to their peer group, and to established criteria.

1. *Individual comparison* helps students to build on their strengths. Their performance is compared to their previous performance. Writing samples can be filed in a folder and reviewed with the student to note progress and growth patterns. Individual goals and objectives are mutually established to plan the teaching and learning process. Conferences with students to discuss their programs can help assess their achievements.
2. *Group comparisons* are also helpful. They can help students compare their work with that of other students in the class or group. Determining the outcome criteria prior to instruction can help students to work individually toward these outcomes.
3. *Criteria comparison* can also be used. Criteria must be specifically identified, and students' work should be assessed in relation to these criteria. Students should also be given the opportunity to designate the work to be compared. Individual conferences throughout the week can help students to progress rapidly.

Self-evaluation is one of the most useful forms of evaluation. Teachers consistently evaluate themselves and their teaching. They also help students generate methods to assess their own development, to know the status of their progress in relation to language and its learning (Goodman, 1986). Self-evaluation provides students with a sense of ownership and motivates their learning, thus leading to self-improvement. Students can learn to think objectively and critically, becoming aware of their strengths and needs and valuing the process, their products, and themselves.

Sometimes the inclusion of formal devices in the assessment process indicates the students' strength and needs. Unfortunately most standardized reading and writing tests focus strongly on isolated skills and words. Although assessing the effectiveness of Whole Language instruction may include some form of standardized testing, it should focus primarily on "authentic evaluation." This would rely heavily on collecting qualitative data about what children actually do in the program. Such data could include interviews, discussions, video- or audiorecording of children's reading, and selected samples of children's compositions, handwriting, and artwork. Such an evaluation would indicate that those doing the evaluating understand the Whole Language concept prior to incorporating their assessment methods incorporating it in.

CONCLUSION

The Whole Language approach to teaching language and literacy is one that is consistent with acceptable early childhood practices. It is an activity-based program that is integrated with other aspects of the curriculum. It allows children to create their own knowledge about written and spoken language. It also allows children to learn how language is used in many different contexts.

While no one methodology can be identified as Whole Language, there is a set of underlying beliefs and values that should be reflected in the classroom practices that the teacher adopts. The forms of evaluation used in the classroom should also reflect those beliefs and values.

In judging the effectiveness of Whole Language instruction, teachers might include some form of standardized testing. However, scores on such tests should not be used alone to make judgments about the program's effectiveness. Assessment should also rely heavily on qualitative data, for the process of learning language is as important as the outcomes.

REFERENCES

Altwerger, B., Edelsky, C., & Flores, B. M. (1987). Whole language: What's new? *The Reading Teacher, 41*(2), 144–154.

Anderson, R. C., Hiebert, E. H., Scott, J. A., & Wilkerson, I. A. G. (1985). *Becoming a nation of readers: The report of the Commission on Reading.* Washington, DC: National Institute of Education.

Bloome, D., & Slosken, J. (1988, November). *Cultural and political agendas of literacy learning in two communities: Literacy is a verb.* Paper presented at the annual meeting of The American Anthropological Association, Phoenix, AZ.

Britton, J. (1987, August). *Writing and reading in the classroom* (Technical Report No. 8). Berkeley: Center for the Study of Writing, University of California.

Butler, A., & Turbill, J. (1984). *Towards a reading-writing classroom.* Portsmouth, NH: Heinemann.

Calfee, R. C., & Drum, P. A. (1985). Research in reading. In M. C. Wittrock

(Ed.), *Handbook on research on teaching* (3rd ed.) (pp. 804–849). New York: Macmillan.

Chall, J. S. (1989). Learning to read: The great debate 20 years later: A response to "debunking the phonics myth." *Phi Delta Kappan, 70,* 521–538.

Clarke, M. A. (1987). Don't blame the system: Constraints on "whole language" reform. *Language Arts, 64,* 384–396.

Clay, M. M. (1990). Research currents: What is and what might be in evaluation. *Language Arts, 67,* 288–298.

Dickinson, D. K. (1987). Oral language, literacy skills, and response to literature. In J. R. Squire (Ed.), *The dynamics of language learning: Research in reading and English* (pp. 147–183). Urbana, IL: ERIC/RCS.

Doake, D. (1985). Reading-like behavior. In A. Jaggar & M. Smith-Burke (Eds.), *Observing the language learner* (pp. 82–89). Newark, DE, and Urbana, IL: International Reading Association and National Council of Teachers of English.

Duffy, G. G., & Roehler, L. R. (1986). *Improving classroom reading instruction: A decision-making approach.* New York: Random House.

Dutcher, P. (1989, April). *The development of the new MEAP reading tests.* Paper presented at the annual meeting of the American Educational Research Association, San Francisco.

Edelsky, C. (1990). Whose agenda is this anyway? A response to McKenna, Robinson, and Miller. *Educational Researcher, 19*(8), 3–6.

Edelsky, C., Altwerger, B., & Flores, B. (1991). *Whole language: What's the difference?* Portsmouth, NH: Heinemann.

Edelsky, C., & Draper, K. (1989). Reading/"reading"; writing/"writing"; text/ "text." *Reading-Canada-Lecture, 7,* 201–216.

Ehri, L. C. (1987). Learning to read and spell words. *Journal of Reading Behavior, 19*(1), 5–31.

Farr, R., & Carey, R. F. (1986). *Reading: What can be measured?* (2nd ed.). Newark, DE: International Reading Association.

Fountas, I. C., & Hannigan, I. L. (1989, June). Making sense of whole language: The pursuit of informed teaching. *Childhood Education, 39,* 133–137.

Ganopole, S. (1988). Reading and writing for the gifted: A whole language perspective. *Roeper Review, 11*(2), 88–92.

Gibson, R. (1986). *Critical theory and education.* London: Hodder & Stoughton.

Goelman, H., Oberg, A. O., & Smith, F. (Eds.). (1984). *Awakening to literacy.* London: Exeter.

Goodman, K. S. (1986). *What's whole in whole language?* Portsmouth, NH: Heinemann.

Goodman, K. S. (1989). Whole-language research: Foundations and development. *The Elementary School Journal, 90,* 207–221.

Grundin, H. (1985). A commission of selective readers: A critique of *Becoming a nation of readers. The Reading Teacher, 39,* 262–266.

Harris, A. J., & Sipay, E. R. (1990). *How to increase reading ability: A guide to developmental and remedial methods.* New York: Longman.

Harste, J. C. (1985). Becoming a nation of readers: Beyond risk. In J. C. Harste (Ed.), *Toward practical theory: A state of practice assessment of reading comprehension instruction* (pp. 227–353). Bloomington, IN: Language Education Department, Indiana University.

Harste, J. C., & Woodward, V. A. (1989). Fostering needed change in early literacy programs. In D. S. Strickland & L. M. Morrow (Eds.), *Emerging literacy: Young children learn to read and write* (pp. 147–159). Newark, DE: International Reading Association.

Jaggar, A. M., & Harwood, K. T. (1989). Suggested reading list: Whole language theory, practice and assessment. In G. S. Pinnell & M. L. Matlin (Eds.), *Teachers and research: Language learning in the classroom* (pp. 142–177). Newark, DE: International Reading Association.

Johnston, P. H. (1983). *Reading comprehension assessment: A cognitive basis.* Newark, DE: International Reading Association.

Klesius, J. P., Griffith, P. L., & Zielonka, P. (1991). A whole language and traditional instruction comparison: Overall effectiveness and development of the alphabetic principle. *Reading Research and Instruction, 30*(2), 47–61.

Linek, W. M. (1991). Grading and evaluation techniques for whole language teachers. *Language Arts, 68*(2), 125–132.

MacGinite, W. H. (1991). Reading instruction: Plus ca change . . . *Educational Leadership, 48*(6), 55–58.

McKenna, M. C., Robinson, R. D., & Miller, J. W. (1990). Whole language: A research agenda for the nineties. *Educational Researcher, 19*(8), 3–6.

McNeil, J. D. (1984). *Reading comprehension: New directions for classroom practice.* Glenview, IL: Scott, Foresman.

Newman, J. M. (1985). *Whole language: Theory and use.* Portsmouth, NH: Heinemann.

Peters, C. W., & Wixson, K. K. (1989). Smart new reading tests are coming. *Learning, 17*(8), 43–44, 53.

Prenn, M. C., & Scanlan, P. A. (1991). Teaching as we are taught: A model for whole language inservice. *Reading Horizons, 31*(3), 189–198.

Rentzel, D. R., & Hollingsworth, P. M. (1988). Whole language and the practitioner. *Academic Therapy, 23*(4), 405–416.

Rich, S. J. (1985). Restoring powers to teachers: The impact of "whole language." *Language Arts, 62,* 717–724.

Richgels, D. J., McGee, L. M., & Slaton, E. A. (1988). Kindergartners' attention to graphic detail in functional print: Letter name knowledge and invented spelling ability. In J. Readence et al. (Eds.), *Dialogues in literacy research* (37th Yearbook of the National Reading Conference, pp. 77–84). Chicago, IL: National Reading Conference.

Rosenblatt, L. (1985). Transaction versus interaction — A terminological rescue operation. *Research in the Teaching of English, 19,* 96–107.

Shepard, L. (1991). The influence of standardized tests on early childhood curriculum, teachers, and children. In B. Spodek & O. N. Saracho (Eds.), *Issues in early childhood curriculum: Yearbook in early childhood education* (Vol. 2) (pp. 166–189). New York: Teachers College Press.

Slaughter, H. B. (1988). Indirect and direct teaching in a whole language program. *The Reading Teacher, 42*, 30–34.

Smith, F. (1988). *Understanding reading: A psycholinguistic analysis of reading and learning* (4th ed.). Hillsdale, NJ: Erlbaum.

Smith, J., & Heshusius, L. (1986). Closing down the conversation: The end of the quantitative-qualitative debate among educational researchers. *Educational Researcher, 15*, 4–12.

Smith-Burke, M. T. (1987). Classroom practices and classroom interactions during reading instruction: What's going on? In J. R. Squire (Ed.), *The dynamics of language learning: Research in reading and English* (pp. 226–265). Urbana, IL: ERIC/RCS.

Stahl, S. A., & Miller, P. D. (1989). Whole language and language experience approaches for beginning reading: A quantitative research synthesis. *Review of Educational Research, 59*(1), 87–116.

Valencia, S., & Pearson, P. D. (1987). Reading assessment: Time for a change. *The Reading Teacher, 40*, 726–732.

Watson, D. J. (1989). Defining and describing whole language. *The Elementary School Journal, 90*, 129–141.

Weaver, W. C. (1989). The basalization of America: A cause for concern. In *Two reactions to the "report card on basal readers"* (pp. 4–7, 14–22, 31–37). Bloomington, IN: ERIC Clearinghouse on Reading and Communication Skills.

Wollman-Bonilla, J. E. (1991). Shouting from the topics of buildings: Teachers as learners and change in schools. *Language Arts, 68*(2), 114–120.

CHAPTER 4

Assessing Young Children's Language and Literacy: Tests and Their Alternatives

Celia Genishi

The term *assessment* calls to mind an assortment of items or images such as the following:

A. Adult says to a 4-year-old child as they sit in a testing room: "Listen carefully and do just what I say: 'Go to the chair, pick up the piece of paper, and bring it to me.'"

B. Teacher says to Natalia, a crying 3-year-old: "Want to tell me why you're sad?" "I want my daddy," responds the child.

C. Teacher says to her kindergarten class: "Look at the pictures [of a doll, a bike, and a house], and circle the one that starts with the same sound as *boy*."

D. Teacher in a bilingual first/second grade looks at the written work of her class. She chooses samples that show progress over the last two months to include in the children's portfolios.

Each of these examples depicts an aspect of assessment, and together they reflect the limitations and possibilities of current means for assessing children's language and literacy. Each serves a different purpose: Example A resembles an item on a standardized test of general intelligence, and example C, an item on a standardized reading achievement test. In contrast, examples B and D are informal, teacher-based assessments that focus on individual children's behavior and learning in school. Each example incorporates language, as understood and used by child and teacher, as well as information about experiences and feelings. The four examples will reappear in this chapter as I consider *assessment*, which includes *standardized testing*, and, more importantly, informal or alternative assessment, *adults' everyday observations and documentation of what children know and do*. Although I provide an overview of both standardized and alternative assessment, I argue that the latter is more appropriate for young children.

CHILDREN, LANGUAGE, AND TESTING: A PORTRAIT OF MISMATCHES

Current controversies about standardized testing highlight mismatches between (1) the positions of professional organizations and educational researchers and practices in schools, (2) the nature of tests and the nature of children, and (3) the nature of tests and the nature of language.

The Stance of Professional Early Childhood Organizations

Since the early 1900s standardized tests have been used as an objective, efficient, and practical way to assess general intelligence or sets of skills. They have become such an integral part of public schooling that about 100 million tests are now sold each year (Medina & Neill, 1990), and many administrators have come to rely on the results to see which schools or teachers are more "successful" than others. Moreover, recent recommendations from the federal government for educational reform include proposals for national testing, beginning in the primary grades (Howe, 1991; see Darling-Hammond, 1991, and Lieberman, 1991, for critiques of standardized testing as a key to reform).

Although national tests have not yet been established, testing at all age and grade levels has increased and led many early childhood educators and professional organizations to take official positions against the use of standardized tests for young children. In general, tests are not developmentally appropriate: They do not take into account the nature of children, their ways of learning and developing, and their ways of responding to particular situations. The National Association for the Education of Young Children, for example, opposes the use of such tests, *except* for developmental screening and assessment measures when they help detect the need for special services (Bredekamp & Shepard, 1989; Meisels, 1987; National Association for the Education of Young Children & National Association of Early Childhood Specialists in State Departments of Education, 1991). Those services should *benefit* children with particular conditions, disabilities, or gifts that require special classroom facilities or individualized curricula and help to move children forward in their development and learning. Tests should not be misused for purposes of excluding children from programs or schools. (See Chittenden & Courtney, 1989; Chapter 1 in Genishi, 1992b; Teale, Hiebert, & Chittenden, 1987, for further discussion of the misuse of tests and the need for alternatives to formal tests.)

The Nature of Children

Despite the change in testing practices, the nature of young children has remained in essence the same. As they develop and grow, children are often *not consistent* in their day-to-day behavior, and they are *in flux*, changing and developing more rapidly than they will in later childhood. Thus a test score might reflect a child's performance or demonstration of knowledge on a given day, but on another day the same child's performance might change noticeably. Also, individual children respond differently to testing situations; lack of familiarity with a tester leads some children to withdraw or be nonresponsive, whereas others react confidently. The supposed strength of standardized tests is their blindness to this individual variability. When strictly administered, the tests are to be given in the same way to everyone, regardless of children's unique responses or past experiences. Further, the increased use of readiness and achievement tests of reading in kindergarten and the primary grades has presented children just in the process of becoming literate with testing material that is appropriate for *conventional readers*, those who are already literate. For young children, paper-and-pencil tests made up of multiple-choice items are often abstractions, puzzling questions presented in an unfamiliar format. In summary, then, the nature of young children often leads them to be "bad test takers." Taking the test may itself be a negative experience, and the resulting scores may not be reliable, not an accurate measure of what they know or can do.

The Nature of Language

Just as standardized tests may not capture important aspects of children's learning and development, they also do not adequately assess what children know about language. Language is a complex and multilayered system that relates symbols (sounds, words, gestures) to meanings; it is something all normally developing people acquire within the social and cultural networks of their families and communities. How children learn language depends on many factors, such as attention, memory, and the kinds of life experiences they have had within their own cultures. Thus tests of language cannot assess either the totality of what children know about language or an isolated slice of language. Example A shows the impossibility of separating characteristics of children's language "by itself" from their "intelligence," what they know and how they make sense of the world. The item illustrates the constant overlapping of a child's prior experience, for example, in listening to and following verbal instructions, with ways of attending and remembering, and knowledge of language.

In their attempts at assessment, educators are interested in both what children *know about language* (its multitude of tacit rules for combining sounds, words, and sentences into meaningful utterances or text) and what children *do with language* (establish social relationships, play, control their own and others' behaviors, reveal what they know, solve problems, and so on). In their "doing with language," children demonstrate their *communicative competence*, their abilities to use language appropriately in different situations, to accomplish different purposes. (See Dyson & Genishi, in press; Garvey, 1984; Genishi, 1992a; Lindfors, 1987, for extended discussions of children's language in use.) The fact that human beings respond and speak differently according to who is present, where they are, and why they are there has been well documented by sociolinguists, who focus on language in social contexts (Cazden, John, & Hymes, 1972; Ervin-Tripp & Mitchell-Kernan, 1977; Labov, 1970; Schieffelin & Ochs, 1986).

Thus for adults to fully assess a child's language, they need to take a *sociolinguistic perspective*: to observe what the child does and says in a variety of situations. *Assessing a single situation — for example, that of a standardized test — is only one sample, a partial representation of children's knowledge and abilities.* The remainder of this chapter addresses tests and alternatives that we need to describe fully what children know about and do with language.

TESTS OF LANGUAGE AND LITERACY

Despite flaws in tests and testing practices and the mismatches between children and tests, tests continue to be used and educators are asked to make decisions about them. This section contains guidelines for selecting tests, along with reminders of their limitations. The large number of standardized tests to assess children's spoken and written language (Chapter 9 in Lund & Duchan, 1988; Mitchell, 1985) are designed with specific abilities or purposes in mind. Educators select among them by matching their own purposes with those of available tests, as they keep in mind that tests usually have a narrow focus; they do not span a broad sociolinguistic spectrum. For example, the often-used Peabody Picture Vocabulary Test (Dunn & Dunn, 1981) tests only *comprehension* of words in standard English. Further, standardized tests are designed primarily to compare performances of *groups*, so that their usefulness to teachers who wish to know about individuals is often limited.

In a comprehensive review of means for assessing language and literacy, Nurss (1992, p. 229) provides criteria for selection of tests. Specifically, any test should be: (1) reliable, (2) valid, (3) practical, (4) culturally sensitive, and (5) congruent with the curriculum it is intended to assess. These are strict criteria, which only some assessment tools fulfill. Standardized tests need at least to be reliable (accurate and consistent in what they measure) and valid (able to measure what they are intended to measure, such as vocabulary knowledge). Moreover, they should be practical, easy to administer in a relatively short period of time. A test that is practical from a teacher's point of view also provides accessible information to improve learning and instruction. The phrase "culturally sensitive" refers to whether the test is responsive to social and cultural differences among test takers. Because tests of language always reflect aspects of culture and children in early childhood settings belong to increasingly diverse cultures, it is impossible to construct a single test that is "culturally sensitive," that incorporates aspects of all the cultures to which children belong. Many tests have been written with middle-class children in mind as the "typical" test takers. Educators are able to make fair decisions about which tests are appropriate only when they know how norms for a test have been established, or what groups of children took the test when reliability and validity judgments were made. (Mitchell, 1985, provides this information when available.)

Tests of language and literacy, as Nurss (1992) points out, should also be compatible with the curriculum they are to assess. For example, a reading/language arts program that includes a focus on skills, presented in sequence from a published textbook series, is congruent with tests (teacher-made, publisher-made, or standardized) that assess the skills that are taught and practiced. But they are not compatible with holistic programs that are less predictable in content and may not focus on skills. Moreover, a curriculum that places a premium on many forms of oral language is not easily tested since many language tests are designed with delayed development in mind.

Tests of Early Literacy

Among the best-known diagnostic measures of early literacy are reading-readiness tests. These aim to assess whether children have the skills and knowledge needed for beginning reading instruction and are most often administered to groups of children. They consist of multiple-choice items, arranged in subsections of vocabulary knowledge, visual and auditory discrimination, letter recognition, and letter–sound correspondence. That structure reflects a particular view of reading, one that breaks reading down into components, each of which children can learn through systematic instruction. Reading achievement tests reflect the same view. In fact, instruction has often mirrored the content of tests when teachers have used published materials, basal readers and their accompanying workbooks, as the basis of their reading program (Stallman & Pearson, 1990). Example C illustrates this mirroring: We could find items asking children to find pictures of objects that begin with a certain sound both on an achievement test and on a child's classroom worksheet.

When Language Development Lags

When the language of young children is notably different from their age- or grademates, adults often consult with speech–language pathologists who can help remediate the difficulty and who are familiar with the numerous, wide-ranging measures available for assessing disorders (see van Kleeck & Richardson, 1990, for a thorough review). Identifying a "language disorder," however, can be more complicated than assessing oral language in children whose development seems typical, largely because children vary so much among themselves. For example, what looks to some like a "delay" or possible "disorder" may actually be an *individual difference*, as in a child who says his or her first word at 26 months, instead of the more usual 12 to 18 months, of age. This child's language is not disordered; the rate of development is simply different. Children vary not only in terms of *when* they learn aspects of language, but also in how able or willing they are to demonstrate what they know — in other words, to respond or talk in testing situations. Further, *differences in ways of speaking* — a dialect (a social or regional variety of language) or the language itself (as in non-English-speakers) — sometimes are misjudged as disorders.

Specialists who aim to identify and then alleviate language disorders acknowledge that these individual and cultural differences add to the challenge of defining and identifying disorders, or "learning disabilities," even in the middle elementary grades when children are assumed to be more reliable test takers. Standardized measures are routinely used with these learners to separate the "disabled" from others, but again, even with these measures, it is difficult to determine which students show an individual difference in learning, not a disability. Thus there is still "the serious problem of misclassification" (Silliman & Wilkinson, 1991, p. 4) that has led speech–language pathologists — like educators in regular class-rooms — to recommend more *ecologically valid* methods of assessing both abilities and disabilities, or methods that describe how children and teachers use language in ordinary classroom settings. Specialists strongly recommend that educators take the same cautious approach in assessing potential disabilities as they take in assessing typical development (Bloom & Lahey, 1978; Lund & Duchan, 1988). These experts emphasize the importance of the following:

Understanding fully the purpose of each means of assessment
Determining that the procedure or test is necessary, that is, there is no other way of obtaining the information
Determining that the information is useful and beneficial enough to the child to warrant possible stress on child and parent
Ensuring that the child is observed (not tested) in as many situations as possible when judgments are made about language use

RESPONDING TO CHILDREN: ALTERNATIVE ASSESSMENTS FOR ALTERNATIVE CURRICULA

As stated earlier, an adequate means of assessment is compatible with the curriculum it is to assess. *Curriculum* in this chapter refers to a range of opportunities for learning: not only published curricula and plans made in advance, but also whatever occurs as children and teachers interact and enact plans together. Those opportunities may develop out of children's interests and experiences (Dewey, 1938/1963; Katz & Chard, 1989; Snyder, Bolin, & Zumwalt, 1992) and may be negotiated among children, teachers, and administrators (Lester & Onore, 1990). Assessment that matches this kind of curriculum, which is dynamic and experiential, is also dynamic. It attempts to answer adults' questions about how well the curriculum is working, how much children are learning, or how engaged children are with classroom activities.

In classrooms where plans and activities are flexible and molded to suit individual children, teachers find standardized tests of language and literacy learning inadequate, even irrelevant. For these teachers a curriculum based on skills and traditional ways of learning about language and print conflicts with their own beliefs. In their view, often referred to as that of "emergent literacy" (Clay, 1966; Teale & Sulzby, 1989), language and literacy are seen as more than the sum of their component skills.

Rather than an accomplishment of early schooling, literacy learning is a long *developmental process* that begins early in life and is grounded in the language of varied situations in and out of school. Also, early in life children begin to use symbols, as in symbolic play, and continue to use them in more complex ways as they come to know print and other symbols in their everyday lives (Dyson, this volume, Chapter 2). Given the variation among children as they become orchestrators of meaning through talk and print, early childhood educators need means for assessment that are more flexible than standardized tests and that can describe the *processes* of change and development over time in *individual* children. From this point of view, teachers, not standardized tests or outside experts, should have the power to create means of assessment and be the *primary instruments* of assessment. Ways in which teachers use themselves and their own abilities to tap learners' development follow.

Observation: The Essential Skill

Teachers' and other adults' judgments about a child's progress in all areas of development have always been based on their observational skills, which are especially essential while children are *becoming* speakers, writers, and readers (see Almy & Genishi, 1979; Boehm & Weinberg, 1987; Genishi & Dyson, 1984). For teachers, the overall purpose of observation and assessment is to take note of what children do so that learning can be enhanced. Since observations can be fleeting and memories imperfect, teachers use a number of ways to record what they see and hear.

Anecdotal Records. When Natalia's teacher in example B reflected on the events of the day, she wrote a note about this brief exchange: "Want to tell me why you're sad?" followed by, "I want my daddy." The teacher decided to be attentive to Natalia's talk and behavior after her arrival for the rest of the week, as a way of assessing the 3-year-old's adjustment to daycare. Like many of her colleagues, this teacher used the anecdotal record, a popular way of recording observations, often written on an index card or on a piece of paper showing a grid, or boxes for comments on individual children. Teachers are as objective as possible as they write; they *describe* what they see and hear and separate their feelings from descriptions so that each child can be viewed fairly. In their notes they might separate *children's behaviors*, for example, "Sullah hit Billy," from *teacher interpretation* ("this is a constant power struggle") by placing parentheses around interpretations. The length of each anecdote varies, depending on the child, the style of the teacher, and the amount of time available for note writing. Often anecdotes are short and telegraphic. For example, preschool teachers wrote about 4-year-olds Philip and Cathleen:

> Philip: Sad about Liah. Looking for friend — played. Wrote–dictated story.
> Cathleen: More outgoing. Had a house with Lavonne and Kristina. Talked to her, said "what happened?"

Teachers at this school used their anecdotes for two main purposes: for discussion at staff meetings and for discussion of children's progress with parents. So in both cases, the anecdotes jogged their memories to allow a more elaborate oral description of children's behaviors and feelings, strengths and weaknesses. Teachers who rely on anecdotes usually develop methods for making their note taking efficient, for example, they carry small notebooks or Post-it pads in their pockets or leave cards or paper and pencils in assigned places of the classroom or center.

Longer anecdotes are written when teachers want more information about particular children or when enough adults are available to spell each other and teachers have the luxury of writing extended anecdotes or narratives. Some teachers use a "double-entry" system for extended note taking, creating two columns on a sheet of paper, writing anecdotes in one column, and later writing their interpretations or feelings in the other blank column.

In assessing language and literacy, anecdotes are especially helpful during the first years of life, when children are not yet speaking or using print in conventional ways. How children respond to conversation, whether or not they seem to hear and vocalize as other children do, what their first babbling sounds or words are, or what they attend to as they hear a story — we can note all these behaviors as aspects of language use.

Checklists. Particularly in settings with large numbers of children, teachers use shortcuts to record their observations. Checklists are an efficient and versatile form of record keeping that are most useful when teachers create or modify them to suit their own purposes. A teacher who is focusing on the development of spoken language might develop a checklist that he or she fills in once a week, noting whether — and in what situations — individual children are talking when observed (see Figure 4.1). A similar checklist could be used by the teacher who is interested in children's reading during partner or buddy reading time.

Teachers in a bilingual second grade developed an extensive checklist to document children's writing (Fournier, Lansdowne, Pastenes, Steen, &

North Street Day Care Center

Observer_____   Date_____ Time_____

Name	Talking?	With Whom		Where	Comments
		Child	Adult		
Ruby A.					
Darron C.					
William C.					
Alice D.					
Kiko E.					
...					

Figure 4.1. Checklist to document spoken language.

Hudelson, 1992; see Figure 4.2). They believed that the skills listed were important for children's literacy learning, regardless of the language they spoke and wrote. By presenting features of "writing quality," such as selecting topics and experimenting with style, at the top of the list the teachers also implied that these broad qualities are more important than the narrower mechanics of writing. There are many published checklists and forms available that teachers have used and adapted to record multiple aspects of children's language and literacy, for example, the *Primary Language Record* (Centre for Primary Language Education/Inner London Education Authority, 1988) and Goodman, Goodman, and Hood's (1989) *The Whole Language Evaluation Book*.

SECOND GRADE WRITING RECORD
Wm. T. Machan Elementary School

Student _____   Year _____
Teacher _____   Date of Entry into Classroom_____
Primary Language_____   Secondary Language_____

CODES: NE = no evidence, D = developing, C = controls

	DATE	DATE	DATE	COMMENTS
WRITING QUALITY:				
Self selects topic				
Uses expansive vocabulary				
Experiments with style				
Uses revision strategies				
WRITING MECHANICS:				
Handwriting				
Uses periods				
Uses question marks				
Uses quotation marks				
Uses exclamation points				
Uses capitalization				
Uses comma/ apostrophe/accents				
Grammar usage				
% Invented spelling				
% Conventional spelling				

Figure 4.2. Checklist to document writing.

Audiotape Recordings

For those with a particular interest in what children say, audiotape recorders are a valued tool (see Genishi & Dyson, 1984, pp. 84–85, for more detailed guidelines). Although listening to and transcribing the recordings is time consuming, teachers find that listening to conversations away from the busyness of the center or classroom allows assessment of children's uses of language, their interests and ways of thinking, and of the teacher's own language, how he or she uses it to respond to children, prompt or clarify thinking, and so on.

Teacher–researchers whose careful listening has led to published stories about life in their classrooms demonstrate how much can be learned from recordings. Paley (1981), for example, has made visible the thinking of her kindergartners in discussions such as the following:

> *Andy:* My father has two cactus plants in the big windows in his office. You know why? When robbers come in at night they touch the cactus plants and have to go back where they came from. To get the prickles out. They's why my daddy has those plants.
> *Deana:* What if you got stuck in the desert when you weren't stealing anything?
> *Eddie:* What if he stoled the whole cactus plant?
> *Andy:* Then he might fall on it and get stuck by it.
> *Tanya:* How about if the robber came in another way except by the way the cactus are?
> *Andy:* He can't. The doors are locked. (p. 61)

These kindergartners not only display what they know about language, they also show how it is used to discuss a problem, one about which they have ideas even though they have not experienced cactus prickles or robberies.

First graders reading together can record themselves. Here Daryll, Tahrique, and Justin read *The Napping House* (Wood, 1984), quietly but playfully, after practice-reading it once:

> *Daryll:* (reading) There is a house a napping house where everyone is sleeeeeeping (giggles from Daryll and Tahrique).
> *Tahrique:* (reading) And in that red house there is a bed a cozy bed in a napping house where everyone is sleeping! (singing the repeated refrain)
> *Justin:* (laughing and moving to join the reading) My turn. Where are we, right here? Right here? (general discussion of where they are and whose turn it is)
> *Justin:* And in (much laughter)
> *Tahrique:* And IN!

Justin: And in that bed there is a gr — (again much laughter)
Tahrique and Daryll: A granny. . . . (Merritt & Dyson, 1992, p. 114)

They continue reading and later improvising and joking until Ms. Merritt, their teacher, intervenes. Justin, who is better known for singing rap than reading, has managed to shift the direction of the session away from reading. His teacher is able to use the taped documentation from such interactions to see how these boys are progressing, not just in reading, but also in larger groups and on the playground. The *composite* portraits of the boys as talkers, readers, singers, and players help the teacher plan activities that enhance their literacy learning. For Justin she later included lyrics to songs in reading lessons, integrating his interests with the instructional goal of improved reading and writing after thoughtful observation in varied social contexts.

Portfolios: A Metaphor for Orchestrating Assessment

The recent work of Gardner and his collaborators (Gardner, 1991; Wolf, Bixby, Glenn, & Gardner, 1991) provides a psychological framework for multifaceted assessment. Through their Project Spectrum they have put into practice aspects of Gardner's theory of *multiple intelligences* (Gardner, 1983), which proposes that traditional views of intelligence are inadequate. According to Gardner, there are intelligences beyond the traditionally emphasized verbal and mathematical, including the social, artistic, musical, kinesthetic, and scientific. In verifying the theory, Gardner and others have sought out manifestations of the various intelligences in early childhood classrooms, asking children to demonstrate their competencies by, for example, singing "Happy Birthday." Thus earlier conceptions of children as "little linguists" or "little scientists" are now expanded to include budding musicians, negotiators, or dancers.

Evidence of children's progress reflecting different intelligences may be documented in *portfolios*, collections of work that serve multiple purposes. Like artists' portfolios, they contain examples of a range of children's work, not necessarily their most flawless, but representations of learning — notable shifts in content and style. Although they may seem initially like "places" for storage, they stand for — are a *metaphor* for — a theory of assessment that claims assessment is valid only when it reflects the learning that occurs over time as children and teachers enact the curriculum. Embedded in this theory is the view that teachers' and learners' own assessments are important, that they have both the right and the responsibility to make their own judgments. Thus in some classrooms adults and children select what work should be saved, what shows the greatest change, what is aesthetically pleasing, what is characteristic of the child, and so on. Learner-centered teachers at all age levels have espoused this general theory for decades, along with more recent supporters of Whole Language. (The works of Carini, 1982; Harp, 1991; and Heald-Taylor, 1989, are illustrative.) And although in the elementary grades some portfolios focus on writing (Tierney, Carter, & Desai, 1991), multiple intelligences may be represented: artwork, math work, child-done checklists, audiotaped stories or readings, letters, child-written songs, videotapes, and so on. Also, in some places, portfolios accompany children from grade to grade; they become cumulative records that are of greater value than test scores.

Theory and practice, then, merge in intriguing ways to support a device such as the portfolio to house examples of children's language and literacy that include but also go beyond the traditional, as illustrated by the following tasks and products.

Classroom Dramas: Story Playing, Dictating, and Retelling. Ways of capturing children's literary voices, dramatic play, dictations, and oral retellings have traditionally revealed what children know about their own and others' stories. The daily "social work" of negotiation, of children choosing and assigning roles in dramatic play is a prime example of a growing understanding of characters, plot, place, and the ways they fit together (Genishi & Galvan, 1985; Schickedanz, 1978). Paley (1990) has richly illustrated the enactment of such stories over time in her preschool classroom, where stories are told, heard, dictated, acted out, and talked about often. They are the basis for a curriculum centered on children's unbounded interests and their ongoing social lives.

Storytelling and retelling can also be straightforward ways of assessing both oral language and individuals' understandings of stories. For example, during the time that a class project was about castles, two kindergartners responded to their teacher's drawing of a medieval castle by dictating stories. One child said:

> There is a black drawbridge below the orange lines. There is a pink dungeon with a bad knight in it. There are lots of knights in the castle. There is a big storm coming. There is water around the castle.

And the second said:

> Welcome to my castle. This is a gold castle. That's why the ghost likes to travel around the castle to see if there are any gold pieces loose. The bad knight was walking near the drawbridge. He wasn't looking and he fell into the moat and the shark came and ate him up. That was the end of that bad knight.

Keeping these dictations in portfolios, along with the two kindergartners' own drawings of castles, provides a record of a number of things: their ways of representing castles; the first storyteller's accurate description; and the second's placement of himself in the story ("Welcome to my castle"), his recognition of intention ("to see if there are any gold pieces loose"), and his sense of closure ("That was the end of that bad knight").

When reviewing children's retellings based on books, a teacher in a classroom or center might note the presence or absence of such features as

> Descriptive words
> Literary language
> Elements of the book's plot
> The child's own phrasings and interpretations
> Short or elaborated sentences

Children use a range of details in their stories and retellings, and teachers' checklists and anecdotes help preserve the uniqueness of each version (see Chapter 6 in Genishi & Dyson, 1984, for further discussion and checklists).

Children's Written Stories. As children begin to write, rather than tell, their stories, their written products become key parts of portfolios, as in example D. Samples of a bilingual first grader's writing (see Figures 4.3 and 4.4) show not only greater sophistication over time, but also Jeanevie's attempt at figuring out differences between Spanish (her native language) and English (her second language). For example, in Figure 4.3 Jeanevie writes "mi and may bonny" ("me and my bunny"), using Spanish vowel sounds to guide her spelling. Just below, though, when writing "bi bay," Jeanevie seems to be using the English sound of the letter *I* in "bi" and the Spanish sound /ay/ immediately afterwards in "bay." Two months later, her caption in Figure 4.4 is longer and more sophisticated, and she uses mainly English spellings. Whether or not they are familiar with Spanish, teachers can see from Jeanevie's invented spellings that she is attempting her own "balancing act," her way of orchestrating the details of two different orthographic systems, based on what she knows about both. A portfolio allows the seeming inconsistencies in children's work (the word "bi" next to "bay") to stand, awaiting the next acts, later samples of writing that show progress toward conventional spellings.

Stories and Music: Other Ways of Orchestrating Print. Most examples in children's portfolios fall within traditional boundaries; they are pieces of writing, drawing, perhaps recordings of talk. Of course there are other forms of expression, as Gardner (1983) reminds us, and other ways

Photo by Joyce Culver

Figure 4.3. Jeanevie's drawing, November 1991.

of coming to understand print. Steedman (1985) depicts one of these ways as she tells a poignant tale of Amarjit, a 9-year-old East Indian girl whose first language was Punjabi. In the setting of an urban school in England, as Amarjit was becoming bilingual, she began to read a book called *The Green Man and the Golden Bird* (McCullagh, 1976). It contained the story of a mother who bought her children a caged golden bird at the market and whose daughter begged her to free it. Over time, often at home in bed, Amarjit created a song for her adaptation of part of the text:

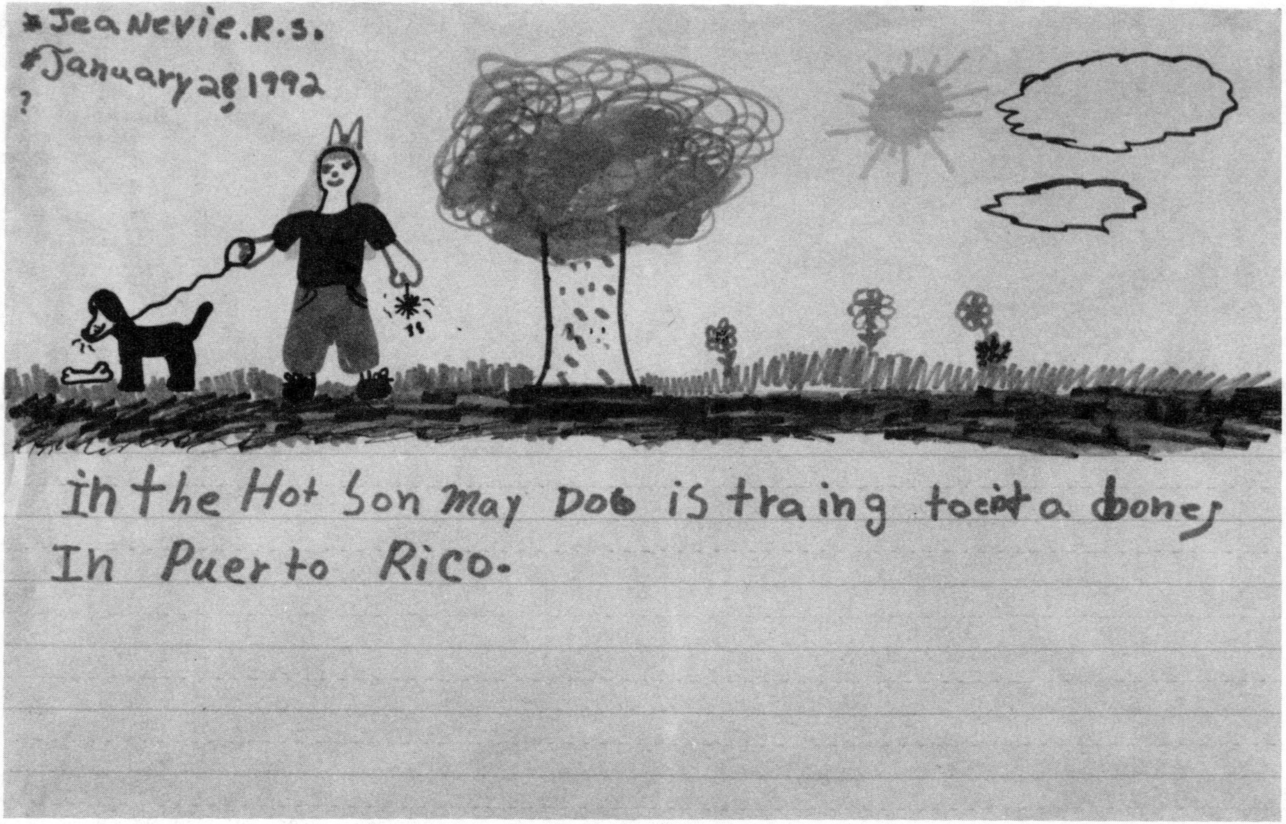

Figure 4.4. Jeanevie's drawing, January 1992.

Photo by Joyce Culver

The song is so sad I can't bear to listen to it.
The bird wants to get out and fly away.
"Don't be silly," replies the mother.
"That bird cost me a lot of money."
(Steedman, 1985, p. 139)

Steedman, Amarjit's teacher, recognized the accomplishments that the song documented: A few of these were an understanding of a poetic tale written in her second language, an ability to select a personally meaningful segment, and a musical talent for setting English words to music. Although other children's response to Amarjit's lyrical song at a school assembly was laughter, her teacher knew how it captured the girl's intelligences and her ability to orchestrate print with feeling and song. Earlier we encountered a more receptive classroom as Merritt and Dyson (1992) showed how three first-grade boys—Daryll, Tahrique, and Justin—read *together* and blended their stories with music as reading became a shared musical event (see also Dyson, 1992, for the story of Jameel, another first grader with a gift for orchestrating tunes and print).

Children with experiences and talents like those of Amarjit, an East Indian immigrant, and Daryll and his friends, African Americans in California, not only stretch the shape of "typical" portfolios, they also compel us to appreciate again the link between assessment and curriculum. These children in schools distant from each other had teachers who assumed the curriculum could be stretched and reshaped to accommodate varied intelligences and individual styles. A "good story" may take the form of a written retelling for one child and a musical performance for another. For other children, videotape may preserve their ability to move with grace; for still others, photographs of block constructions or maps document spatial intelligence. Assessment that is responsive to children—observation and documentation of what they can and cannot do over time—follows the unique shape of the curriculum. Teachers can orchestrate the varied ways of assessing their curricula by means of flexible and selective portfolios.

CONCLUSION: A VISION OF ALTERNATIVE ASSESSMENT AS TEACHER-LED CONVERSATIONS

The topic of this chapter was assessment of language and literacy, standardized assessment and alternative means. The purposes for these contrasting approaches differ, and I have argued that alternative ways of assessing are most appropriate for classrooms where children and teachers together enact a learner-focused and dynamic curriculum. Unlike test scores, these alternative ways are not efficient statements about how children compare with others at a given point in time. Instead, they help adults see multiple aspects of children's growth, multiple intelligences played out in each child's story of development. These alternatives have the greatest potential for affecting children's daily experiences in early childhood settings and thus great appeal for learner-centered teachers.

The assortment of items in the chapter's introduction represents a narrow slice of what children can do. The imagined scenes that I close with are fuller, revealing groups of people as they discuss individuals' progress and development. A group might start by looking at a photograph of a child on a swing; teachers talk of how this is typical of her, how she likes to pump hard, how she cheerfully shouts at kids nearby. A parent asks what other things she does, and the conversation continues as drawings and stories in which she has written her own and her brother's names emerge from a portfolio; more questions are asked and answered by parents and others. Scenes like this one might be played out often as parents, teachers, aides, directors, or principals discuss children's strengths and weaknesses (Martin, 1988). Some children's portfolios are thin, supporting the idea that less can be more, whereas others are bulging. Other children's progress is presented through conversations without portfolios, but with written anecdotes, a few children's products, or teacher-developed assessment guidelines that summarize their curriculum (Waters, Frantz, Rottmayer, Trickett, & Genishi, 1992). These talk-filled assessment scenes capture just some of the ways that children and teachers have orchestrated the balancing acts that occur daily in classrooms and centers, balances between watching and participating, dramatizing and writing, being alone and being in a group, talking and listening, painting and reading, dancing and block building, playing outdoors and singing. The power to envision these and other ways of assessing such an extensive curriculum should fall to the adults who so carefully shape it.

Acknowledgments. I am grateful to Beverly Falk Feigenberg, Luz Gonzalez, Janis Koeppel, and Mari Mori, teachers who graciously shared their ideas and their children's work with me; and to Gwendolyn Strassner, a future teacher, for calling my attention to our need for songs like Amarjit's.

REFERENCES

Almy, M., & Genishi, C. (1979). *Ways of studying children* (rev. ed.). New York: Teachers College Press.

Bloom, L., & Lahey, M. (1978). *Language development and language disorders.* New York: Wiley.

Boehm, A. E., & Weinberg, R. A. (1987). *The classroom observer: Developing observation skills in early childhood settings* (2nd ed.). New York: Teachers College Press.

Bredekamp, S., & Shepard, L. (1989). How best to protect children from inappropriate school expectations, practices, and policies. *Young Children, 44*(3), 14–24.

Carini, P. (1982). *The lives of seven school children*. Grand Forks: University of North Dakota Press.

Cazden, C. B., John, V. S., & Hymes, D. (Eds.). (1972). *Functions of language in the classroom*. New York: Teachers College Press.

Centre for Primary Language Education/Inner London Education Authority. (1988). *Primary language record*. Portsmouth, NH: Heinemann.

Chittenden, E., & Courtney, R. (1989). Assessment of young children's reading: Documentation as an alternative to testing. In D. S. Strickland & L. M. Morrow (Eds.), *Emerging literacy: Young children learn to read and write* (pp. 107–120). Newark, DE: International Reading Association.

Clay, M. M. (1966). *Emergent reading behavior*. Unpublished doctoral dissertation, University of Auckland, New Zealand.

Darling-Hammond, L. (1991, November). The implications of testing policy for quality and equality. *Phi Delta Kappan, 73*, 220–225.

Dewey, J. (1963). *Experience and education*. New York: Collier. (Original work published 1938)

Dunn, L., & Dunn, L. (1981). *Peabody Picture Vocabulary Test–Revised (PPVT–R)*. Circle Pines, MN: American Guidance Service.

Dyson, A. H. (1992). The case of the singing scientist: A performance perspective on the "stages" of school literacy. *Written Communication, 9*, 3–47.

Dyson, A. H., & Genishi, C. (in press). Visions of children as language users: Research in language and language education in early childhood. In B. Spodek (Ed.), *Handbook of research on the education of young children*. New York: Macmillan.

Ervin-Tripp, S. M., & Mitchell-Kernan, C. (1977). *Child discourse*. New York: Academic Press.

Fournier, J., Lansdowne, B., Pastenes, Z., Steen, P., & Hudelson, S. (1992). Learning with, about, and from children: Life in a bilingual classroom. In C. Genishi (Ed.), *Ways of assessing children and curriculum: Stories of early childhood practice* (pp. 126–162). New York: Teachers College Press.

Gardner, H. (1983). *Frames of mind: The theory of multiple intelligences*. New York: Basic Books.

Gardner, H. (1991). *The unschooled mind: How children think and how schools should teach*. New York: Basic Books.

Garvey, C. (1984). *Children's talk*. Cambridge, MA: Harvard University Press.

Genishi, C. (1992a). Developing the foundation: Oral language and communicative competence. In C. Seefeldt (Ed.), *The early childhood curriculum: A review of current research* (2nd ed., pp. 85–117). New York: Teachers College Press.

Genishi, C. (Ed.). (1992b). *Ways of assessing children and curriculum: Stories of early childhood practice*. New York: Teachers College Press.

Genishi, C., & Dyson, A. H. (1984). *Language assessment in the early years*. Norwood, NJ: Ablex.

Genishi, C., & Galvan, J. (1985). Getting started: Mexican-American preschoolers initiating dramatic play. In J. L. Frost & S. Sunderlin (Eds.), *When children play* (pp. 23–30). Wheaton, MD: Association for Childhood Education International.

Goodman, K. S., Goodman, Y. M., & Hood, W. J. (1989). *The whole language evaluation book*. Portsmouth, NH: Heinemann.

Harp, B. (Ed.). (1991). *Assessment and evaluation in whole language programs*. Norwood, MA: Christopher-Gordon.

Heald-Taylor, G. (1989). *The administrator's guide to whole language*. Katonah, NY: Richard C. Owen.

Howe, H., II. (1991). America 2000: A bumpy ride on four trains. *Phi Delta Kappan, 73*, 192–203.

Katz, L. G., & Chard, S. C. (1989). *Engaging children's minds: The project approach*. Norwood, NJ: Ablex.

Labov, W. (1970). The standard of nonstandard English. In F. Williams (Ed.), *The language of poverty* (pp. 153–189). Chicago: Markham.

Lester, N. B., & Onore, C. S. (1990). *Learning change: One school district meets language across the curriculum*. Portsmouth, NH: Boynton/Cook.

Lieberman, A. (1991). Accountability as a reform strategy. *Phi Delta Kappan, 73*, 219–220.

Lindfors, J. W. (1987). *Children's language and learning* (2nd ed.). Englewood Cliffs, NJ: Prentice-Hall.

Lund, N. J., & Duchan, J. F. (1988). *Assessing children's language in naturalistic contexts* (2nd ed.). Englewood Cliffs, NJ: Prentice-Hall.

Martin, A. (1988). Screening, early intervention, and remediation: Obscuring children's potential. *Harvard Educational Review, 58*, 488–501.

McCullagh, S. (1976). *The green man and the golden bird*. St. Albans, England: Rupert Hart-Davis.

Medina, N., & Neill, D. M. (1990). *Fallout from the testing explosion: How 100 million standardized tests undermine equity and excellence in America's public schools* (3rd ed.). Cambridge, MA: National Center for Fair and Open Testing (FairTest).

Meisels, S. J. (1987). Uses and abuses of developmental screening and school readiness testing. *Young Children, 42*(2), 4–6, 68–73.

Merritt, S., & Dyson, A. H. (1992). A social perspective on informal assessment: Voices, texts, pictures, and play from a first grade. In C. Genishi (Ed.), *Ways of assessing children and curriculum: Stories of early childhood practice* (pp. 94–125). New York: Teachers College Press.

Mitchell, J. V., Jr. (Ed.). (1985). *The ninth mental measurements yearbook* (Vols. 1 & 2). Lincoln: Buros Institute of Mental Measurements, University of Nebraska Press.

National Association for the Education of Young Children & National Association of Early Childhood Specialists in State Departments of Education. (1991). Guidelines for appropriate curriculum content and assessment in programs serving children ages 3 through 8. *Young Children, 46*(3), 21–38.

Nurss, J. R. (1992). Evaluation of language and literacy. In L. O. Ollila & M. I. Mayfield (Eds.), *Emerging literacy: Preschool, kindergarten, and primary grades* (pp. 229–252). Needham Heights, MA: Allyn & Bacon.

Paley, V. G. (1981). *Wally's stories*. Cambridge, MA: Harvard University Press.

Paley, V. G. (1990). *The boy who would be a helicopter: The uses of storytelling in the classroom*. Cambridge, MA: Harvard University Press.

Schickedanz, J. A. (1978). "You be the doctor and I'll be sick": Language arts for preschoolers. *Language Arts, 55*, 713–718.

Schieffelin, B. B., & Ochs, E. (Eds.) (1986). *Language socialization across cultures*. New York: Cambridge University Press.

Silliman, E. R., & Wilkinson, L. C. (Eds). (1991). *Communicating for learning: Classroom observation and collaboration*. Gaithersburg, MD: Aspen.

Snyder, J., Bolin, F., & Zumwalt, K. K. (1992). Curriculum implementation. In P. W. Jackson (Ed.), *Handbook of research on curriculum* (pp. 402–435). New York: Macmillan.

Stallman, A. C., & Pearson, P. D. (1990). Formal measures of early literacy. In L. M. Morrow & J. K. Smith (Eds.), *Assessment for instruction in early literacy* (pp. 7–44). Englewood Cliffs, NJ: Prentice-Hall.

Steedman, C. (1985). "Listen, how the caged bird sings": Amarjit's song. In C. Steedman, C. Urwin, & V. Walkerdine (Eds.), *Language, gender, and childhood* (pp. 137–163). Boston, MA: Routledge & Kegan Paul.

Teale, W. H., Hiebert, E. H., & Chittenden, E. A. (1987). Assessing young children's literacy development. *The Reading Teacher, 40*, 772–777.

Teale, W. H., & Sulzby, E. (1989). Emergent literacy: New perspectives. In D. S. Strickland & L. M. Morrow (Eds.), *Emerging literacy: Young children learn to read and write* (pp. 1–15). Newark, DE: International Reading Association.

Tierney, R. J., Carter, M. A., & Desai, L. E. (1991). *Portfolio assessment in the reading–writing classroom*. Norwood, MA: Christopher-Gordon.

van Kleeck, A., & Richardson, A. (1990). Assessment of speech and language development. In J. Johnson & J. Goldman (Eds.), *Clinical child psychology: A handbook* (pp. 132–172). New York: Pergamon.

Waters, J., Frantz, J. F., Rottmayer, S., Trickett, M., & Genishi, C. (1992). Learning to see the learning in preschool children. In C. Genishi (Ed.), *Ways of assessing children and curriculum: Stories of early childhood practice* (pp. 25–57). New York: Teachers College Press.

Wolf, D., Bixby, J., Glenn, J., III, & Gardner, H. (1991). To use their minds well: Investigating new forms of student assessment. In G. Grant (Ed.), *Review of research in education* (Vol. 17) (pp. 31–74). Washington, DC: American Educational Research Association.

Wood, A. (1984). *The napping house*. San Diego: Harcourt Brace Jovanovich.

CHAPTER 5

Biliteracy and the
Language-Minority Child

Kris D. Gutierrez

The demographic shift in the past few years has virtually changed the complexion of our school's population, with elementary schools experiencing the most significant changes. Today, in some of the nation's largest school districts minority groups are the majority, of whom some estimated 3,600,000 are language-minority students. This significant shift in student enrollment has made the schooling of language-minority children increasingly problematic for an educational system that is essentially unprepared and, perhaps, even reluctant to insure the success of this important student population. Not only have schools had tremendous difficulty understanding and dealing with the wide range of cultural and social experiences these children bring to the school setting, but they have also found themselves virtually unprepared to deal with the vastly different linguistic experiences and abilities of this increasingly large student population.

While there has been a major thrust in educational reform to improve education and equity for school-aged children from diverse ethnic and linguistic backgrounds, to a large extent, these reforms have not worked. In particular, their underachievement and poor performance on measures of literacy development, chronicled by local, state and national assessments, have persisted (Applebee, Langer, Jenkins, Mullis, & Foertsch, 1990). The continued educational vulnerability of culturally and linguistically diverse children has highlighted the importance of effective early childhood school programs in children's literacy development, particularly in light of the well-documented long-term academic and social benefits of early education programs for at-risk young children (Lazar, 1983).

Yet as the number of ethnic- and language-minority children participating in early childhood programs grows, the degree of congruity between the school curriculum and what children know and how they learn decreases, as does their success in school (Shepard & Smith, 1988). This disparity may be attributed in part to the changing curriculum and function of early childhood programs—kindergarten in particular—as early childhood programs become part of the public rather than private school domain (Hymes, 1988; National Association for the Education of Young Children, 1986; Silvern, 1988). Previously, the emphasis in kindergarten had been on developing social competence and responsibility (Hiebert, 1988; Spodek, 1988). The new academic focus of the kindergarten curriculum serves as evidence that preschool programs are now being modeled after primary school programs (Gallagher & Siegel, 1987). This curricular change has also affected teacher attitudes and beliefs. Expectations of what children should know when they enter and leave kindergarten, for example, have increased significantly in the last 20 years (Shepard & Smith, 1987, 1988).

These changes have created significant debate about the nature of early childhood programs. The debate centers around the following questions:

1. What should be taught; that is, what is developmentally appropriate?
2. What should be the focus? That is, should the emphasis be on developing social competence or on the acquisition of academic knowledge and skills?
3. When should formal instruction begin and what should be the role of the teacher and the students in learning activities? That is, how will teachers know when, how, and to what extent children should participate?

This chapter will discuss the development of early childhood literacy programs for language-minority students in the context of the ongoing debate. It is assumed that the case for using the child's home language as the medium of instruction has been sufficiently made (California State Department of Education, 1986; Wong-Fillmore & Valadez, 1986). In this chapter I will suggest a reconceptualization of bilingual programs in early childhood education, specifically kindergarten. I will discuss the importance of developing early literacy, not just linguistic skills—"biliteracy," not simply bilingualism—in the language-minority child. I will embed this discussion in a theoretical framework that defines literacy as a meaning-making process that is simultaneously sociocultural, cognitive, and linguistic and that redefines bilingualism as biliteracy, or the acquisition of a more comprehensive set of literacy skills, including knowledge of and experimentation with both oral and written forms of language.

This reconceptualization requires a reexamination of early literacy programs, teachers' beliefs, and current instructional practices in the context of the following questions:

1. What do we know about how children learn and acquire literacy in particular?
2. Are early literacy programs based on what and how children have previously learned?
3. What contexts foster literacy development?
4. What, then, should be the nature of literacy instruction in the early childhood classroom?

Current estimates of the number of entering kindergarten children likely to be at risk for educational failure are nearly 20% (Children's Defense Fund, 1987). A growing number of these are language-minority children. The critical need for early intervention is obvious. How literacy learning is defined in early childhood education learning experiences may significantly influence how children come to know literacy in the native and second language. However, the importance of developing effective biliteracy programs for language-minority children should not be solely an educational and social policy issue. Literacy practices in early childhood programs should also be research-driven. Such practices should be based on what we know about language-minority children as we continue to observe them in the everyday routines of home and school life.

FROM BILINGUALISM TO BILITERACY

There appears to be no one comprehensive definition or commonly used set of criteria for identifying linguistically diverse students. At the most simplistic level, these students may be so identified because they come from homes in which English is not spoken. Or they may be identified and defined by their low performance on a standardized test of language competence. Although the range in language abilities among children within the same ethnic or racial group may be as disparate as that found between groups, they nevertheless are generally defined in terms of the language-minority groups to which they belong.

Language-minority students, however, are not members of monolithic groups and, thus, may fit into a variety of categories. Most often, though, the labels used to describe these students are generalized to mean "at risk" (Cazden & Snow, 1990). Consider, for example, the label "limited," used to describe oral English-language skills, or the terms "basic," "developmental," "inexperienced," or "remedial," used to characterize the writing and reading abilities of many language-minority children. Implicit in the use of such labels is the assumption that linguistic and cultural differences can be equated with knowledge and skills that need to be "remediated." These descriptions or classifications do not account for the rich sociocultural and linguistic experiences children bring to school.

How children are defined and labeled, even at the earliest stages of their schooling experience, is not an insignificant issue. These labels may have implications for the ways these children come to know and acquire literacy from the instruction they receive. Here, language-minority children are defined as students who

1. Participate extensively in non-English-speaking social and cultural contexts out of school
2. Have developed the communicative competence required for participation in those sociocultural contexts
3. Are being introduced, in substantive ways, to an English speaking environment (Garcia, 1991).

The process of becoming bilingual and biliterate is a highly variant and complex phenomenon that cannot be characterized by simple labels and definitions. Our inability to understand the complexity of the acquisition of these skills, as well as the importance of producing biliterate students, has contributed to a wide range of definitions of bilingualism. On one end of this definitional continuum, bilingualism is defined as having nativelike control of two languages. Bilingualism has also been understood more broadly to include the "circumstances surrounding the creation of bilingualism and its maintenance or attrition" (Hakuta, 1986, p. 4). The conceptualization of "biliteracy" builds on Hakuta's more developmental and sociocultural definition of bilingualism. It can be distinguished from bilingualism insofar as it requires, both theoretically and in classroom practice, the acquisition of a more comprehensive set of language skills or literacy in both the first and second languages. This constellation of early literacy abilities, initially developed in the child's first language, includes, for example, talking, sharing, telling and retelling jokes and stories, drawing, playing with written and oral forms of language, extending discussion and asking questions, and assisting oneself and other children. From this perspective, biliteracy in the early childhood classroom necessarily includes developing emergent understandings of both oral and written language and the social knowledge needed to use various forms of language and to participate in particular discourse communities — most notably the early childhood classroom community.

Numerous instructional interventions have been designed to ameliorate the educational circumstance of primary school–aged language-minority children. One of the primary goals of these programs has been to help these children acquire the language skills needed for successful participation in academic contexts. Common to most of these intervention programs, regardless of the language of instruction, is an emphasis on "bilingualism," that is, language programs designed to help children develop oral language fluency in the native language, the second language, or both. However, the degree to which these programs address the continued development of the child's first-language skills varies considerably. For example, nearly one-third of the primary school programs for language-minority students surveyed in one study reported no use of native language instruction (O'Malley, 1981). Thus many students have little or no opportunity to build on their knowledge of the native language as they develop second-language skills; they have limited opportunity to become truly "bilingual." Not only have many "bilingual" programs focused primarily on the acquisition of second-language skills, but they have also emphasized oral language fluency and have not fully incorporated writing instruction (Edelsky, 1986). In other words, early language instruction in many bilingual programs has been too narrowly defined as developing oral language skills or has focused around language activities that do not acknowledge the social nature of bilingualism, the wide range of language abilities among bilinguals, the various dimensions and conditions of bilingualism, or the full range of literacy skills needed for bilingualism and biliteracy (Duran, 1987; Hornberger, 1989; Wong-Fillmore, 1983).

Some programs have emphasized the importance of building on the children's native-language skills and sociolinguistic experiences and have been successful in assisting children's development of important language skills (Cardenas, 1986; Cummins, 1986). Too often, though, even these bilingual programs have not addressed all those components of literacy that indeed are needed for biliteracy (Flores et al., 1985). These practices have limited students' opportunities to develop emergent understandings of a more comprehensive view of literacy, as well as to appropriate the social knowledge needed to understand the communicative contexts of the early childhood classroom and the rules and roles of participation. Without full participation in meaningful learning activities that require the use of a variety of forms of language, language-minority children will have difficulty understanding the function of literacy and the ways literacy can mediate their learning across a variety of academic contexts (Altwerger, Edelsky, & Flores, 1987; Goodman, Goodman, & Flores, 1979).

While the emphasis on oral language development is certainly appropriate in the early childhood literacy program, these programs have not included opportunities for children to experiment and play with written language and to integrate the various components of literacy in everyday language activities. Such programs, then, have been built around instructional practices that do not account, in full, for the cognitive and social nature of literacy and for the larger repertoire of literacy skills young children possess (Dyson, 1985; Genishi, 1988b; Genishi & Dyson, 1984).

Until recently, little emphasis has been placed on developing more comprehensive literacy skills, particularly writing, in kindergarten literacy programs. In fact, writing is still not a regular part of the language curriculum of many first- or second-language programs for ethnic- and language-minority students. Not surprisingly, many students from diverse linguistic and cultural backgrounds ultimately leave schools without ever acquiring the abilities of written academic discourse (Farr, 1986). There are, of course, many reasons that this phenomenon occurs across K–12 classrooms. In general, the value of writing in promoting literacy and critical thinking is not fully appreciated; consequently, it is not emphasized in regular literacy routines for either traditional (Applebee et al., 1990) or ethnic- and language-minority students (Farr & Daniels, 1986). Thus these students, like many mainstream students, receive inadequate writing instruction and practice. When they do write, they are rarely given opportunities to produce whole texts or elaborated pieces of discourse, to experiment with language, to become critical readers of their own writings, or to develop sustained arguments and marshal evidence to support these arguments (Farr, 1986; Gutierrez, 1987).

There is, then, reluctance to incorporate writing into the early childhood literacy program. In a recent year-long ethnographic study of the social contexts of literacy learning in three early childhood classrooms, the nature of teaching and learning literacy was studied (Gutierrez, in preparation). Across these classrooms, teachers' beliefs about learning in general and learning literacy in particular shaped the instructional contexts. In general, these teachers held several major assumptions about young children's knowledge of oral and written language and about the nature of early literacy instruction, that is, the kinds of literacy tasks in which children could engage:

1. Most young children have limited experiences with the forms of written discourse and the function of written texts when they enter the early childhood classroom.
2. Children will come to literacy, particularly writing, when they are developmentally ready, and they will come to know literacy without the formal inclusion of regular and varied opportunities to experiment with written forms of language.

3. Literacy instruction should not precede the developmental level.
4. Young children are not developmentally ready to engage in the writing process.

These classroom literacy practices revealed teachers' strict adherence to their conceptualizations of Piagetian notions of development. Because they believed that writing was a developmentally inappropriate task for young children, these teachers did not construct literacy tasks that encouraged the use and development of various kinds of writing skills. Instead, literacy tasks that involved writing were teacher defined and tightly managed. Children had limited opportunities to construct literacy activities or to co-construct such activities with their peers. Consequently, teachers had few occasions to know what students knew and could do with and without teacher assistance. The teachers' assessments of what children could do were frequently based on informal assessments of how children performed on teacher-constructed and -managed activities.

The contexts for learning were informed by teachers' well-articulated but unexamined assumptions about the teaching and learning of literacy — assumptions that were not necessarily well grounded in theory and research or that did not emerge from systematic observation or study of children. These teachers generally relied on anecdotal experience, on their own experience as teachers and learners, and on local folk theories of literacy learning to explain or describe children's performance. These were very good teachers; their willingness to open up their classrooms to intensive study was indicative of their desire to improve literacy instruction. However, the teachers' beliefs about what the children knew about written language, how they acquired written language, what kinds of literacy tasks were developmentally appropriate, and how to assist children's literacy development precluded the implementation of a biliteracy program.

Experimenting with written forms of language is not an unnatural act for language-minority children who are still mastering oral language skills. Edelsky (1986), for example, found that the bilingual children she studied were able to participate in the various language arts and read and write in English without having "total control" over oral English (1986, p. 78). In her study of young children's writing abilities, Dyson (1984b; this volume, Chapter 2) found that the nature of the context influenced children's writing. She cites the importance of providing children multiple opportunities to control the writing process and to interact with one another. These interactions with peers greatly influenced the nature of the children's writing strategies and the content of their final drafts.

Some second-language researchers suggest that there may well be no single best program for all children and all schools (Cazden & Snow,

1990; McLaughlin, 1985; Reyes, 1991). These researchers point out that although schools should build on the native-language strengths of language-minority children, the teaching of English should not always be taboo. These researchers argue against literacy instruction as a linear accumulation of skills or against the conceptualization of literacy as only oral language and reading skills development (Edelsky, 1989; Reyes, 1991). While all second-language learners benefit from opportunities to participate in meaningful literacy activities, when and how children approach the learning of English varies widely (Genishi, 1988a; Wong-Fillmore, 1983). Garcia (1991), for example, argues for nurturing first-language environments that introduce English literacy skills on an individual basis and that take into account the various contexts in which the child participates and uses language.

In order to make informed decisions about the nature of literacy instruction in early childhood classrooms, to know both individual and whole-class needs, educators must become careful observers of what children do and say and should know much more about what English-language skills and knowledge children have when they enter the classroom (Dyson & Genishi, 1988; Genishi, 1988b). This requires examining existing assumptions that currently underlie beliefs about how early literacy is taught and learned.

Few native- or second-language early literacy programs, however, introduce children to a larger view of literacy and, thus, a more comprehensive set of literacy skills. There are a number of possible reasons for this dearth in practice, including a number of existing assumptions, folk theories, or teaching lore about how language is taught and learned (Goldenberg & Gallimore, 1991; Gutierrez, 1991). Some assumptions are based in cultural explanations of how language is best acquired and about the roles of families in the literacy learning process. Others are based on understandings of how children learn oral and written discourse, about which contexts facilitate learning, and about the order in which literacy skills should be taught. It is important to examine whether these beliefs and practices enhance the acquisition of literacy and biliteracy for language-minority students. Several of these major assumptions and their implications are discussed below.

Understanding Home–School Relationships

Some educational practices have been built on the assumption that low-income, non-English-speaking families cannot provide environments that facilitate the acquisition of academic literacy. Several researchers have argued that middle-class children are more socialized to academic discourse than are lower-income students (Cummins, 1979). Other researchers, however, have pointed out that there need not be a connection between social class and the role and uses of literacy in the home (Delgado-Gaitan, 1991; Moll, Amanti, Neff, & Gonzalez, 1992; Trueba & Delgado-Gaitan, 1991). Wells (1981), for example, found that entry-level knowledge of the purposes and mechanics of literacy, not social class, was the single best predictor of literacy acquisition after two years of formal schooling for the monolingual children he studied. In other words, the extent to which children were socialized to the uses and forms of written text influenced later literacy learning.

In their study of the reading development of low-income, immigrant Latino children, Goldenberg and Gallimore (1991) found that literacy practices varied significantly among this seemingly homogeneous population. Their study, which debunked several strongly held beliefs about the tremendous incongruity between the home and the school, revealed that there was significant congruity between teachers' and families' beliefs about how literacy should be taught. What differed was the way in which individual families implemented these educational values. For this Latino population, the degree to which literacy was required by the father's job served as the best predictor of children's success in reading (Reese, Balzano, Gallimore, & Goldenberg, 1991).

These researchers' findings also challenge another commonly held myth, that is, that Latino parents do not value education in the same way that Anglo or middle-class parents do. These Latino parents "placed more value on educational achievement — and its importance for social and economic mobility — than the school staff seemed to realize" (Goldenberg & Gallimore, 1991, p. 9). Many of the parents they studied expressed the belief that "educational attainment was the key to a good job and a more secure future" (p. 9). Instead of attributing the differences in how values were implemented across families to cultural or educational deficits, this study identified the highest rates of literacy learning among those families who successfully implemented traditional Mexican values (Goldenberg, Reese, & Gallimore, in press; Reese et al., 1991). Such studies strongly challenge deficit-model explanations that tie literacy development to social class rather than explore the unique contexts in which these children live and the everyday practices of their families. They also suggest that schools need to tap the underutilized resource of the Latino parent.

Some primary school literacy educators have acknowledged the "funds of knowledge" (Moll, 1991) that exist among parents and have extended instruction beyond the classroom walls. Reyes and Laliberty (1992), for example, found that both Anglo and Latino parents demonstrated cross-cultural appreciation of the literacy skills their children displayed at a Young Author's Conference organized by one classroom teacher. During this literacy event, children read favorite stories they had written throughout the year. Some pieces were read in Spanish, others in English, all without translation. Both groups of parents participated enthusiastically, even when they did not understand the language in which the child was reading. Moreover, all parents wrote comments (in their native language) about work collected in prepared booklets by all the children. One Latino parent, for example, commented on a story written by an Anglo student: "Bueno, no le entendi pero me gustaron sus dibujos. [Well, I didn't understand it, but I liked his illustrations]" (p. 272). Such examples challenge practices and beliefs that do not recognize that the social interaction required for literacy learning can be extended beyond the traditional classroom.

Accounting for Culture

The schooling of children whose culture and language differ dramatically from that of traditional students is a complex process. Certainly, the ambiguity surrounding our understanding of bilingualism adds to its complexity (Cazden & Snow, 1990). The difficulty in understanding and valuing the linguistic and social differences of language-minority children may be compounded by the fact that the profile of today's teachers is in sharp contrast to that of their students. Cazden and Mehan (1986) describe the typical beginning teacher of the 1990s as an Anglo female in her early to mid-twenties who comes from a lower-middle to middle-income family. Most of these novice teachers will be confronted with teaching urban or inner-city students whose languages and sociocultural experiences vary dramatically from their own. Of particular importance is that this disparity may have significant consequences in the way classroom instruction is organized and implemented and, consequently, on the nature of learning experienced by students (Cazden, 1988; Mehan, 1979). If we accept Clyne's (1987) notion that discourse norms are culture-bound, then we might also suspect that the ways in which instructional events and discourse patterns are constructed in the classroom are also bound by the culture of the classroom.

From this perspective, a study of linguistic and cultural incongruity in the education of ethnically and linguistically different populations must move beyond broad theoretical explanations that focused primarily on macro features of the culture (e.g., sociological, historical, and economic factors) to explain the academic underachievement of diverse student populations (Ogbu, 1978). More recently, researchers have examined how context and the social organization of instruction influence literacy learning for ethnic- and language-minority children (Au, 1980; Au & Mason, 1981–1982; Gutierrez, 1992; Heath, 1986; Moll, 1989; Trueba, 1987). In these studies the various aspects of context — the literacy events or activities themselves, the talk or discourse used in those activities by students and teachers, and the ways in which students and teachers participated in these instructional contexts — were found to play a significant role in shaping children's perceptions and uses of literacy. This kind of contextual analysis focuses on the nature of the learning event rather than on a decontextualized set of skills or macro features of culture (Trueba, 1988). From this culturally sensitive theory of learning, development is examined within contexts of activity, and socially constructed activities are identified as the units of analysis for study. In this way, researchers and practitioners can observe the relationship between development and context and better understand that development cannot be understood apart from the context in which it occurs.

Further research that focuses specifically on the early childhood classroom, however, is needed to better understand how to construct appropriate contexts for early literacy development. What kinds of learning environments take account of cultural and linguistic differences important to the acquisition of literacy? What kinds of literacy practices provide students opportunities to develop their own skills, to appropriate the discourse of the classroom and its various participation structures?

Dissecting the Literacy Process

There are several commonly held assumptions about the appropriate instructional sequence for teaching literacy skills. One is centered around the belief that oral language fluency in either the native or second language must precede reading and writing instruction. First-language researchers of children's writing and reading have long argued that young writers and readers need to engage in meaningful literacy activities before they fully understand the writing and reading processes (Altwerger et al., 1987; Graves, 1978). The focus of these classrooms is not on teaching isolated writing, reading, and speaking skills; instead, the emphasis is on creating contexts of use for meaningful discourse. According to Goodman, Smith, Meredith, and Goodman (1987), "Oral language is learned holistically in the context of speech acts; written language is learned holistically in the context of literacy events" (p. 398).

Edelsky (1986) argues for a holistic presentation of literacy and discusses how this approach promotes general literacy development. She defines writing development, for example, as a "reorganization of a child's literacy knowledge [which occurs when] a child has the chance to orchestrate the demands of multiple systems" (p. 84). The process of simultaneously negotiating multiple systems promotes this reorganization or development. Teaching literacy holistically allows children to draw from and use their various literacy skills simultaneously. As Farr and Daniels (1986) have proposed, "speaking and writing are alternate ways of using one's language capacities, and very often both modes are used within a single speech or literacy event" (p. 27).

Researchers studying the early literacy development of young children, including ethnic- and language-minority children, provide rich accounts of the ways children come to know literacy. When children have multiple opportunities to experience literacy in a variety of contexts, to experience holistic presentations of literacy, they begin to understand the function and power of literacy and to use different forms of literacy (Dyson, 1984a). Learning literacy is not simply learning a particular set of skills in a particular sequence; it involves learning how a particular community uses and values literacy (Gutierrez, in press). Being socialized to literacy also means developing literacy behaviors, such as knowing how and when to ask questions, how to hold a book or listen to a story, and when and how to participate (Gutierrez, 1992). As Dyson (1984a) suggests, "[The] mundane particulars of school functioning are influenced by and influence children's understandings of what [literacy] is and how it is used in schools" (p. 262).

This view of literacy learning as language socialization represents a major shift in how language instruction is being conceptualized in some bilingual programs across the country. It is a view of learning that differs from that actually practiced in literacy activities in most classrooms. This view suggests that learning both written and oral forms of language requires the learning of a new culture (Ochs, 1988; Ochs & Schieffelin, 1984; Schieffelin & Ochs, 1986). It requires learning not only linguistic features and knowledge of the language but simultaneously learning the social knowledge needed to participate effectively in the new discourse community (Mehan, 1980). In this way, the language-minority child must also be socialized to the classroom norms in everyday communicative contexts.

Building on the work of first-language researchers, second-language researchers have also developed compatible theories for the importance of teaching second-language learners whole language (Edelsky, 1989; Garcia, 1991; Moll, 1989; Reyes, 1991; Urzua, 1987). The point here is not to debate whether oral language fluency enhances the learning of other literacy skills but rather to challenge the practice of delaying the introduction of reading and writing instruction and of using an atomistic approach to teaching literacy in either first- or second-language instruction. A parts-to-whole approach to teaching literacy has been widely challenged by theories of language acquisition and learning. From a Vygotskian or sociohistorical perspective, the teaching of literacy must be considered in terms of whole activities rather than from a reductionist position. Vygotsky (1978) has argued that "until now, writing has occupied too narrow a place in school practice as compared to the enormous role that it plays in children's cultural development" (p. 105).

A reductionist theory of teaching literacy violates the fundamental Vygotskian principle that development occurs within the contexts of whole activities. Cole and Griffin (1983) suggest that a sociohistorical approach talks about basic activities instead of basic skills and "instantiates those that are necessary and sufficient to carry out the whole process of [literacy] in the general conditions of learning" (p. 73). Central to this redefinition is a view of literacy as a whole, undissected activity.

This holistic and more comprehensive view of literacy and biliteracy is best understood in a conceptualization of literacy and learning as socially constructed and mediated processes — processes that are shaped and influenced by the nature of the contexts in which learning occurs. These understandings of human and language development have important implications for helping language-minority children become successful biliterates.

DEVELOPING BILITERACY

Beginning literacy instruction has too often been constrained by excessive emphasis on implementing "developmentally appropriate" activities or by overemphasizing what the child must learn to succeed in the first grade. The emphasis in children's biliteracy programs should not be on "the sooner the better," on upgrading the kindergarten curriculum; after all, 4- and 5-year-old children are different from 9- and 10-year-olds. Instead, studies of young children's literacy development suggest that what is appropriate depends on what and how prior literacy learning has occurred, how literacy was used and valued, and the nature of current literacy instruction (Dyson, 1984a).

Fostering biliteracy in young children depends on teachers' willingness to learn from their students, to acknowledge and incorporate what children already know, and to transform the contexts for learning and interacting. Examining our own assumptions about literacy learning is the first step toward transforming the classroom contexts in which we embed literacy learning. This kind of reflective, critical teaching will help teachers distinguish between those beliefs that are part of the folk knowledge and other beliefs that are well grounded in both empirical and practical studies of how children learn and develop literacy. Reflective practice is the first step in transforming the contexts in which children learn.

The Social Contexts of Literacy Learning

Careful examination of the contexts in which students learn — that is, what students learn, how that knowledge is transmitted, who is present in the learning activity, and which goals and motives drive the learning event and the larger curriculum — suggests that the process of learning in general and the acquisition of literacy in particular is a socially mediated process (Gutierrez, 1992; Tharp & Gallimore, 1988). This view of literacy learning is one that characterizes language as inherently dialogic and interactive and considers language acquisition from the perspective of language socialization (Ochs, 1988).

Studying language in the classroom is studying a particular discourse community in a particular social context; it is studying the ways in which people use and understand language, the ways in which they interact and participate in communicative events constructed in the classroom. It is a study of how linguistic, social, and cultural practices shape classroom instruction.

Language acquisition is more than learning to speak; it is a process through which a child becomes a competent member of a community by acquiring both the linguistic and sociocultural knowledge needed to learn how to use language in that particular community. Throughout this process members of communities are both socialized to use language and socialized through language (Ochs, 1988). In this way, children's knowledge and use of language are both socially and culturally organized (Schieffelin & Ochs, 1986).

Thus the contexts in which learning and interactions are embedded are important to the process of both oral and written language development. From this perspective, effective instruction for language-minority children requires an understanding of the acquisition of biliteracy as a process of language socialization that takes place in the culturally and socially organized activities in which children participate, interact, receive assistance, and experiment and play with both oral and written forms of their home language.

This understanding of language as a socially constructed and mediated phenomenon has profound implications for understanding how written and oral language are learned, for understanding how learning can be facilitated in the classroom, and for recognizing the importance of context and the nature of interaction within those contexts in the language learning process. Educators need to rethink current instructional practices that are developed without consideration of the social nature of language learning, the contexts in which language learning takes place, and the ways in which participation and interaction are organized.

Teaching and Learning

The development of enriched activity settings that promote literacy learning in early childhood classrooms may be facilitated by recognizing the dynamic relationship between teaching and learning, and learning and development. Vygotsky (1978) argues that the developmental processes do not occur simultaneously with the learning process. Instead, learning precedes development, and it is this sequence that creates the "zone of proximal development" (ZPD). From this theoretical position, an important characteristic of learning is that the internalization of developmental processes by the child occurs through meaningful interaction with and assistance from other people.

Using this theoretical framework, Tharp and Gallimore (1988) have called for a redefinition of teaching as "assisting performance through the ZPD. Teaching can be said to occur when assistance is offered at points in the ZPD at which performance requires assistance" (p. 31). This zone of proximal development is a central concept in helping early childhood teachers

1. Assess what a student can perform or understand alone and what he or she can do in collaboration with others
2. Insure that the level of difficulty of instruction slightly precedes actual student development
3. Offer appropriate and maximum assistance to facilitate and scaffold learning
4. Create instructional contexts and interactions that mediate students' learning
5. Redefine the role of the teacher and student in the learning process.

Of importance to the teaching process is that the cognitive, social, and linguistic skills children acquire are directly related to the nature of the contexts for learning and the ways they interact and participate in those contexts. This understanding of the social nature of language learning offers early childhood educators a template for constructing and examining the contexts in which literacy is taught and learned and for implementing literacy programs that promote the development of cognitive, social, and linguistic skills in children's native and second languages. First- and second-language literacy programs developed around this theoretical framework design instruction based on the following premises:

1. Learning is a highly social and mediated process.
2. Language acquisition involves language socialization and requires the acquisition of linguistic, cognitive, and sociocultural knowledge and skills.
3. Literacy instruction should include opportunities to use, develop, and appropriate speaking, listening, reading, writing, and performance skills.
4. The nature of the context in which children learn influences language learning.
5. Children must participate in contexts in which they can use and ultimately appropriate the cultural tool of literacy.
6. Children's learning must be regularly assisted.
7. Children need to actively participate in contexts within which they can interact with peers and more expert others.
8. Children need opportunities to develop literacy skills in both the native and second languages.

Finally, implementing comprehensive biliteracy programs must also include assisting teachers' performance in regular and meaningful ways. Restructuring language programs must also include regular opportunities for teachers to participate in activities in which they can acquire better understandings of how children develop literacy skills in both first and second languages. It also requires further investigation of the sources of teacher beliefs about literacy learning in the first and second language and about the role teacher-education programs play in constructing, reinforcing, or revising beliefs and practices.

REFERENCES

Altwerger, B., Edelsky, C., & Flores, B. (1987). Whole language: What's new? *Reading Teacher, 41*, 144–154.

Applebee, A., Langer, J., Jenkins, L., Mullis, I., & Foertsch, M. (1990). *Learning to write in our nation's schools: Instruction and achievement in 1988 at grades 4, 8, and 12.* Princeton, NJ: National Assessment of Educational Progress, Education Testing Service.

Au, K. (1980). Participation structures in a reading lesson with Hawaiian children: Analysis of a culturally appropriate instructional event. *Anthropology and Education Quarterly, 11*(2), 91–115.

Au, K., & Mason, J. (1981–1982). Social organizational factors in learning to read: The balance of rights hypothesis. *Reading Research Quarterly, 17*, 115–152.

California State Department of Education. (Ed.). (1986). Beyond language: Social and cultural factors in schooling language minority students. Los Angeles: Evaluation, Dissemination, and Assessment Center, California State University.

Cardenas, J. (1986). The role of native-language instruction in bilingual education. *Phi Delta Kappan, 67*, 359–363.

Cazden, C. (1988). *Classroom discourse: The language of teaching and learning.* Portsmouth, NH: Heinemann Educational Books.

Cazden, C., & Mehan, H. (1986). Principles from sociology and anthropology: Context, code, classroom, and culture. In M. C. Reynolds (Ed.), *Knowledge base for the beginning teacher* (pp. 47–57). New York: Pergamon.

Cazden, C., & Snow, C. (1990). *Preface. The annals. The Academy of Political and Social Science* (pp. 9–10). Newbury Park, CA: Sage.

Children's Defense Fund. (1987). *The antecedents of self-esteem.* San Francisco: Freeman.

Clyne, M. (1987). Cultural differences in the organization of academic texts. *Journal of Pragmatics, 11*, 211–247.

Cole, M., & Griffin, P. (1983). A socio-historical approach to re-mediations. *The Quarterly Newsletter of the Laboratory of Comparative Human Cognition, 5*(4), 69–74.

Cummins, J. (1979). Linguistic interdependence in the educational development of bilingual children. *Review of Educational Research, 49*, 225–251.

Cummins, J. (1986). Empowering minority students: A framework for intervention. *Harvard Education Review, 56*, 18–36.

Delgado-Gaitan, C. (1991). Involving parents in school: A process of empowerment. *American Journal of Education, 100*, 20–46.

Duran, R. (1987). Factors affecting development of second language literacy. In S. Goldman & H. Trueba (Eds.), *Becoming literate in English as a second language* (pp. 33–56). Norwood, NJ: Ablex.

Dyson, A. H. (1984a). Learning to write/learning to do school: Emergent writers' interpretations of school literacy tasks. *Research in the Teaching of English, 8*(3), 233–264.

Dyson, A. H. (1984b). "N spell my Grandmama": Fostering early thinking about print. *The Reading Teacher, 38*, 262–271.

Dyson, A. H. (1985). Research currents: Writing and the social life of children. *Language Arts, 62*(6), 632–659.

Dyson, A. H., & Genishi, C. (1988). Research currents: Paradoxes in classroom research. *Language Arts, 65*(8), 788–798.

Edelsky, C. (1986). *Writing in a bilingual program: Habia una vez.* Norwood, NJ: Ablex.

Edelsky, C. (1989). Bilingual children's writing: Fact and fiction. In D. M. Johnson & D. H. Roen (Eds.), *Richness in writing: Empowering ESL students* (pp. 165–176). New York: Longman.

Farr, M. (1986). Language, culture, and writing: Sociolinguistic foundations of research on writing. In E. Z. Rothkopf (Ed.), *Review of research in education* (Vol. 13) (pp. 195–224). Washington, DC: American Educational Research Association.

Farr, M., & Daniels, H. (1986). *Language diversity and writing instruction*. Urbana, IL: ERIC Clearinghouse on Reading and Communications Skills, National Council of Teachers of English.

Flores, B., Garcia, E., Gonzales, S., Hidalgo, G., Kaczmarek, K., & Romero, T. (1985). *Holistic bilingual instruction strategies*. Chandler, AZ: Exito.

Gallagher, J. M., & Siegel, I. E. (Eds.). (1987). Introduction to special issue: Hot-housing of young children. *Early Childhood Research Quarterly, 2,* 201–202.

Garcia, E. E. (1991). *The education of linguistically and culturally diverse students: Effective instructional practices*. Santa Cruz, CA: Center for Research on Cultural Diversity and Second Language Learning.

Garcia, E. E. (1991). Effective instruction for language minority students: The teacher. *Journal of Education, 173*(2), 130–141.

Genishi, C. (1988a). Observing the second language learner: An example of teachers' learning. *Language Arts, 66*(5), 509–515.

Genishi, C. (1988b). Research currents: What Maisie knew. *Language Arts, 66*(5), 872–882.

Genishi, C., & Dyson, A. H. (1984). *Language assessment in the early years*. Norwood, NJ: Ablex.

Goldenberg, C., & Gallimore, R. (1991). Local knowledge, research knowledge, and educational change: A core study of early Spanish reading improvement. *Educational Researcher, 20*(8), 2–14.

Goldenberg, C., Reese, L., & Gallimore, R. (in press). Effects of school literacy materials on Latino children's home experiences and early reading achievement. *American Journal of Education*.

Goodman, K. S., Goodman, Y., & Flores, B. (1979). *Reading in the bilingual classroom: Literacy and biliteracy*. Rosslyn, VA: National Clearinghouse for Bilingual Education.

Goodman, K. S., Smith, E. B., Meredith, R., & Goodman, Y. M. (1987). *Language and thinking in school: A whole-language curriculum*. New York: Richard C. Owen.

Graves, D. (1978). *Balance the basics: Let them write*. New York: Ford Foundation.

Gutierrez, K. D. (1987). *The composing process of four college-age ethnic minority basic readers and writers*. Unpublished doctoral dissertation, University of Colorado, Boulder.

Gutierrez, K. D. (1991, April). *The effects of writing process instruction on elementary school-aged Latino children*. Paper presented at the annual meeting of the American Educational Research Association, Chicago.

Gutierrez, K. D. (1992). A comparison of instructional contexts in writing process classrooms with Latino children. *Education and Urban Society, 24*(2), 244–262.

Gutierrez, K. D. (in press). Unpackaging academic literacy. *UCLA Journal of Education*.

Gutierrez, K. D. (in preparation). When Piaget meets Vygotsky: The social context of literacy in the early childhood classroom. Unpublished manuscript, Graduate School of Education, UCLA.

Hakuta, K. (1986). *Mirror of language: The debate on bilingualism*. New York: Basic Books.

Heath, S. B. (1986). Sociocultural contexts of language development. In Bilingual Education Office, California State Department of Education (Ed.), *Beyond language: Social and cultural factors in schooling language minority students*. Los Angeles: Evaluation, Dissemination, and Assessment Center, California State University.

Hiebert, E. H. (1988). The role of literacy experiences in early childhood programs. *Elementary School Journal, 89*(2), 161–172.

Hornberger, N. (1989). Continua of biliteracy. *Review of Educational Research, 3*, 271–296.

Hymes, J. L., Jr. (1988). Public school for four-year-olds. In J. S. McKee & K. M. Paciorek (Eds.), *Early Childhood Education* (pp. 106–107). Guilford, CT: Dushkin.

Lazar, I. (1983). Discussion and implication of the findings. In Consortium on Longitudinal Studies, *As the twig is bent . . . Lasting effects of preschool programs* (pp. 561–566). Hillsdale, NJ: Erlbaum.

McLaughlin, B. (1985). *Second language acquisition in childhood: Vol. 2. School-age children* (2nd ed.). Hillsdale, NJ: Erlbaum.

Mehan, H. (1979). *Learning lessons: Social organizations in the classrooms*. Cambridge, MA: Harvard University Press.

Mehan, H. (1980). The competent student. *Anthropology and Education, 11*, 131–152.

Moll, L. (1989). Teaching second language students: A Vygotskian perspective. In D. M. Johnson & D. H. Roen (Eds.), *Richness in writing: Empowering ESL students* (pp. 55–69). New York: Longman.

Moll, L. (1991, October). *Funds of knowledge for change: Developing mediating connections between homes and classrooms*. Paper presented at conference on "Literacy, Identity, and Mind," University of Michigan, Ann Arbor.

Moll, L., Amanti, C., Neff, D., & Gonzalez, N. (1992). Funds of knowledge for teaching: Using a qualitative approach to connect homes and classrooms. *Theory into Practice, 31*(2), 132–141.

National Association for the Education of Young Children. (1986). NAEYC position statement on developmentally appropriate practice in early childhood programs serving children from birth through age 8. *Young Children, 41*(6), 4–29.

Ochs, E. (1988). *Culture and language development*. Cambridge, England: Cambridge University Press.

Ochs, E., & Schieffelin, B. B. (1984). Language acquisition and socialization: Three developmental stories and their implications. In R. Schweder & R. LeVine (Eds.), *Culture theory: Essays on mind, self, and emotion* (pp. 276–320). Cambridge: Cambridge University Press.

Ogbu, J. (1978). *Minority education and caste: The American system in cross-cultural perspective*. New York: Academic Press.

O'Malley, M. J. (1981). *Children's and services study: Language minority children with limited English proficiency in the United States.* Rosslyn, VA: National Clearinghouse for Bilingual Education.

Reese, L., Balzano, S., Gallimore, R., & Goldenberg, C. (1991, November). *The concept of educación: Latino family values and American schooling.* Paper presented at the annual meeting of the American Anthropological Association, Chicago.

Reyes, M. (1991). *The "one size fits all" approach to literacy.* Paper presented at the annual conference of the American Educational Research Association, Chicago.

Reyes, M., & Laliberty, E. (1992, April). A teacher's "Pied Piper" effect on young authors. *Education and Urban Society, 24*(2), 244–262.

Schieffelin, B. B., & Ochs, E. (1986). *Language socialization across cultures.* Cambridge, England: Cambridge University Press.

Shepard, L. A., & Smith, M. L. (1987). Effects of kindergarten retention at the end of first grade. *Psychology in the Schools, 24,* 346–357.

Shepard, L. A., & Smith, M. L. (1988). Escalating academic demand in kindergarten: Counterproductive policies. *Elementary School Journal, 89*(2), 135–146.

Silvern, S. B. (1988). Continuity/discontinuity between home and early childhood education environments. *Elementary School Journal, 89*(2), 147–160.

Spodek, B. (1988). Conceptualizing today's kindergarten curriculum. *Elementary School Journal, 89*(2), 203–212.

Tharp, R., & Gallimore, R. (1988). *Rousing minds to life: Teaching, learning, and schooling in social context.* Cambridge, England: Cambridge University Press.

Trueba, H. T. (1987). Organizing classroom instruction in specific sociocultural contexts: Teaching Mexican youth to write in English. In S. Goldman & H. Trueba (Eds.), *Becoming literate in English as a second language* (pp. 235–253). Norwood, NJ: Ablex.

Trueba, H. (1988). Culturally based explanations of minority students' academic achievement. *Anthropology and Education Quarterly, 19,* 270–287.

Trueba, H., & Delgado-Gaitan, C. (1991). *Crossing cultural borders: Education for immigrant families in America.* London: Falmer.

Urzua, C. (1987). "You stopped too soon": Second language children composing and revising. *TESOL Quarterly, 21,* 270–304.

Vygotsky, L. S. (1978). *Mind in society: The development of higher psychological processes.* Cambridge, MA: Harvard University Press.

Wells, G. (1981). *Learning through interaction.* Cambridge, England: Cambridge University Press.

Wong-Fillmore, L. (1983). The language learner as an individual: Implications or research on individual differences for the ESL teacher. In M. A. Clarke & J. Handscombe (Eds.), *On TESOL '82: Pacific perspectives on language learning and teaching* (pp. 157–174). Washington, DC: TESOL.

Wong-Fillmore, L., & Valadez, C. (1986). Teaching bilingual learners. In M. S. Wittrock (Ed.), *Handbook on research on teaching* (pp. 648–685). New York: Macmillan.

CHAPTER 6

Reading Recovery: A Literacy Program for At-Risk Children

Gay Su Pinnell

Reading Recovery was designed exclusively for at-risk children. This early intervention, based on a robust theory of literacy learning, has had documented success in helping struggling young readers. This chapter describes the program and presents a summary of research results.

A DEFINITION OF READING RECOVERY

Reading Recovery is based on the premise that early, high-quality help has the greatest potential for lasting impact and for reducing the need for continued compensatory help. Originally developed by New Zealand psychologist Marie M. Clay, the program has been adapted and tested for eight years in the United States and Canada. It now exists in 42 U.S. states and 4 Canadian provinces.

The theoretical base for Reading Recovery was developed through Clay's observational studies of young children learning to read. In Reading Recovery, reading is viewed as a complex process involving internal operations such as using information from a range of sources (including world knowledge, the syntactic structure of language, and visual information contained in the print) to monitor, search, and check. As they encounter written text, readers construct meaning by bringing their own knowledge to the process. Learning to read involves learning to use all sources of information in an orchestrated way. Clay (1991) suggests that "out of early reading and writing experiences the young learner creates a network of competencies which power subsequent independent literacy learning" (p. 1). Using meaning to control the process, children use in-the-head problem-solving strategies while working on print; eventually, they develop what Clay has called a self-extending system for reading, one that allows them to continue to learn.

Significant in the process is an adult (parent, teacher, or other caregiver) who interacts with the child during literacy events. Children learn within social contexts. The meaningful literacy events they experience — such as early writing for different purposes, hearing stories read, or trying to "read" themselves — help them build the knowledge they need. They receive feedback and observe demonstrations from more knowledgeable adults; conversations surrounding reading events illustrate processes. Adults share the task; with help, the children can do more reading and writing than they can alone, and they can engage in the searching and checking operations that will build the system. The adult helps the child work in what has been called the "zone of proximal development" (see Clay & Cazden, 1990; Wood, 1988).

Reading Recovery teachers work specifically with children who are having difficulty. They see their role as engaging children in rich literacy events and providing the kind of support necessary to help even those having difficulty to bring their own knowledge to this problem-solving event and to construct the internal operations they need to become independent readers.

The intensive one-to-one intervention is designed for children who are having difficulty in reading and writing after one year of school. In New Zealand, where children enter school on their fifth birthday, the poorest readers are identified at age 6. In the United States, Reading Recovery is recommended for the lowest-achieving 15% to 20% of a first-grade classroom. As to need and timing of the intervention, local judgment is required because of differences in policy and curriculum.

Children are selected using multiple indicators, including teacher judgment and individually applied observational measures, that are described later in this chapter. The primary goals of Reading Recovery are to reduce the instance of reading failure and to help children become independent readers. The goals are accomplished by

1. Bringing children who are considered at risk of failing up to average range in their classes so that they profit from ongoing classroom instruction
2. Providing an instructional context that makes accelerated progress possible so that children can catch up rather than just make progress
3. Helping each child develop a self-extending system that allows for continued progress without help beyond good classroom teaching.

In other words, Reading Recovery's purpose is not only to help or serve at-risk children; it is to remove the conditions that place these students in risky situations. It modifies the school environment and the school support system to provide the level and kind of help each child needs.

AT-RISK CHILDREN IN TODAY'S SCHOOLS

The term *at risk* can have several meanings, but the most general educational definition refers to children not profiting from the schooling they receive. The term usually refers to characteristics in the students themselves, a misleading designation because it suggests that the fault or deficiency lies within the individuals or families rather than in the interaction of home and school factors. At-risk characteristics are not necessarily problematic. They become so only if circumstances in the school interact with the characteristics to create risky situations.

Any child, whatever the economic circumstances, could be considered to be in a risky situation if he or she is not making steady progress toward the development of school-based literacy. For economic and social reasons, whole populations of children are considered to be more likely to be inadequately served by our educational system. Natriello, McDill, and Pallas (1990) have provided a thorough discussion of the term, which they say implies a look to the future, a suggestion that such students may have certain characteristics that make them more vulnerable to difficulty. They cite poverty, family composition, mother's education, racial and ethnic identity, and language background as factors that have high correlation with poor performance in school. They estimate that approximately 40% of the population under 18 possesses at least one of these characteristics; and, while many children are resilient enough to succeed in spite of vulnerability, there is the potential for large proportions of children to have problems in school.

The population of children with at-risk characteristics is increasing dramatically. Over the next 40 years, the number and proportion of minority-group children will increase; by 2020, the number of children in poverty is expected to rise to 16.5 million, an increase of 33%. Both the number and the proportion of children with a primary language other than English, with mothers who have not completed high school, or who are not living with both parents will also increase dramatically (see Hodgkinson, 1985, 1988). Clearly, these social problems are relevant to educational planning.

Even children without obvious difficulties may be considered at risk in certain educational contexts. In the 1960s Fantini and Weinstein (1968) suggested that being at a disadvantage simply means being blocked from attaining human potential and that such failure is actually a reflection of institutional failure.

Failure to learn to read in a timely enough manner to enable the use of reading in other learning creates a gap that is increasingly difficult to surmount during the following years. Furthermore, as Clay (1985) says, "there are consequences for the child's personality and confidence" (p. 11). School literacy instruction must be based on the knowledge and ways to learning that children have acquired through their preschool experiences. Children entering school have had very different prior experiences; and, according to Clay (1991), these differences may be traced not only to different home backgrounds but to the fact that children have selectively attended to their home and community learning experiences.

For most children, a rich literacy environment, with good teaching in the first year, will provide the support necessary to make the transition between home and school literacy learning. Some, however, seem to operate marginally in classroom situations. However hard they try, they cannot fully participate in the ongoing activities. Even if the environment is accepting and benevolent, they ultimately realize that they are not fully part of the culture that surrounds them daily.

They may listen to and delight in stories but pay little attention to print; they may not initiate the problem solving that moves a child from approximated versions of a story to actually reading for a precise message. Or, as a response to instruction, they may look hard at the letters and words but treat them as isolated items unrelated to their existing knowledge of language. If such circumstances exist, there is the potential that reading and reading instruction may be empty exercises that make little sense.

Extra time and extra help are the two most common approaches to reading problems. Perhaps children need more time either to mature or to build the appropriate foundation of knowledge that would make literacy learning easy. Wouldn't it make sense just to allow children to spend an extra year or two in school? The research on retention, however, does not support this view (Johnson, 1984; Walker & Madhere, 1987). A history of research (Arthur, 1936; Coeffield & Bloomers, 1956; Farley, 1936; Goodlad, 1954; Hall & Demarest, 1958) suggest that retention does not work to students' advantage. Special "transition rooms" designed to disguise retention by placing slower-moving children in one room, sometimes with decreased class size, also are problematic, leading to labeling and low expectations.

A pragmatic approach would suggest that these children need some extra help. Classroom teachers can adjust their plans to provide some individual assistance, but this minimal help may be inadequate for those having the most difficulty. Traditional solutions to providing extra help have brought their own problems. Remedial programs, both pull-out (see Johnston, Allington, & Afflerbach, 1985) and in-class (Slavin & Madden, 1987) models, do not fully meet children's needs. Such programs have the disadvantage of labeling children and entering them into a long-term compensatory education situation. Typically, learning tends to be slowed down, with drill and piecemeal learning being the norm (see Astrein, Fraser, & Steinberg, 1984). Meanwhile, usually on a long-term basis, students are missing classroom instruction, which puts them at a further disadvantage (Allington, McGill-Franzen, 1989; Good, 1986). Further, there is no evidence of long-term gains from the typical compensatory programs provided for high-risk students (Carter, 1984; Savage, 1987; Slavin, 1987).

Educators also have chosen to wait for maturity to solve the child's problems. However sensible the "wait and see" approach may appear on the surface, the evidence suggests that the issues are more complex. Students who have not had the literacy experiences necessary to provide a framework for the instruction they receive in school may find the classroom literacy activities confusing no matter what kind of curriculum they encounter (Heath, 1983; Mason, 1984; Teale & Sulzby, 1986; Wells, 1985). For example, high-risk children in a systematic, structured phonics program may find such a curriculum bewildering. They are required simultaneously to learn to distinguish the visual features of print and to link this knowledge to the systems of oral language they have learned. They may memorize items of knowledge but not know how to use these bits in orchestrated ways while problem solving on text. In more holistic curricula, children may focus on meaning but neglect detail and move along trying to "remember" texts or construct them solely from pictures. Whatever the situation, children cannot be expected to sort out confusions alone, and they do not remain "on hold."

In fact, they are learning within their social world. They listen to and notice what the teacher emphasizes; they watch others write and read. They construct new knowledge in the light of what they already understand, and for some, the process goes wrong. In Clay's (1985) view, there is a period, around the second year of schooling, when it is necessary for some children to have individual time with a teacher who tries to see from their point of view and then engages them in ways that will help to untangle confusions and recover the trajectory of progress toward effective, strategic reading. Reading Recovery is this kind of temporary extra help.

READING RECOVERY AS A SYSTEM INTERVENTION

In terms of the system, Reading Recovery is a "first net." Children selected for the program are the lowest achievers in reading. The idea is to identify young readers so that they can be helped but not to unnecessarily label and categorize them for long-term services. Daily, children are engaged in intensive reading and writing activities. Through careful selection from a repertoire of interactional procedures, the Reading Recovery teacher provides an individual program for each child. Designed to be supplementary to the classroom reading instruction, the program should exist "against the backdrop of a sound general programme" (Clay, 1985, p. 48).

Implementers of Reading Recovery are required to take a systemic view of change. Clay (1987) has said that "an innovation cannot move into an educational system merely on the merits of what it can do for children" (p. 38). The innovation must be designed to take into account the preexisting organization as it interacts in complex ways with the new model (see Sarason, 1991). Reading Recovery is designed as a series of interlocking interventions that support one another. The program design includes specified roles for administrators and the training and support of a special staff developer, called a teacher leader in the United States and Canada and a tutor in New Zealand, Australia, and England. To succeed, innovation designs must have a redirecting system that continually solves the problems that inevitably arise during the process of change. For Reading Recovery, the key person in the redirecting system is the teacher leader. The leader receives special preparation for one year in an intensive, university-based course that includes learning to teach children as well as how to work with adults and teach the teacher course.

Implementing Reading Recovery depends on three tiers of educational programs:

1. The daily tutorial program for children
2. The year-long inservice course for teachers, held at school district, regional, or university sites
3. The year-long course for teacher leaders held at university sites

Teachers, teacher leaders, and university personnel work together, each with different roles and responsibilities. They have in common their daily teaching of children; leaders in Reading Recovery are required to remain daily practitioners. They are also required to participate in ongoing staff development as long as they remain associated with the program.

Surrounding these educational programs is a network of communication and support that provides for continual renewal of the educational programs. For example, a newsletter containing theoretical articles and new research as well as notices of common events is circulated to all Reading Recovery teachers. Conferences provide updates on research and refinements or changes in instructional techniques. Teacher leaders attend annual institutes; people at all levels participate in collegial visits with one another to refine their skills.

A final element is the rigorous data-collection procedures that provide a way of accounting for every child served in the program. Data are collected at sites, sent to a central university location for analysis, and then returned to sites so that teacher leaders can prepare a yearly research report. Reading Recovery is a developer/demonstrator project of the National Diffusion Network (NDN), a division of the U.S. Department of Education that works to disseminate excellent programs. Aggregated data are reported each year to NDN.

THE READING RECOVERY PROCESS

For each child, participation in Reading Recovery represents a temporary adjustment in his or her educational process. Individual help is provided for a relatively short period of time, between 12 and 20 weeks. A specially trained teacher works with the child outside the classroom environment for 30 minutes each day. Accelerated learning is the goal. When the child shows behavioral evidence of an independent system of strategies that will result in further learning and can read and write within average range for the school or classroom, the extra help is withdrawn. An independent assessor helps the teacher make the decision to discontinue extra help.

Accelerated Progress

The theoretical concept of accelerated progress is basic to the process described above. Acceleration is achieved not by pushing the young student through levels of skills to "mastery." Instead, children are involved in successful reading and writing while a knowledgeable adult supports the process. Through carefully selected teacher–child interactions, children are assisted in constructing the networks of understandings that they need to develop effective reading strategies. They learn to use their knowledge of the world and of language as they check it against the visual information contained in print. The teacher carefully observes the child's behavior, noting evidence of such strategies as searching and checking; often the teacher complements the reader's moves or engages the child in conversation that makes processes more explicit. This productive conversation helps the young reader do much more than could be accomplished alone; it supports independent problem solving. Reading Recovery teachers call this process teaching for strategies.

Strategies

Clay (1985) says that strategies are in-the-head operations that cannot be directly observed or taught. Good readers apparently orchestrate a range of effective strategies (see Bussis, Chittenden, Amarel, & Klausner, 1985; Clay, 1991). They are flexible, using information from any level of language (the meaning system, the syntactic system, or the phonemic system) in concert with perceptual information. They have learned to attend to and use information efficiently as needed. Poor readers, on the other hand, seem to operate in more rigid ways. Initially, they may try to use what they know but find the task so complex that they have little success and resultantly become passive. Such children may be vulnerable to instruction (see Board, 1982) in that they follow instructions but do not actively work to fill in the gaps for themselves and use information other than that provided by the teacher. They may continue to invent text long beyond the emergent literacy period, neglecting to check their language predictions with visual information. They may take on some of the directions of their teachers (such as "sounding out" by using the first letter) but not use this information in orchestrated ways. They are content to produce what Smith (1978) called "nonsense" instead of constructed renditions of meaningful text.

The children I have described above are highly dependent on school for their literacy learning experiences. They need expert help embedded within meaningful reading and writing. Reading Recovery teachers talk about "teaching *for* strategies" because they realize that they cannot directly communicate the kind of in-the-head operations that good readers use. They can, however, watch carefully for evidence of productive strategies and encourage the significant behaviors. The feedback from sensitive and systematic observation helps teachers shape their teaching moves. They decide, as a result of analyzing observational data, what they will attend to and point out to children. They can provide demonstrations and suggest actions that might be productive. Teaching, for Reading Recovery teachers, "can be likened to a conversation in which you listen to the speaker carefully before you reply" (Clay, 1985, p. 6).

Observing and Analyzing Children's Behavior

At the heart of Reading Recovery is observing children while they read, talk, and write. An observational survey, consisting of six individually applied instruments, has been developed to provide an initial assessment of children's literacy knowledge. These assessments, along with the judgment of the classroom teacher, are used as criteria for admitting children to the program. The observational procedures are also helpful to classroom teachers and are extensively used in New Zealand to assess the progress of primary school children. They offer a useful, systematic way of inventorying students' strengths. On each measure, the student receives a score; however, Reading Recovery teachers interpret the results based on all the evidence, including observation of behavior during the tasks. The six measures are described below:

1. *Letter identification.* Children are asked to identify, in any way they can, the 54 characters [upper- and lowercase letters, including two varieties of two letters, a/ɑ and g/g) of the alphabet. Teachers notice students' attempts and substitutions as signs of growing ability to distinguish features of letters.
2. *Word test.* Children are asked to identify a list of words drawn from a basic word list. The assessment provides important information about how children approach this most difficult task. Teachers note not only words identified but also important attempts. Even children who refuse to attempt some words are displaying knowledge; they know that they do not know.
3. *Concepts about print.* Teachers read a short storybook and ask children to interact with the print in various ways. This observational task measures children's knowledge of the print conventions; for example, knowing which way to go, that print (rather than pictures) carries the primary message, or that space is used to designate words.
4. *Writing vocabulary.* Children are asked to write all the words they can within a 10-minute maximum limit. Accurately spelled words are scored; teachers also note strengths and knowledge revealed by approximations.
5. *Dictation task.* The teacher reads a sentence containing 37 phonemes and asks the child to try to write it. The objective is to determine how many phonemes the child can represent with an appropriate letter.
6. *Running record of text reading.* The running record, a way of recording reading behavior, is a powerful tool for guiding instruction. To take a running record, the teacher sits beside the student, who is reading orally from a selected text. Both teacher and student can view the

material being read. The teacher acts as a neutral observer, helping the student only when necessary to move the reading along. While the student reads, the teacher records significant reading behavior (for example, words read accurately, substitutions, omissions, repetitions) using a coding system. In the initial assessment, the running record provides an estimate of the level of text difficulty a student can read with 90% or greater accuracy. More important, it provides a precise description of reading behavior that the teacher can use as evidence of knowledge. Besides the beginning assessment with reading level, the running record is used every day to analyze the child's progress in the program.

Roaming Around the Known

Data from all assessments provide information that establishes a beginning point for the teacher and child. Reading Recovery teachers are required to conduct an ongoing quest for information about each of the children they teach. The first 10 days of the students' programs involve reading, writing, and language activities that allow exploration of the individual's knowledge base. During this period, in which the teacher does not try to introduce new learning, children become fluent and flexible with what they already know. Teachers discover strengths that were not evident in responses to the original assessments. A typical activity might be collaboratively writing books, with children providing the words or letters they can write and teachers writing the rest.

Reading Recovery Lessons

Reading Recovery procedures specify a lesson framework that assures a combination of oral reading and writing activities during the 30-minute period. These components are:

1. Rereading books that the student has previously read
2. Reading a book that was new the previous day while the teacher takes a running record
3. Composing and then writing a brief story or message
4. Putting together a cut-up version of that same message
5. Attempting, with support, a new book that has been introduced by the teacher

What is read and written and the types of teacher–child conversations that take place are not specified. Those factors are shaped by the teacher's analysis of the individual child's strengths and his or her predictions concerning where the young learner needs to go next. The teacher follows a recommended framework and sequence of activities but within that must adjust to each child. Following the child means that the teacher makes choices that are most productive for that learner and that allow the child to engage in problem-solving work while maintaining comprehension and fluency. To illustrate this process, and also to display the lesson framework, a sample lesson, with typical examples drawn from our experiences in Reading Recovery, is presented below.

Jon's Reading Recovery Lesson

When Jon entered the Reading Recovery program, he could recognize 39 letters and could write his name and the words *a* and *I*. He knew that print contained the message and that readers move left to right across the line of print. He did not have control of word-by-word matching but could distinguish words and letters. On the dictation task, he could represent *k* with the appropriate letter. When faced with a reading task, he could invent stories that were consistent with the pictures but did not attempt to check with the visual information. By his thirty-fifth lesson, Jon had full control of word-by-word matching and was reading most material without using his finger to point. He could write 36 words and was reading books on Reading Recovery level 11 (roughly equivalent to a third preprimer).

Jon's thirty-sixth lesson began with familiar reading. All reading in Reading Recovery lessons is oral. He first read *When Lana Was Absent* (1984), a book at about preprimer level that he could easily read without using his finger. He read fluently, with phrasing, and then quickly read another at about the same level of difficulty about what animals wear on a cold day. In this book, he noticed that *goats* and *coats* looked alike. On another page, the text said, "On a cold, cold day, kittens wear mittens." Jon noticed the word *mitten*, saying, "If that was a *k* it would be 'kittens wear kittens.'" Finally, he read *Oh No* (Cairns, 1987), a book at about the same level that he had read twice before. His teacher helped him use magnetic letters to work out *there* and *there's* from *the*, a word he knew well. Throughout the reading, his teacher talked with him about the stories and praised his efforts. She especially commented on his fluency and noticed that he was discovering aspects of print and beginning to analyze words. An ongoing conversation surrounded the reading.

Next, Jon read *Ten Little Bears* (Ruwe, 1976), a more difficult book that had been introduced the day before, while his teacher took a running record. A segment from the record illustrates the productive problem solving this child was doing (see Figure 6.1).

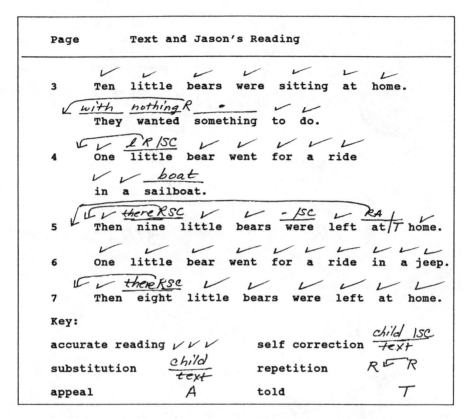

Figure 6.1. Jon's reading of *Ten Little Bears* (Ruwe, 1976).

Jon operated independently during the reading, allowing his teacher to observe. She noticed that he made predictions based on meaning and knowledge of language syntax and consistently checked his attempts with visual information. He read the book at 96% accuracy with a self-correction ratio of 1 : 2. More important, it was evident that he was monitoring his own reading. For example, on line five, he read, "Then there . . . then nine little bears left." Then, he returned to the beginning of the line, reading accurately to the end. His teacher commented on Jon's ability to check on himself, pointing out places where he had worked to make it "sound right."

Jon decided to write a story based on *Oh No*, currently his favorite book. His writing is shown in Figure 6.2. The writing book is a blank book turned sideways so that a "practice page" is available at the top and a "story page" is below. The child and teacher collaboratively write the

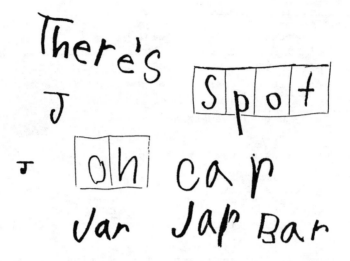

Figure 6.2. Jon's writing.

child's story on the bottom page, providing both the opportunity to write and a finished story that can be read. The top half, or practice page, provides a space to work out words and practice writing them. The child and teacher move back and forth between the story page and the practice space as indicated by problems and opportunities in the child's story. Jon knew how to write "Oh no," which he wrote quickly on the story page, adding an exclamation point for emphasis. Then, he worked out *there's* on the practice page. First, he wrote the known word *the* and then added *r* and *s* by linking sound to letters. The teacher added the *e*, and Jon wrote *there's* on the story page.

A technique called hearing sounds in words helps young writers learn to construct words by accessing their knowledge of sound-letter relationships. The teacher draws a series of boxes, one for every phoneme, and asks the child to say the word slowly while pushing a marker into the visual frame provided by the drawn boxes. The practice page is used to work out words using this technique. With the teacher's help, Jon used boxes to write *Spot* and *on*. He surprised his teacher by writing the *c* for *car* and then saying, "Oh, that has *ar*." As Clay (1985) says, "The child will want to hurriedly write down the clusters he knows, resisting a teacher's attempts to get him to work letter by letter. And rightly so" (p. 78). At his teacher's suggestion, he wrote *jar* and *bar*. No further practice will be needed because the substitution principle is well established.

Jon read the sentence several times during its construction and when it was finished. Then, the teacher quickly wrote it on a sentence strip that was cut apart for him to reconstruct. He was ready for some words—for example, *car* and *there's*—to be cut apart for reconstruction. The sentence was read again in its entirety and then placed in an envelope for Jon to take home and remake.

His new book was *Saturday Morning* (Moyes, 1983). The teacher talked through the pictures of the book and used some of the language, for example, *hosed the car*. She was careful to leave some problem solving for Jon to do, though, because one of her goals was to help him become more independent. On his first attempt, Jon needed little help. He did not pause or self-correct on errors that made no difference, but he consistently checked on his reading, repeating lines when necessary to work out a line of text. He used cues from pictures and print in a orchestrated way, and his teacher kept up a supportive conversation during the reading. Tomorrow, he will read this book independently, while the teacher takes a running record. At the end of the lesson, Jon chose *Oh No* to take home.

The lesson framework includes writing and reading at several levels of difficulty. The idea is to make it possible for the student to do "reading work" as independently as possible. We could describe the teacher's role as helping the child to work at a level difficult enough to present opportunities for problem solving but not so difficult that meaning is lost.

Studies of Reading Recovery lessons (see Pinnell, DeFord, Lyons, Bryk, and Seltzer, 1991) indicate that almost every minute of the lesson is engaged time; the student is involved in reading and writing extended text. The lesson framework is a powerful combination of activities, but teacher decision making on a moment-to-moment basis is the most powerful component in the lesson.

RESEARCH ON STUDENT OUTCOMES

Research supports the effectiveness of the Reading Recovery model. This research includes replications of the program in New Zealand, Australia, and the United States. It also includes a statewide experimental study.

Studies and Replications

Studies of Reading Recovery represent 16 years of research, beginning with Clay's six projects between 1976 and 1981 (see Clay, 1985, 1990) and also including Australian studies (Wheeler, 1984) and the Ohio State studies beginning in 1984 (see DeFord, Lyons, & Pinnell, 1991; Pinnell, 1989). In addition, Reading Recovery has been implemented at 137 sites. Each site represents replication of the process with different teachers, different leaders, and different children. In 1990–1991, an average of 87% of students were successfully discontinued at U.S. and Canadian sites. The 9,486 students who received Reading Recovery lessons for at least 60 days were used as a basis for that figure.

A Statewide Study

A statewide study[1] (see Pinnell, Deford, et al., 1991) addressed some specific questions about Reading Recovery, for example:

1. Wouldn't any one-to-one program work just as well?
2. Is the year-long training program really necessary or would a summer workshop do as well?
3. Can you do Reading Recovery in groups and achieve the same results?

Reading Recovery seemed to work; practitioners were interested in finding out *what* it was that was effective and what could be changed to adapt it

---

[1]This research was conducted at The Ohio State University through a grant from the John D. and Catherine T. MacArthur Foundation.

to local conditions or to make the program less costly or less troublesome to implement. For this study, researchers looked at the various program characteristics, for example, the individual nature of the program and the long-term training. They examined the relative effectiveness of these components when used together and separately.

From 33 schools serving low-income populations, first-grade low readers ($n = 403$) were selected and assigned to one of four intervention programs or to a control group that represented traditional extra help. The first intervention program was traditional Reading Recovery with a fully trained teacher. The second method, called Reading Success, was modeled on Reading Recovery; however, Reading Success teachers were provided with a condensed version of the training. Another one-to-one intervention, Direct Instruction Skills Plan, was provided by experienced reading teachers who did not use Reading Recovery's procedures. In the fourth, called Reading Writing Group, trained Reading Recovery teachers led group sessions instead of private lessons. The fifth, the control group, represented typical group remediation classes in the state.

Each of the four interventions was compared with its own control group in one of the project schools. The lowest-achieving first-grade students ($N = 324$) were randomly assigned either to a treatment or a control group; thus the study controlled for the variation in students that exists across schools and school districts. Remedial instruction lasted 70 days for each of the first four groups and throughout the entire school year for the control classes. At the end of their special classes, students took five tests covering a range of literacy skills. To measure the lasting powers of the different forms of instruction, the students repeated some of the tests at the end of their first-grade year and again at the beginning of second grade.

Analysis of the data showed that Reading Recovery children performed significantly better than an equivalent control group and three other special-treatment groups. Reading Recovery was the only group that was better on all tests, showing long-term effects in reading. Reading Recovery children were reading the equivalent of the primer in February and were independently and comfortably reading the first-grade reader at the beginning of second grade. Children receiving other treatments, on average, were lagging far behind in reading level. An interesting follow-up to this research project was found in the children who received Reading Recovery services *after* the experiment was over (in February, March, or April). These children were three reading levels ahead of children who had received regular remedial reading after they were tested in the autumn. So they, too, were reading within the average as beginning second graders.

This study supported several program components that apparently strengthen one another: (1) individual lessons, (2) the instructional approach, and (3) long-term teacher development. The results suggest, however, that the success of Reading Recovery goes beyond the individual factor and the instructional emphasis factor. The time allocations for Reading Recovery and Reading Success were quite similar, and they used the same framework for instruction; but as a group, the Reading Recovery teachers had higher student outcomes. It is clear that another factor made the difference: the intensity and effectiveness of teaching within the Reading Recovery framework. This research suggests that the training program has an impact.

A PROFESSIONAL DEVELOPMENT
PROGRAM FOR TEACHERS

The professional development course for teachers is one academic year in length (see Alverman, 1990; Clay & Watson, 1982; Pinnell, Fried, & Estice, 1990; Pinnell, DeFord, & Lyons, 1988; Pinnell, Fried, Estice, & Powell, 1991). Teachers begin immediately to work with children. First, they learn to use the observational survey to select children for the program. Then, after writing an observational summary that synthesizes their beginning observations, they begin seeing children for 30 minutes daily and to meet weekly, usually in after-school sessions, for the Reading Recovery training class. In the United States, the course is nine quarter hours (six semester hours) of graduate credit. Teachers must be able to teach four Reading Recovery children daily at a school site. Typically, they work one half-day in Reading Recovery and the other half-day at another assignment, such as teaching remedial reading or classroom teaching. The course is conducted by a teacher leader who has received a full-time training course for one year at one of the national training sites.

After the assessment training, getting underway with the lesson framework, that is, with the activities, is the first task for teachers. They quickly learn to efficiently apply the framework of the 30-minute lesson. The real challenge for teachers is to reflect on and analyze their interactions with students so that they can select and attend to the kind of memorable examples that will help children increase their power over the tasks of reading. The teacher leader's job is to assist teachers in learning this complex teaching process.

Each week, two members of the class teach their students in regular lessons behind a one-way glass. The rest of the group observe closely, developing the ability to notice minute shifts in children's behavior and to quickly make inferences about the internal processing that the behaviors might signal. The observation is not silent. While they observe, teachers in the class engage in an extended conversation during which they are encouraged to think out loud, describe behavior, and try out their inferences and generalizations about instruction. They intimately participate in the lesson and the inherent instructional decisions without having to assume the responsibility for acting; thus they can concentrate on the development of their thinking as teachers. The idea is to describe what is going on in the lesson and to engage in ongoing analysis while the lesson proceeds. The leader guides the process by questioning and challenging group members to formulate hypotheses and back them up with evidence.

Afterwards, the group meets with the teachers who provided the two demonstration lessons. The purpose of this reflective discussion is to provide cases for group discussions. The model helps teachers build a system of understandings out of which they act. This system is generative in that it helps them learn more about teaching with each student they encounter. At every level in Reading Recovery, educators participate in behind-the-glass sessions, working to build their theories of how children learn and strengthening their observational and decision-making power.

SUMMARY

Reading Recovery goes beyond the piecemeal approaches of the past by providing a program designed to meet the complexity of human learning and of system change. The program for children immerses individual learners in reading and writing experiences and allows them to engage at the level of their own knowledge. Teachers must learn to analyze behavior and to follow the child's lead in order to help young learners attend to productive demonstrations of processes. This powerful teaching is developed through a staff development program that recognizes the complexity of instructional decision making. Teachers develop the theoretical base for instruction in a setting that is close to their daily work. From their observation of ongoing lessons, they develop analytic skills. At the system level, structures are in place to assure continuing quality and a network of communication that both supports and challenges. Research indicates that Reading Recovery has promise for reducing reading failure. As a coordinated set of innovations, Reading Recovery provides a powerful demonstration of new possibilities in meeting the needs of at-risk children.

REFERENCES

Allington, R. L., & McGill-Franzen, A. (1989). Different programs, indifferent instruction. In D. Lipsky & A. Gartner (Eds.) *Beyond separate education* (pp. 3–32). New York: Brookes.

Alverman, D. E. (1990). Reading teacher education. In W. R. Houston, M. Haberman, & J. Sikula (Eds.), *Handbook of research on teacher education: A project of the Association of Teacher Educators* (pp. 687–704). New York: Macmillan.

Arthur, G. A. (1936). A study of the achievement of sixty grade-one repeaters as compared with that of nonrepeaters of the same mental age. *Journal of Experimental Education, 5,* 203–205.

Astrein, B., Fraser, J. W., & Steinberg, A. (1984). *Our children at risk: The crisis in public education* (Report of hearings conducted by the Massachussetts Advocacy Center, Boston).

Board, P. E. (1982). *Toward a theory of instructional influence: Aspects of the instructional environment and their influence on children's acquisition of reading.* Unpublished doctoral dissertation, University of Toronto.

Bussis, A. M., Chittenden, E. A., Amarel, M., & Klausner, E. (1985). *Inquiry into meaning: An investigation of learning to read.* Hillsdale, NJ: Erlbaum.

Cairns, S. (1987). *Oh no!* Crystal Lake, IL: Rigby Education.

Carter, L. F. (1984). The sustaining effects study of compensatory and elementary education. *Educational Researcher, 13,* 4–13.

Clay, M. M. (1985). *The early detection of reading difficulties.* Portsmouth, NH: Heinemann.

Clay, M. M. (1987). Implementing educational Reading Recovery: Systematic adaptations to an educational innovation. *New Zealand Journal of Educational Studies, 22,* 35–58.

Clay, M. M. (1990). The Reading Recovery programme, 1984–1988: Coverage, outcomes and education board district figures. *New Zealand Journal of Educational Studies, 25,* 61–69.

Clay, M. M. (1991). *Becoming literate: The construction of inner control.* Portsmouth, NH: Heinemann.

Clay, M. M., & Cazden, C. (1990). A Vygotskian interpretation of Reading Recovery. In L. Moll (Ed.), *Vygotsky and education: Instructional implications and applications of sociohistorical psychology* (pp. 206–222). New York: Cambridge University Press.

Clay, M. M., & Watson, B. (1982). An inservice program for Reading Recovery teachers. In M. M. Clay (Ed.), *Observing young readers* (pp. 192–200). Portsmouth, NH: Heinemann.

Coeffield, W. H., & Bloomers, P. (1956). Effects of non-promotion on educational achievement in the elementary school. *Journal of Educational Psychology, 32,* 281–287.

DeFord, D. E., Lyons, C.A., & Pinnell, G.S. (Eds.). (1991). *Bridges to literacy: Learning from Reading Recovery.* Portsmouth, NH: Heinemann.

Fantini, M. D., & Weinstein, G. (1968). *The disadvantaged: Challenge to education*. New York: Harper & Row.

Farley, E. S. (1936). Regarding repeaters: Sad effect of failure upon the child. *Nation's Schools, 18*, 37–39.

Good, T. L. (1986). What is learned in elementary schools. In T. Tomlinson & H. Walberg (Eds.), *Academic work and educational excellence* (pp. 87–114). Berkeley, CA: McCutchan.

Goodlad, J. I. (1954). Some effects of promotion and nonpromotion upon the social and personal adjustment of children. *Journal of Experimental Education, 22*, 301–328.

Hall, W. F., & Demarest, R. (1958). Effect on achievement scores of a change in promotional policy. *Elementary School Journal, 58*, 204–207.

Heath, S. B. (1983). *Ways with words: Language, life and work in communities and classrooms*. New York: Cambridge University Press.

Hodgkinson, H. (1985). *All one system: Demographics of education, kindergarten through graduate school*. Washington, DC: Institute for Educational Leadership.

Hodgkinson, H. L. (1988). The right schools for the right kids. *Educational Leadership, 45*, 10–14.

Johnson, J. R. (1984). Synthesis of research on grade retention and social promotion. *Educational Leadership, 41*, 66–68.

Johnston, P., Allington, R., & Afflerbach, P. (1985). The congruence of classroom and remedial reading instruction. *Elementary School Journal, 85*, 465–477.

Lyons, C. A. (1991). A comparative study of the teaching effectiveness of teachers participating in a year-long or two-week inservice program. In J. Zutell & S. McCormick (Eds.), *Learner factors/teacher factors: Issues in literacy research and instruction* (Fortieth Yearbook of the National Reading Conference, pp. 357–365). Chicago, IL: National Reading Conference.

Mason, J. M. (1984). Early reading from a developmental perspective. In P. D. Pearson (Ed.), *Handbook of reading research* (pp. 505–544). New York: Longman.

Moyes, L. (1983). *Saturday morning*. Wellington, New Zealand: Department of Education, School Publications Branch.

Natriello, G., McDill, E. L., & Pallas, A. M. (1990). *Schooling disadvantaged children: Racing against catastrophe*. New York: Teachers College Press.

Pinnell, G. S. (1989). Reading Recovery: Helping at-risk children learn to read. *The Elementary School Journal, 90*, 161–183.

Pinnell, G. S., DeFord, D. E., & Lyons, C. A. (1988). *Reading Recovery: Early intervention for at-risk first graders*. Arlington, VA: Educational Research Service.

Pinnell, G. S., DeFord, D. E., Lyons, C. A., Bryk, A., & Seltzer, M. (1991). *Studying the effectiveness of early intervention approaches for first grade children having difficulty in reading*. Columbus, OH: The Ohio State University, Martha L. King Language and Literacy Center.

Pinnell, G. S., Fried, M. D., & Estice, R. M. (1990). Reading Recovery: Learning how to make a difference. *The Reading Teacher, 43*, 282–295.

Pinnell, G. S., Fried, M. D., Estice, R. M., & Powell, D. (1991). *Teaching for problem solving in reading*. Paper presented at the 1991 National Reading Conference, Palm Springs, CA.

Ruwe, M. (1976). *Ten little bears*. Glenview, IL: Scott Foresman.

Sarason, S. (1991). *The predictable failure of educational reform*. New York: Free Press.

Savage, D. G. (1987). Why Chapter 1 hasn't made much difference. *Phi Delta Kappan, 68*, 581–584.

Shulman, L. S. (1987). Knowledge and teaching: Foundations of the new reform. *Harvard Educational Review, 57*, 1–22.

Slavin, R. E. (1987). Making Chapter 1 make a difference. *Phi Delta Kappan, 69*, 110–119.

Slavin, R. E., & Madden, N. A. (1987). *Effective classroom programs for students at risk*. Baltimore: Johns Hopkins University, Center for Research on Elementary and Middle Schools.

Smith, F. (1978). *Reading without nonsense*. New York: Teachers College Press.

Teale, W. H., & Sulzby, E. (Eds.). (1986). *Emergent literacy: Writing and reading*. Norwood, NJ: Ablex.

Walker, E. M., & Madhere, S. (1987). Multiple retentions: Some consequences for the cognitive and affective maturation of minority elementary students. *Urban Education, 22*, 85–102.

Wells, G. (1985). *The meaning makers: Children learning language and using language to learn*. Portsmouth, NH: Heinemann.

Wheeler, H. G. (1984). *Reading Recovery: Central Victorian field trials*. Victoria, Australia: Bendigo College of Advanced Education.

When Lana was absent. (1984). Crystal Lake, IL: Rigby.

Wood, D. (1988). *How children think and learn*. Cambridge, MA: Blackwell.

CHAPTER 7

From the Margin to the Center of Curricula: Multicultural Children's Literature

Violet Harris

Many of us are familiar with the picture books and novellas created by poet Lucille Clifton. Her most recognizable character, Everett Anderson, the child hero of six books, reminds us of a younger brother, godchild, son, neighbor, or grandson. We identify with Everett because he is a likeable and loving child. We wait impatiently with Everett as he grows a year older. We share his pain on the death of his father. Some of us were reminded of our feelings about a new stepparent when we read about Everett's new stepfather. We also celebrated the birth of his sister. Clifton captured some essential moments of childhood in *Some of the Days of Everett Anderson* (1970), *Everett Anderson's Year* (1974), and *Everett Anderson's Nine Month Long* (1978). A special delight for readers and listeners is the poetic text. Clifton deliberately wrote the texts in iambic pentameter for those who do not believe that she has control of standard English because some of her books, such as *My Brother Fine with Me* (1975), include black vernacular English (BVE). Children, more than likely, do not care whether iambic pentameter, BVE, or standard English gives voice to Everett's feelings. Nor does it matter that Everett Anderson is African American. Unfortunately, the race and gender of Lucille Clifton matter to some.

Consider, for instance, the experience she related at the spring conference of the National Council of Teachers of English (Clifton, 1992). Clifton spoke of her elation at being part of a celebration of the life of poet Walt Whitman. Some of that elation dissipated momentarily when a reporter asked her why she was included as an invited guest reader. Evidently, the reporter could not imagine that a poet who is an African

American woman would find some pleasure in Whitman's work, discover her dreams and feelings in his poems, or see herself in his word images. Like some of us, the reporter lacked knowledge and information and reduced individuals to stereotypes. That kind of thinking could prevent children from discovering Ms. Clifton's books or those of other writers like her. Why shouldn't Clifton find enjoyment, comfort, and inspiration in Whitman's poetry? Conversely, why shouldn't a Chicana, disabled Native American, or white child find similar literary and artistic moments in Clifton's work or that of others who share her ethnicity, gender, or class? To paraphrase Langston Hughes, Clifton, too, sings America. Just as the world has more than one recipe for bread, authors have more than one way of telling a story. Sometimes the stories they weave are filtered through a particular cultural perspective; other times they are rendered through the writer's unique perspective.

In this chapter I examine the literature created by Clifton and other "people of color"; that is, literature written by African, Asian, Latino, and Native Americans. Lately, these authors have been placed under the rubric of multiculturalism. Specifically, I discuss multiculturalism; detail the current status of children's literature and multiethnic literature; examine multiethnic literature from the perspectives of African, Asian, Latino, and Native Americans; and identify some of the implications for early childhood education.

MULTICULTURALISM:
CELEBRATING AND VALUING DIVERSITY

Multiculturalism is adherence to the ideology that diversity enriches and contributes to the development of a group or a society (Banks, 1988; Sleeter & Grant, 1988). Proponents believe that multiculturalism will result in a more just and equitable society. Achieving the ideals of multiculturalism, however, requires continuous and consistent struggles. Ultimately, these struggles involve the reformation of societal institutions and of society itself. Several groups, attributes, and ideologies are categorized under the multicultural rubric. These include race, gender, and class as well as disability, age, language, sexual preference, religion, environmentalism, and pacifism. Each characteristic exerts varying degrees of influence; in many cases, they overlap. For instance, it is possible to be a Chicana who is upper-middle class, vegetarian, and devoted to environmentalism.

Similarly, multicultural education suggests that schools and curricula will undergo significant restructuring. This educational restructuring should culminate in each child having equal access to educational opportunities (Banks, 1991). Literature offers ideal opportunities to read about the diverse cultures that make up the United States. Children can read books that showcase the similarities and differences that exist among cultures. They can receive an introduction to the beliefs, perspectives, values, and behaviors of other groups. Literature also enables children to understand some of the inequities and problems that remain unresolved. Equally important, literature provides enjoyable moments. Multicultural literature offers this and much more.

CHILDREN'S LITERATURE:
INCREASING RESPECTABILITY AND PROFITS

Children's literature acquired increasing social, educational, and economic importance throughout the 1980s; the trend continues into the 1990s. Without a doubt, children's literature experienced tremendous economic growth (Roback, 1992a). Sales reached $1 billion during 1990 and are projected to reach $1½ billion by middecade (Roback, 1990b, 1992a). More than 5,000 children's books were published; there are nearly 69,000 children's books in print (Lindgren, 1991). Roback (1992a) reported the results of a survey that assessed the current status of children's literature. Among the major findings were the following: Growth continued unabated, the number of titles and amount of space devoted to children's literature increased, browsers spent considerable time in stores, adults and children purchased more books, and many best-sellers were older titles. Other indications of the enhanced status accorded children's literature include the increasing visibility of journals such as *The New Advocate*, *Children's Literature Association Quarterly*, and *Booklinks*; the proliferation of children's-only bookstores across the country (they now number over 400); and the importance of book clubs in many elementary literature programs. These observations suggest that children's literature will remain a vital force throughout the decade.

Despite the improved respectability and huge profits, some individuals are sounding alarms (Englehardt, 1991). For example, poet Myra Cohn Livingston (1988) warned against a creeping mediocrity. Whole Language advocate Kenneth Goodman (1988) detailed the basalization of children's literature apparent in some commercial reading programs. Anita Silvey (1989), editor of *The Horn Book Magazine*, directed attention to the basalization of children's literature in a particularly insidious form — the proliferation of study guides many times the length of the original works and replete with examples of "verbosity and inanity" (p. 549). Still others bemoaned the cost of children's books; hardbacks average $17.45 (Roback, 1992a). It is possible that book ownership will become an increasingly class-based phenomenon. In addition, the reduction in library budgets has major consequences. Nonetheless, children's books will continue to bask in adoration. Many remain hopeful that some of the adoration will reflect onto a neglected area, multiethnic children's literature.

LITERARY MOSAIC: MULTIETHNIC LITERATURE

Multicultural literature is literature written by and/or about people of color; children of various classes; girls and women; individuals whose first language is not English; the elderly; the disabled; gays and lesbians; single-parent families; adherents of minority religions such as the Amish, Muslims, or Jews; environmentalists; and pacifists. As indicated previously, many of the categories overlap. The commonality that binds each group is the marginalized status of its members. The groups are not full participants in cultural institutions. Their participation is or has been limited by law and custom. Further, each group does not experience the same degree of marginalization. The literature examined in the remaining sections of this chapter is the multiethnic component of multicultural literature. In this case, multiethnic literature is that written by or about people of color. Multiethnic literature was selected because many of the authors and illustrators produce work of exceptional quality. The books entertain, educate, and inform all children, but they are particularly welcomed by children of groups generally stereotyped or ignored in literature. However, the literature does not remain in print for significant amounts of time, and it is unknown to most parents, teachers, and students. Yet multiethnic children's literature, which has existed since the 1800s, is a part of the nation's cultural heritage and has earned inclusion in literary canons. Demand, though unmet, has always existed for it (Harris, 1990a, 1992).

Recent Market for Multiethnic Books

Roback (1990a, 1990b) detailed two contradictory themes in multicultural publishing as the 1990s commenced. Publishers and others recognized the need to publish more books related to multicultural populations. In contrast, a survey of booksellers and subscribers to *Publishers Weekly* revealed that only 4.5% of respondents reported a strong demand for multicultural titles (Roback, 1990b). Typical factors cited for these contradictory perspectives include

1. The belief that a market—that is, a white market—does not exist for the books
2. The inability of small presses, which publish some of the books, to create ties with distributors and chain and regional bookstores
3. The reluctance of bookstores to stock a variety of titles rather than a few titles of well-known authors
4. The inappropriate marketing of the books (for instance, the majority of purchasers for multiethnic literature are not necessarily those who read *Booklist*)
5. The scheduling of release dates for Black History or Latino History Month, which results in a torrent of books in one month and a relative dearth in the remaining eleven

Roback (1992b) reported that publishers seem to have responded to the need for multicultural literature by releasing many more books in the fall publishing cycle. Goddard (1992) documented some additional trends that suggest improved sensitivity. Among those cited are:

1. The number of booksellers concentrating on children's literature increased from a dozen or so to more than 200.
2. At least six African American book distributors are in business.
3. Two new publishing and bookseller groups, African American Publishers and Booksellers Association and the Multicultural Publishers Exchange, were established.
4. A new organization, Black Board's African American Bestsellers Inc., was formed to chart sales figures of books written by African Americans.
5. New genres—for example, romance series such as Odyssey Books and Romance in Black—appeared on the scene.

Another sign of improvement is the republication of previously out-of-print children's books, such as *Three Wishes* (Clifton, 1992). Other groups— Asian, Native, and Latino Americans—saw a minor increase in the numbers of titles published, but most were for adults.

Most of the books, however, have not become national best-sellers, with the exception of three books, two of which were not written by a person of the culture depicted. One, *Brother Eagle, Sister Sky* (Seattle, 1991), was the center of a minor controversy (Dooley, 1991; Jeffers, 1991). Another, *Amazing Grace* (Hoffman, 1991), garnered critical praise for its narrative and the quality of its illustrations. The third, *Tar Beach* (Ringgold, 1991), introduced a new narrative form, the story quilt. These statistics are slightly better than those for 1990, when only one book for early childhood readers was a best-seller. While most books are not best-sellers — 75,000 hardbacks and 100,000 paperbacks — several sell quite well, as evidenced by the figures compiled by Black Board. For instance, *Nathaniel Talking* (Greenfield, 1988) has 40,000 copies in print (Maughn, 1992). This feat is all the more remarkable given that *Nathaniel Talking* is a book of poetry.

Issues of Authenticity and Authorial Identity

The two types of books that are current best-sellers — the two written by authors not members of the culture depicted and the one written by a member of the group depicted — highlight two of the major issues in multiethnic literature: authenticity and authorial identity. Both are inter-related and complicated.

The question of authenticity or, more correctly, what constitutes an accurate portrayal of a culture, has plagued children's literature for dec-ades. Consider for example, the scorn heaped on books such as *The Story of Little Black Sambo* (Bannerman, 1899), *The Five Chinese Brothers* (Bishop & Wise, 1938), and others of that ilk. In each case, members of the group portrayed — quite justifiably — sought to replace these books with images they deemed more accurate, truthful, and positive in books such as *Gladiola Garden* (Newsome, 1944) and *My Happy Days* (Shackel-ford, 1938), but these authors and their publishers did not possess the cultural or economic power needed to eradicate stereotyped and inauthen-tic literature.

What, then, are the characteristics that define authentic literature?

1. The literature should include the range of character types or people found within the culture, though not necessarily in one book. The characters should not be idealized, but neither should stereotypes pre-dominate. There should be doctors, teachers, truck drivers, cooks, and individuals with other occupations.
2. The illustrations should not consist of caricatures of a group's physical features. Rather, the illustrations should reflect the variety found among members of any group.
3. The speech adopted by characters should have linguistic authenticity. Many members of a group speak standard English and can use and understand various dialects within the group as well. Vernacular lan-guage and casual, informal dialects are appropriate to some characters some of the time, but not all characters all of the time.

4. The names of the characters should reflect the cultural traditions of a group.
5. Food should not be used as a shorthand signifier of a group; for example, *rice* is not a code word for Asian or Asian American.
6. The beliefs and values of characters as well as their worldviews should reflect the diversity found in the groups' communities. Some will be conservative, others liberal, and a few radical.
7. Writers should understand the pivotal roles families play in these groups and the family configurations that exist within the groups.
8. Authors should portray members of the groups as intelligent problem solvers who are not dependent on the intervention of a kindly white for redemption, salvation, or mediation.

Authenticity derives from insider knowledge about a culture acquired as a member or through extensive study, observation, and interaction. A number of authors and critics tackled the issue of who should write about a culture and drew varying conclusions (Clifton, 1981, 1992; Howard, 1991). An example illustrates the problems that can arise when one is not part of a culture that one writes about or includes in illustrations: Susan Jeffers received criticism (Dooley, 1991) for using the stereotype of Native Americans fixed in popular culture in *Brother Eagle, Sister Sky* (Seattle, 1991).

Author Virginia Hamilton reacted to an aspect of authenticity and authorial freedom in another way. An interviewer posed this question, Do you consider yourself a black writer? And she responded in this manner: "And an American writer. And a woman. I'm all those things. It doesn't matter to me . . . I'm sure that the categories people use for me depend on their own consciousness. It all depends on how you see things. My themes are universal" (Rochman, 1992, p. 1021). She continued and spoke about the strictures placed on African American writers, restrictions that force them to write solely about that which is deemed African American.

Rudine Sims-Bishop (Sims, 1982) has developed a typology for analyzing literature written by and about African Americans. Her scheme has applications for other cultures as well and provides some theoretical basis for determining authenticity. She identified three categories of fiction — melting pot, social conscience, and culturally conscious — and three issues that determine in which category an author wrote (Sims, 1982, 1983). Those issues were (1) the primary audience the author intended to reach, (2) the author's interpretation of African American experiences, and (3) the author's perspective as an insider or outsider in relation to the cultural group portrayed.

Social conscience books were seen as "well-intentioned." The goals of

the author seemed to be the creation of a social conscience in white readers. Sims-Bishop contended that many of these books supported old stereotypes or evidenced a patronizing or paternal attitude. Melting pot books
began appearing in the 1940s. Most were picture books and presented a
monolithic depiction of America. They contained no racial conflicts, ignored racial differences, promoted racial integration, and emphasized
middle-class nuclear families. Sims-Bishop (1990) indicated that the melting pot category might need redefining in order to acknowledge that some
of the books depicted universal activities, beliefs, or interactions.

Culturally conscious books came closest to constituting a body of literature created especially for African American children (Sims, 1982, 1983).
These stories are always told from the perspectives of African Americans,
are placed within the context of African American families and communities, and reflect the language, rituals, cultural artifacts, and beliefs of
African Americans. Moreover, Sims-Bishop argued that culturally conscious literature was crucial in order to ameliorate and eradicate the effects of stereotyped literature and omissions from literature. Among the
negative effects were lowered self-esteem and lessened self-worth of African American children and the perpetuation of undeserved feelings of
superiority among white children (Sims, 1983). Culturally conscious literature and the philosophies of its creators are examined in the next section.

CULTURALLY CONSCIOUS CHILDREN'S LITERATURE: STORIES FROM THE SOURCE

Nearly 69,000 children's books remain in print; more than 5,000 were
published in 1990 and 1991 (Lindgren, 1991). Only 51 of the total published in 1990 featured or were written by African Americans (Lindgren,
1991). Far fewer books concentrating on Asian, Latino, or Native Americans were published. Not all of the 51 books meet the criteria for being
culturally conscious. Those that do, however, are often exceptional artistic
and literary products. First, African American children's literature is examined.

African American Literature

African American children's literature has at least a hundred-year
history (Harris, 1990). The first examples were race-neutral and resembled
other literature of the era. Today, most of the examples are race-specific;
indeed, they evoke a certain amount of racial consciousness and racial
pride. This is not to suggest, however, that other children cannot find

something of interest in the literature. Some of the authors who create culturally conscious literature for early childhood include:

Arnold Adoff	Eloise Greenfield	Frané Lessac
Albert Burton	Elizabeth Howard	Sharon B. Mathis
Joyce Barrett	Virginia Hamilton	Patricia McKissack
Ashley Bryan	Angela Johnson	Faith Ringgold
Jeanette Carnes	Dolores Johnson	Irene Smalls
Lucille Clifton	Lynn Joseph	John Steptoe

A few of the authors — for example, Clifton, Greenfield, and Steptoe — have established literary careers. The others are developing stellar reputations, as evidenced by the enthusiastic reviews of their work and awards won, such as the Caldecott Honor Medal.

Angela Johnson is a newcomer whose work has won considerable critical praise. Johnson's five books — *Tell Me a Story, Mama* (1989), *Do Like Kyla* (1990a), *When I Am Old with You* (1990b), *One of Three* (1991), and *The Leaving Morning* (1992) — depict children engaged in everyday or commonplace activities with family members. The language in these books is poetic and suggestive of natural conversations or story-sharing situations. The stories are universal, but pictorial elements place them within African American families. For example, the young boy in *When I Am Old with You* sports dreadlocks, a hairstyle associated with Rastafarians. Yet the culturally specific art does not prevent children from identifying with the love of an older sibling, joyous times spent with a grandfather, or the nightly bedtime story ritual.

Johnson has written that storytelling was important to her development. Although she has not delineated her literary philosophy, some indications of her beliefs are implicit in her works. Her worldview seems optimistic; family is central to the lives of children, and children are valued, loved, and nurtured. If not happily-ever-after tales, her stories are at least hopeful and happy.

Johnson's words are given life in the illustrations that accompany the text. The illustrator of four of the books, David Soman, although not African American, possesses the sensitivity and cultural knowledge needed for authenticity. For example, he recognizes the diversity in skin color and hair texture. Again, the humanity of African Americans emanates from the text and illustrations.

Nowadays, individuals warn that the African American male is an endangered species (Madhubuti, 1991). His media image as an athlete, criminal, or juvenile delinquent has become entrenched. The work of the late John Steptoe contradicts these images. Steptoe burst onto the children's literature scene as a teenager. His first book, *Stevie* (1969), generated considerable critical praise; it was also the first book published in its entirety in *Life* magazine, an unparalleled feat then. Steptoe wrote the text and illustrated each of his books. He had a progressive aesthetic philosophy culled from experiences as an African American male and member of the working class (Natov & De Luca, 1987).

Steptoe attempted to give voice to African American males and members of the working class through five picture books — *Stevie* (1969), *Uptown* (1970), *Train Ride* (1971), *My Special Best Words* (1974), and *Daddy Is a Monster . . . Sometimes* (1980). His other picture books depicted the playful interference of a toddler as his older brother plays with building blocks, *Baby Says* (1988), and two folktales, *The Story of the Jumping Mouse* (1984) and the extraordinary *Mufaro's Beautiful Daughters* (1987), a Caldecott Honor book.

Those who read and share these books and others reflective of the culture can interact with literature that engages their cognitive and aesthetic abilities. They can begin to understand that many African Americans are similar to them and that certain values, worldviews, and behaviors are found in many cultures. This understanding can be acquired from sharing Asian American literature, too.

Asian American Literature

The ritual is commonplace: A mother tucks her children into bed each night. Loh reinterprets that ritual in a manner relatively rare in children's literature: an Asian American family are the featured characters in *Tucking Mommy In*. This depiction of a universal ritual helps dispel the images of Asian Americans as a monolithic, robot-like, model minority engaged in solving math problems, running a restaurant, or washing laundry. *Tucking Mommy In* and other books fulfill a crucial need in this era of Japan-bashing. At the very least, the books will broaden children's knowledge base and inform them that not all Asian Americans are of Japanese descent. They or their ancestors immigrated from North and South Korea, China, Vietnam, Laos, Cambodia, Thailand, India, the Pacific Islands, and other countries.

Author–illustrator Allen Say (1991) captures the cultural dualities faced by some Asian Americans. The United States is his adopted country, but he understands the ostracism individuals face because they are different.

My earliest understanding of a stereotype was pounded into me by my parents. It was that of artists-painters in particular. They were poor, unkempt, and irresponsible, my mother told me. They were sissies who didn't know right from wrong, my father added, and those who gained fame did so only after their death. . . . So my fight against stereotypes began at home, and continued in the back alleys and school yards of postwar Tokyo because I had a Korean father, and at age 16 I came to the United States and instantly turned into a walking stereotype. I was a Jap in high school, an inscrutable Oriental in college, a Chinaman in the army laundry detail. (p. 45)

His books transcend the mere dispelling of stereotypes. They are artistic masterpieces that combine an exceptional use of color and light in order to enhance stories about uncommon heroes and everyday rituals. For example, *El Chino* (1990) chronicles the trials and ultimate triumph of the first Chinese bullfighter, Billy Wong. Wong grew up believing in the dream of hard work leading to success. He became an engineer, but remained dissatisfied. He would later leave Arizona for Spain in order to pursue his dream of athletic prowess. Other Say books explore the relationships between child and parent. They are portraits of Asian Americans engaged in activities familiar to most.

Other authors variously highlight or hint at their Asian heritage. They should have that artistic freedom. For instance, *How My Parents Learned to Eat* (Friedman, 1984) positively explores the cultural differences that are breached when individuals court, marry, and have children. The Children's Book Press published several folktales in bilingual editions: *Aekyung's Dream* (Paek, 1989), *The Little Weaver of Thai-yen Village* (Tuyet, 1987), and *Nine-in-One, Grr! Grr!* (Xiong, 1989). These tales entertain and inform. *Silent Lotus* (Lee, 1991) features a deaf girl who achieves her dream of becoming a dancer under the tutelage of a master teacher. Many girls will identify with and share this desire. Children will occasionally face the problem of fitting into a new neighborhood, class, or school. They can bring questions about that situation or experiences to *Angel Child, Dragon Child* (Surat, 1983). Finally, *Lon Po Po* (Young, 1989) continues the tradition of creating a variant of a well-known folktale, in this instance Little Red Riding Hood. The sisters in this version outwit the wolf and save their lives. Surely, children will enjoy the suspense and the triumph of the sisters.

Latino Literature

Sims-Bishops (1990) reports that only six children's books about Latinos appeared in 1989. The numbers have improved, thanks to efforts of authors such as Alma Ada, Arnold Adoff, Rudolfo Anaya, Byrd Baylor,

Martel Cruz, Lulu Delacre, Arthur Dorros, Carmen Lomas Garza, and others. Latinos have cultural antecedents in a variety of Central and South American countries as well as Caribbean islands. These rich heritages are brought to life in several picture books. For instance, *Abuela* (Dorros, 1991) and *Family Pictures* (Garza, 1990) portray children engaged in fantastic and ordinary familial activities. In both books, the illustrators adopted a "primitive" or untrained style that is colorful, detailed, and inviting.

Several books — for example, *Con Mi Hermano* (Roe, 1991), *Yagua Days* (Cruz, 1976), *Arroz Con Leche* (Delacre, 1989), and *Las Navidades* (Delacre, 1990) — include Spanish words and phrases that can provide a literary bridge for bilingual students and introduce monolingual students to another language. These books incorporate Spanish, both standard and vernacular, in a natural way, unlike some of the recent translations of children's classics into Spanish (Zwick, 1991). Equally important, the books present enjoyable rhymes, songs, and stories in a pleasing fashion. Picture-book biographies appear with increasing frequency. A few chronicle the lives of Latinos. For example, *Henry Cisneros* (Roberts, 1991) and *Diego* (Winter & Winter, 1991) are informative and written at levels comprehensible to many primary-age children.

The philosophical diversity exists among Latino authors (Barbuto, 1991). For instance, Nicholasa Mohr, who writes primarily for readers in the middle grades, captured a common perspective with these thoughts: "The Hispanic experience is really an American experience . . . American/Hispanic, Hispanic American, Latino — all these labels! My books are very Latino, but they're not written for Latinos. I write from the heart about what I know and feel strongly about" (Barbuto, 1991, p. 20). Others see their primary audience as Latinos and all others as a secondary audience. The full range of voices will become apparent as authors from other than the Chicano or Puerto Rican majorities write books.

Native American Literature

In February 1992, *Brother Eagle, Sister Sky* (Seattle, 1991) was the number-one best-selling picture book in the country. *The Education of Little Tree* (Carter, 1986), a novel for older readers, enjoyed a similar status. Both became the object of controversy (Dooley, 1991). Carter was denounced as an archsegregationist and the intellectual force behind the policies of former Alabama governor George Wallace, while Susan Jeffers was criticized because her illustrations included artifacts and symbols from a variety of Native American groups although Chief Seattle was a member of a northwestern coastal nation. Herein lies a major problem:

Native Americans are the central characters in hundreds of books, most written by non–Native Americans and marred by stereotypes. A few authentic books are published, but they are obscured by novels such as *The Secret of the Indian* (Banks, 1989).

Virginia Driving Hawk Sneve articulated the need to portray Native Americans in authentic ways:

> In my writing, both fiction and non-fiction, I try to present an accurate portrayal of American Indian life as I have known it. I also attempt to interpret history from the viewpoint of the American Indian and in so doing I hope to correct the many misconceptions and untruths which have been too long perpetuated by non-Indian authors who have written about us. (Commire, 1976, pp. 193–194)

Sneve set about engendering a new tradition with *Jimmy Yellow Hawk* (1972), the winner of the first book prize offered by the Council on Interracial Books for Children. The book explores a range of issues, some of which, such as the bequeathing of historical memories, are appropriate for children in primary grades. Sneve continued her efforts with *Dancing Teepees* (1989), an anthology of poetry by Native American youth. The introduction to this anthology explains the sacred nature of the spoken word to Native Americans.

Where Did You Get Your Moccasins? (Wheeler, 1986) grew out of a Native writers' workshop sponsored by the Native Education Branch of Manitoba Education. It is but one example of the efforts of Native peoples and small presses. The book features a multiracial group of students who question another child about his moccasins. Thus begins a cumulative tale that has a bit of a surprise. Each succeeding question results in an elaborate response that explains the processes of beading, tanning hides, and hunting deer. The children are satisfied with Jody's answer, and the cycle starts again when the teacher arrives and asks about the shoes. Wheeler manages to convey the tone of a folktale and basic information without becoming didactic.

Some non–Native American authors have acquired the respect of Native Americans. Among these authors are Byrd Baylor, Paul Goble, and Gerald McDermott. Baylor in books such as *Hawk, I'm Your Brother* (1976) conveys the interests of children who are connected to their culture but not forced to be models of it. Goble and McDermott concentrate on folktales. These works prove that you can engage children without resorting to stereotypes.

These brief overviews of the literature of African, Asian, Latino, and Native Americans demonstrate the availability of literature that will appeal to many children. The appeal for some will emanate from the colorful and technically proficient illustrations. Others will find pleasure in the text. Many lucky ones will find pleasure in both. That pleasure will remain unrealized unless educators take some actions.

IMPLICATIONS FOR EARLY CHILDHOOD EDUCATION

Many early childhood educators are aware of the changing demographic pattern of the United States. A sort of "browning" of America is taking place. Demographers suggest that people of color will constitute one-third or more of the population by the year 2000, and children of color will account for almost 46% of the enrollment in schools (Banks, 1991). Educators cannot ignore this increasingly diverse student population, which will have complicated educational needs. These children and others need opportunities to read and hear stories that represent the best in children's literature—and that includes multiethnic literature.

A growing number of early childhood educators are familiar with multiethnic children's literature and understand its value (Derman-Sparks & the ABC Task Force, 1989; Schon, 1988). These individuals share the literature with their children, make it available in the classroom or learning center, and seek additional information about its history, current status, and critical reception. Other teachers will need gentle encouragement. Administrators or parents cannot force them to include the literature during story time or within the literacy curricula. They must realize on their own that multiethnic literature is a component of children's, U.S., and world literature. Moreover, teachers and parents will have to recognize that children will be denied essential knowledge and positive, thoughtful, and entertaining literary experiences if they omit multiethnic literature.

The educational, personal, and social benefits that children might derive from reading and listening to multiethnic literature should prompt teachers, parents, and librarians to share it. The cognitive, social, and personal benefits of literature are well known (Cullinan, 1987; Sims-Bishop, 1990; Taylor & Dorsey-Gaines, 1988; Taylor & Strickland, 1989). Multiethnic children's literature provides these as well. Among them are improved vocabulary and comprehension, models of language, visual literacy, critical thinking, aesthetic pleasure, extensive background knowledge, and opportunities to understand individuals unlike ourselves. However, literature cannot solve every problem that confronts children or a society.

After teachers, librarians, and parents decide to include multiethnic literature, they must then seek out knowledge that will guide selection of literature for early childhood education. In addition to general literature guides (Burke, 1990; Glazer, 1991; Rudman & Pearce, 1988), there are several excellent guides that establish criteria for selection and evaluation of multiethnic literature (Harris, 1992; Jenkins & Austin, 1987; Sims, 1982; Slapin & Seale, 1980). These will also acquaint teachers with information about critical topics such as authenticity, authorial freedom, language issues, and controversial topics. Adults might also find it helpful to acquire general historical knowledge about the groups written from the groups' perspectives. Often, these histories include information omitted or given scant attention in general texts.

Finally, one cannot ignore the economics of including multiethnic literature in early childhood education programs. Book buying will become an increasingly middle- and upper-middle-class phenomenon because of cost. Further, news reports indicated that 60% of American families had not purchased a book in the preceding year. All this suggests that educators will have to lead the movement for ensuring that working-class and poor children have opportunities to read and share books that reflect their cultures, that are popular with children, and that are deemed classics.

These issues should not be construed as insurmountable or provide an excuse for not sharing multiethnic literature. Critical examination of the literature and discussions about the literature would bring new visions, vitality, honesty, and richness to the creation of curriculum for all young children.

REFERENCES

Banks, J. (1988). *Multiethnic education* (2nd ed.). Boston: Allyn & Bacon.

Banks, J. (1991). *Teaching strategies for ethnic studies* (5th ed.). Boston: Allyn & Bacon.

Barbuto, J. (1991). Latino writers in the American market. *Publishers Weekly*, *238* (Feb. 1): 18–21.

Burke, E. (1990). *Early childhood literature*. New York: Allyn & Bacon.

Clifton, L. (1981). Writing for black children. *The Advocate*, *1*, 32–39.

Clifton, L. (1992, March). Elementary section keynote address presented at National Council of Teachers of English Annual Spring Conference, Washington, DC.

Commire, A. (1976). Virginia Driving Hawk Sneve. *Something About the Author*, *8*, 193–194.

Cullinan, B. (Ed.). (1987). *Children's literature in the reading program*. Newark, DE: International Reading Association.

Derman-Sparks, L., & the ABC Task Force. (1989). *Anti-bias curriculum: Tools for empowering young children*. Washington, DC: National Association for the Education of Young Children.

Dooley, P. (1991). Letters. *School Library Journal, 37* (Nov.): 88.

Englehardt, T. (1991). Reading may be harmful to your kids. *Harper's Magazine, 276* (June), 55–62.

Glazer, J. (1991). *Literature for young children* (3rd ed.). Columbus, OH: Merrill.

Goddard, C. (1992). Aiming for the mainstream. *Publishers Weekly, 239* (Jan. 20), 28–34.

Goodman, K. (1988). Look what they've done to Judy Blume!: The basalization of children's literature. *The New Advocate, 1*, 29–41.

Harris, V. (1990a). African American children's literature: The first one hundred years. *The Journal of Negro Education, 59*, 540–515.

Harris, V. (1990b). From Little Black Sambo to Popo and Fifina: Arna Bontemps and the creation of African American children's literature. *The Lion and the Unicorn, 14*, 108–127.

Harris, V. (Ed.). (1992). *Teaching multicultural literature in grades K–8*. Norwood, MA: Christopher-Gordon.

Howard, E. (1991). Authentic multicultural literature for children: An author's perspective. In M. Lingren (Ed.), *The multicolored mirror: Cultural substance in literature for children and young adults* (pp. 91–100). Fort Atkinson, WI: Highsmith Press.

Jeffers, S. (1991). Letters. *School Library Journal, 37* (Nov.), 86–87.

Jenkins, E., & Austin, M. (1987). *Literature for children about Asians and Asian Americans*. Westport, CT: Greenwood.

Lindgren, M. (Ed.). (1991). *The multicolored mirror: Cultural substance in literature for children and young adults*. Fort Atkinson, WI: Highsmith Press.

Livingston, M. (1988). Children's literature today: Perils and prospects. *The New Advocate, 1*, 18–27.

Madhubuti, H. (1991). *Blackmen: Obsolete, single, or dangerous?* Chicago: Third World Press.

Maughn, S. (1992). Shortchanging the children. *Publishers Weekly, 239* (Jan. 20), 39–40.

Natov, R., & DeLuca, G. (1987). An interview with John Steptoe. *The Lion and the Unicorn, 11*, 122–129.

Roback, D. (1990a). Bookstore survey: Zeroing In. *Publishers Weekly, 237* (Nov. 30), 36–38, 42–44.

Roback, D. (1990b). Commercial books scored big with kids. *Publishers Weekly, 238* (Mar. 8), 30–35.

Roback, D. (1992a). In space, titles, sales, the trend is still up. *Publishers Weekly, 239* (Jan. 3), 26–31.

Roback, D. (1992b). Spring 1992 children's books. *Publishers Weekly, 239* (Feb. 12), 5, 7–9.

Rochman, H. (1992). The *Booklist* interview: Virginia Hamilton. *Booklist, 89* (Feb. 1), 1020–1021.

Rudman, M., & Pearce, A. (Eds.). (1988). *For the love of reading*. Mount Vernon, NY: Consumers Union.

Say, A. (1991). Musings of a walking stereotype. *School Library Journal, 37* (Dec.), 45–46.

Schon, I. (1988). Hispanic books. *Young Children, 43,* 81–85.

Silvey, A. (1989). The basalization of trade books. *The Horn Book Magazine, 65,* 549–550.

Sims, R. (1982). *Shadow and substance*. Urbana, IL: National Council of Teachers of English.

Sims, R. (1983). What has happened to the all-white world of children's books. *Phi Delta Kappan, 65,* 650–653.

Sims-Bishop, R. (1990). Windows, mirrors, and sliding glass doors. *Perspectives, 6,* ix–xi.

Slapin, B., & Seale, D. (1980). *Books without bias: Through Native American eyes*. Berkeley, CA: Oyate.

Sleeter, C., & Grant, C. (1988). *Making choices for multicultural education*. Columbus, OH: Merrill.

Taylor, D., & Dorsey-Gaines, C. (1988). *Growing up literate*. Portsmouth, NH: Heinemann.

Taylor, D., & Strickland, D. (1989). Family storybook reading. Implications for children, families, and curriculum. In D. Strickland & L. Morrow (Eds.), *Emerging literacy: Young children learn to read and write* (pp. 27–34). Newark, DE: International Reading Association.

Zwick, L. (1991). Letters. School Library Journal, 37 (Nov.), 86.

CHILDREN'S BOOKS CITED

Banks, L. (1989). *The secret of the Indian*. New York: Avon.

Bannerman, H. (1899). *The story of Little Black Sambo*. New York: Stokes.

Baylor, B. (1976). *Hawk, I'm your brother*. New York: Scribner's.

Bishop, C., & Wise, K. (1938). *The five Chinese brothers*. New York: Coward-McCann.

Carter, F. (1986). *The education of Little Tree*. Albuquerque: University of New Mexico Press.

Clifton, L. (1970). *Some of the days of Everett Anderson*. New York: Holt, Rinehart & Winston.

Clifton, L. (1974). *Everett Anderson's year*. New York: Holt, Rinehart & Winston.

Clifton, L. (1975). *My brother fine with me*. New York: Holt, Rinehart & Winston.

Clifton, L. (1978). *Everett Anderson's nine month long*. New York: Holt, Rinehart & Winston.

Clifton, L. (1992). *Three wishes*. New York: Doubleday.

Cruz, M. (1976). *Yagua days*. New York: Dial.

Delacre, L. (1990). *Las Navidades*. New York: Scholastic.

Dorros, A. (1991). *Abuela*. New York: Dutton.

Friedman, I. (1984). *How my parents learned to eat*. New York: Houghton Mifflin.

Garza, C. (1990). *Family pictures*. San Francisco: Children's Book Press.

Greenfield, E. (1988). *Nathaniel talking*. New York: Black Butterfly Children's Books.

Hoffman, M. (1991). *Amazing Grace*. New York: Dial.

Johnson, A. (1989). *Tell me a story, mama*. New York: Orchard.

Johnson, A. (1990a). *Do like Kyla*. New York: Orchard.

Johnson, A. (1990b). *When I am old with you*. New York: Orchard.

Johnson, A. (1991). *One of three*. New York: Orchard.

Johnson, A. (1992). *The leaving morning*. New York: Orchard.

Lee, J. (1991). *Silent Lotus*. New York: Farrar, Straus & Giroux.

Loh, M. (1991). *Tucking mommy in*. New York: Scholastic.

Newsome, E. (1944). *Gladiola garden*. Washington, DC: Associated Publishers.

Paek, M. (1989). *Aekyung's dream*. San Francisco: Children's Book Press.

Ringgold, F. (1991). *Tar beach*. New York: Crown.

Roberts, N. (1991). *Henry Cisneros*. Chicago: Children's Press.

Roe, E. (1991). *Con mi hermano*. New York: Bradbury.

Say, A. (1990). *El Chino*. New York: Houghton Mifflin.

Seattle, Chief (1991). *Brother eagle, sister sky*. New York: Dial.

Shackelford, J. (1938). *My happy days*. New York: Associated Publishers.

Sneve, V. (1972). *Jimmy Yellow Hawk*. New York: Holiday House.

Sneve, V. (Ed.) (1989). *Dancing teepees*. New York: Holiday House.

Steptoe, J. (1969). *Stevie*. New York: Harper.

Steptoe, J. (1970). *Uptown*. New York: Harper.

Steptoe, J. (1971). *Train ride*. New York: Harper.

Steptoe, J. (1974). *My special best words*. New York: Viking.

Steptoe, J. (1980). *Daddy is a monster . . . sometimes*. New York: Viking.

Steptoe, J. (1984). *The story of the jumping mouse*. New York: Lothrop.

Steptoe, J. (1987). *Mufaro's beautiful daughters*. New York: Lothrop.

Steptoe, J. (1988). *Baby says*. New York: Lothrop.

Surat, M. (1983). *Angel child, dragon child*. New York: Scholastic.

Tuyet, T. (1987). *The little weaver of Thai-Yen village*. San Francisco: Children's Book Press.

Wheeler, B. (1986). *Where did you get your moccasins?* Winnipeg: Native Education Branch of Manitoba Education.

Winter, J., & Winter, J. (1991). *Diego*. New York: Knopf.

Xiong, B. (1989). *Nine-in-one, grr! grr!* San Francisco: Children's Book Press.

Young, E. (1989). *Lon Po Po*. New York: Scholastic.

CHAPTER 8

Designing the Early Childhood Classroom Environment to Facilitate Literacy Development

Judith A. Schickedanz

Beginning in the mid-1960s, reports of young children who began to read and write during the preschool years, typically without direct instruction, began to appear in the literature (Durkin, 1966; Read, 1975). These reports indicated that written language could develop simultaneously with oral language, instead of being a "secondary language process," as had been claimed (Mattingly, 1979), and that the acquisition of written language might not be as dependent on direct instruction as had been thought. In addition, the studies called into question the typical practice of excluding the development of written language from the list of goals for preschool programs: If high levels of oral language development were not a prerequisite to initial understanding of many aspects of written language, and if direct instruction of the kind typically associated with reading instruction in the elementary school was not required for beginning literacy development, then there was no rationale for excluding written language development as a goal in preschool programs.

The term *emergent literacy* replaced *reading readiness* to refer to an initial period of literacy development when children's reading and writing behaviors are not yet conventional. For example, children depend on others to provide the first readings of storybooks, which they then reread; they rely too heavily on context to read environmental print; they use incomplete understandings about the nature of the orthography to create their spellings (e.g., "1NS UPON A TIM" for *Once upon a time*); and they violate print conventions, such as putting space between words and writing consistently in one direction.

Research on emergent literacy development has been of several distinct types. There have been descriptive reports of emergent literacy development in the home setting, prior to children's entry into kindergarten and first grade (Anbar, 1986; Baghban, 1984; Bissex, 1980; Clarke, 1976; Durkin, 1966; Schickedanz & Sullivan, 1984; Torrey, 1969). These have included information about the physical contexts associated with high levels of emergent literacy development prior to school entry. By and large, the reports suggest that such children were read to and had easy access to favorite storybooks; were provided with paper and writing tools; owned educational materials, such as magnetic or wooden letters; and typically were surrounded by environmental print in newspapers and magazines, as well as on television, food cartons, storefronts, and road signs.

Other research has documented the young child's emergent literacy behavior in such areas as storybook reading (Rossman, 1980; Sulzby, 1985); word creation, including invented spelling (Ferreiro & Terberosky, 1982; Read, 1975; Schickedanz, 1990a); and print conventions (Clay, 1987). Additional research has attempted to understand how literacy development may depend on specific experiences and how variations in development relate to variations in experience, including adults' styles of reading storybooks (Dunning & Mason, 1984; Heath, 1983; Ninio, 1980) and their ways of providing assistance when children ask questions about spelling (Schickedanz, 1990a, 1990b).

Critical to the questions about variations in experience are considerations about the role adults play in young children's literacy development: Do children construct literacy knowledge and skills naturally, on their own, or is their learning dependent on experience that is at first scaffolded by adults and specific orchestrations of physical contexts? To put it another way, is early literacy learning best explained by a Piagetian (Piaget, 1954, 1952) view of a child in primarily independent interaction with a physical environment, or by a view more consistent with Vygotsky's (1929, 1978) idea that the child is dependent, initially, on social mediation of the physical environment?

The purpose of the chapter is to provide a greater understanding of the undoubtedly complex interplay between the child and his or her environment, both physical and social, that seems to be involved in early literacy learning, in order to make possible the design of preschool and kindergarten programs that are both developmentally appropriate and instructionally powerful.

The chapter will first present a general description of the physical contents of many preschool and kindergarten classrooms. These contents or provisions made their way into preschool and kindergarten classrooms as a result of information derived from the studies of homes in which children either learned to read before going to school or learned with ease soon upon school entry. While these recommendations for physical provisions were based on descriptive studies of home environments (Jewell & Zintz, 1986; Loughlin & Martin, 1987; Schickedanz, 1986; Schwartz, 1988; Strickland & Taylor, 1989), there is general agreement that they are sound and form the substrate upon which additional pedagogical maneuvers depend. This chapter will then review research on the effects of variations in children's literacy behavior that have been associated with variations in the design of the physical environment in classrooms, the design of specific literacy materials, and the social mediation of the literacy environment. The discussion of research will be followed by comments about research that is needed, and about the implications for practice of what is known thus far.

PHYSICAL FEATURES OF PRINT-RICH PRESCHOOL AND KINDERGARTEN CLASSROOMS

Print-rich preschool classrooms are furnished with many literacy-related materials, some of which constitute complete areas. For example, there is typically a library or book corner, filled with picture books to which children have ready access during major portions of the school day. In addition to a library corner, there often is a listening post, which gives children the opportunity to hear taped stories whose texts they can follow in companion storybooks.

In addition to these opportunities to look at or listen to storybooks, classrooms often provide specific materials and settings that encourage children to engage in retellings of familiar stories. For example, teachers often provide felt boards and felt story pieces, puppet theaters with puppets, or story illustrations placed in sequence on a roll of paper that can be unwound inside a box and viewed through one side that has been cut out.

Classrooms also have writing centers, which are stocked with several kinds of paper, a variety of writing tools, and other materials, such as blank books, greeting cards, stationery, envelopes, alphabet stencils, ink stamps, scissors, tape, and string. Children use the materials to explore and play with writing, or to make props needed in play (e.g., tickets, signs for block buildings, money, etc.).

In print-rich classrooms, dramatic play themes are often supported by print-related props (Schickedanz, 1986; Schrader, 1989). For example, for restaurant play, children might be provided with menus; with pads of paper for taking orders, writing bills, and writing down reservations; and with posterboard for creating a "specials" board and "open" and "closed" signs. For hospital play, children might be given health charts and clipboards for use during examinations, a notebook for keeping a log of appointments, slips of paper for writing up prescriptions or lab work, and magazines to read while sitting in the waiting room. For house play, children are often supplied with a pad of paper for taking telephone messages and making shopping lists, storybooks for reading to dolls, and cookbooks to use as they pretend to cook.

Classroom shelves are often labeled to indicate where various items are to be stored, signs are posted to indicate expected behavior, pictures or display objects are labeled, and attendance and helpers' charts are used by teachers and children to keep records and maintain the classroom environment. Print-related manipulatives are often included on the toy shelves. For example, there might be pictures to sort in terms of the consonant phonemes with which their names start, pictures to match with their printed names, or various kinds of alphabet matching materials. In addition, teachers often use instructional signs or posters, such as a list showing the number and name of each kind of item buried in a "treasure hunt" in the sandbox, or the steps to be followed in preparing a batch of play dough or applesauce.

DESIGN AND PROGRAM FACTORS INFLUENCING CHILDREN'S USE OF CLASSROOM LITERACY MATERIALS

Several research studies have indicated that certain program features (e.g., the extent to which books housed in a classroom library area are read during scheduled story times), as well as classroom design features (e.g., the attractiveness of the library area), affect children's literacy behavior in classrooms during free-play portions of the school day. These studies, which will be reviewed here, have focused primarily on children's use of books in library corners and props placed in dramatic play areas.

Use of a Classroom Library Corner

Several studies have investigated the effects of library corner design and specific program characteristics on children's use of a classroom library corner during free play. In one study of kindergarten children, conducted by Morrow and Weinstein (1982), teachers were assigned to one of four conditions. In the design-only condition, teachers organized a library corner that displayed books, included some kind of prop for story retelling (e.g., a felt-board story, a taped story), provided for softness (e.g., pillows, beanbag chairs, carpeting), accommodated at least four children, and contained a display consisting of books and objects relating to books (e.g., a stuffed animal of some book character).

In the design/program condition, teachers made the same physical changes in their library corners as those made by design-only teachers, but, in addition, they also read stories to children on a daily basis and placed the books they had read in the library corner. They also discussed the stories read, both before and after reading them, and they pointed out that the library corner was a play option that could be used during the free-play period of the day.

In the program-only condition, teachers made the same *program* changes required in the design/program condition, but they did not change the physical design of their library corners. Teachers in the control classrooms made no physical changes in their library areas, nor did they make changes in the way they dealt with literature in their daily programs.

Results obtained in the study showed that use of the library corner during free play was significantly greater in all three treatment conditions compared with the control classrooms, but there was no significant difference between treatment conditions.

In a second study (Martinez & Teale, 1988), factors affecting kindergarten children's selection of specific books from a classroom library were isolated. The factors studied included two physical features of books (predictable text and book size), which will be discussed later. The third factor, *familiarity* (the extent to which the book had, or had not been, read by the teacher), is the one of interest here.

Books were categorized as unfamiliar (never read aloud by the classroom teacher), familiar (read aloud once by the classroom teacher), and very familiar (read repeatedly by the classroom teacher). Results showed that children preferred familiar to unfamiliar books at a rate of about 2 to 1 and that they preferred very familiar books to unfamiliar books at a rate of a little more than 3 to 1. This finding indicates that the program feature of reading books that are included in the classroom library affects children's use of library books when they are free to go there to read.

Literacy Behavior During Dramatic Play

A study conducted by Morrow and Rand (1991) demonstrated the effects of physical environment and program features on children's literacy behaviors in dramatic play. Thirteen preschool and kindergarten teachers were assigned to one of four conditions: (1) paper, pencil, and books with adult guidance, (2) thematic materials with adult guidance, (3) thematic materials without adult guidance, and (4) traditional curriculum control group. In the first condition, teachers placed literacy materials (e.g., paper, pencil, markers, crayons, and books) in dramatic play areas, called children's attention to these materials, and mentioned and modeled ways that these materials might be used by the children. In the second condition, teachers set up veterinarian offices. Specific literacy-related materials, such as magazines, books, pamphlets, No Smoking signs, patient sign-in forms, appointment cards, and a calendar, were included in the play offices. Teacher guidance during play consisted of suggestions for using materials (e.g., "You can read to your pet while you wait in the waiting room" or "Be sure to fill out a prescription form for the pet's medicine") and modeling of literacy behavior while joining the children in the dramatic play setting.

In the third condition (i.e., thematic materials without adult guidance), the veterinarian offices contained the same materials as did the offices in the second condition, but teacher suggestions and modeling were absent. In the fourth condition, teachers did not set up a new dramatic play area, nor did they add literacy materials to the traditional dramatic play area (i.e., kitchen).

Results of the study showed that literacy behaviors were significantly higher in both adult guidance conditions than in either the thematic-materials-only or the control conditions, and that a higher number of children engaged in literacy activities in the thematic-materials-only condition than in the control condition. This study, like some others (e.g., Schrader, 1989), indicates that the addition of literacy-related materials in dramatic play areas can prompt literacy-related behavior in children, but it also shows that adult guidance can lead to an even greater increase in children's literacy behavior. Therefore, as shown in the studies on the use of library corners, both physical design factors (e.g., the physical placement of literacy props in dramatic play areas) and programming factors (e.g., teacher modeling of the use of literacy props placed in dramatic play areas) affect children's literacy behavior.

EFFECT OF TEXT PREDICTABILITY ON CHILDREN'S BOOK SELECTIONS

It was noted in the discussion above that their familiarity with books can influence children's library book selections during free play. In addition to the program feature of book familiarity, Martinez and Teale (1988) also studied the effects of the predictability of the text. A book was categorized as *predictable* if it had repetitive sentences, contained a lot of rhyme, or used a sequence with which children already were familiar (e.g., counting or days of the week). The study's results showed that predictable books were preferred to nonpredictable books at a rate of 2 to 1.

If the number of readings of a book by the teacher is held constant, predictable text apparently results in greater familiarity with a book than does unpredictable text, because the predictable text is easier to remember. Without previous readings of a book, there should be no difference in the rate with which predictable versus unpredictable books are selected in a library corner. Therefore the predictability factor should serve as an additional influence on children's book selections only in classrooms where teachers read the books that are contained in the classroom library (Martinez & Teale, 1988).

EFFECTS OF PROGRAM AND BOOK ILLUSTRATIONS ON CHILDREN'S QUESTIONS ABOUT BOOKS

Studies of young children's questions during storybook reading show, in general, that questions about the book's pictures predominate, while questions about the meaning of the story rank second. Questions about graphic form (i.e., questions about letter names, word names, or letter sounds) and about print conventions (i.e., questions about authors or illustrators, the title, or the direction in which a book is read) are relatively rare among preschoolers (Morrow, 1988; Yaden, Smolkin, & Conlon, 1989).

Research indicates, however, that frequency of adult reading of the book influences the kind of questions that children ask. For example, in a home-based study, Yaden (1988) found that rereadings of a book were required to elicit questions about the meaning of words and the story. With just one or two readings of a book, children's questions tended to remain focused on the pictures. With more rereadings, however, questions about word and story meanings began to emerge.

Morrow (1988) found a similar effect with repeated readings of storybooks to children in a daycare center. Print-related questions increased over time in the repeated-book treatment group, but not in the different-book group or in the control group, although picture- and story-related questions still were the most frequent in all groups, even when books were reread frequently to increase their familiarity.

In addition to these program effects, there is some evidence that another aspect of book design, the inclusion of print in illustrations, elicits more questions about print than does confining print to the book's text per se. Smolkin, Conlon, and Yaden (1988) found that children ask more questions about print when print is included as part of the illustrations.

Given that young children focus on the pictures rather than on the text in their storybooks, it is not surprising that print-salient illustrations elicit more print-related questions, especially of the word-meaning type (e.g., "What does that say?"), than do books without print-salient illustrations. In the latter type of book, children probably rarely ask what a word says, because they rarely look at the words. Unless a child actually has started to decode words in books and in the environment, and therefore is likely to be scanning some of the text of the storybook as the adult reads it, it is unlikely that the child will ask print-related questions in the context of storybook reading, except in the case of books with print-salient illustrations.

DESIGN FEATURES OF ENVIRONMENTAL PRINT THAT MAY AFFECT LITERACY LEARNING

There has been almost no research on the effects of variations in the design of other print placed in classrooms for preschool and kindergarten children. Therefore, the discussion here will report informal observations and preliminary data stemming from some manipulations the author has conducted in preschool classrooms. The first observations are of variations in teacher–child interactions about print in connection with attendance charts of different designs, and about changes in the frequency of interactions with print when jobs are assigned for varying lengths of time on a jobs helpers' chart. The second observations are of variations in the designs of poem charts that are available to children for use during free-play periods of the day.

Attendance and Helpers' Chart Design and Teacher–Child Interaction Concerning Print

In many classrooms, children are asked to indicate their presence for the day on an attendance chart. Often, such charts are designed with a photo of the child placed on one side of a card, and the child's name is on the other. Each child's card typically hangs in a specific position on the attendance chart, with the name facing out. Upon arriving for the day, the child flips over the card, exposing his or her photograph.

Another common kind of attendance chart uses pockets in which children place their name cards. But often the child's name card also bears a picture, perhaps of some animal. Because the child cannot yet read his or her name, the pictures are clues indicating to children which name card is theirs. In both of these cases, it is questionable whether children actually inspect the print that makes up their names or the names of other children. In the case of the first chart, the child quickly learns the position of his or her name card, and if an error occurs during the first few days, other cards can be flipped over until the correct photo is found. In the case of the second chart, the child looks for the picture, not the name.

In the Boston University preschool, an attendance chart has been designed with name cards bearing only the child's name. In addition, the loose name cards are arranged differently each morning and are placed on the floor in front of the chart. This design requires children actually to inspect the print when searching for their name cards. Children do, of course, often make some mistakes at first, and a teacher must help children locate the correct name when mistakes occur. The most typical confusion occurs when a child selects another name beginning with the same first letter as his or her own name. This elicits a fairly standard response from the child's parent or from the teacher: "You're right that this name starts with L like your name, but this is Larry's name, not yours." Some adults who give more elaborate responses might go on to say: "Look for the name that starts with L and has a D, not R's, in the middle" (for "Linda").

Other difficulties with this kind of attendance chart involve what might be called search procedures. With 18 or 20 name cards, arranged in three or four rows on the floor, some children do not at first know how to search systematically to find their name. Teachers and parents often model organized search procedures, such as running a finger across one row, then dropping down to the next row to do the same thing, and so on, until the child's name is found. While providing help with the search, teachers and parents might also provide other information. For example, they might read all of the names they pass, or they might say: "No, that's not your name, it starts with S, not L. Not that one; it starts with P. Let's see. We're looking for one that begins with L. Not that one, not that one. Oh, this one could be it."

Also, apparently depending on their perception of the child's skill, adults might begin to pronounce the names they pass, perhaps hanging on for a long time to the first phoneme in the name, as if trying to provide a helpful hint to the child who is looking at the name. Children are often able to "read" the name with this type of hint from an adult, probably because their classmates' names are in their oral vocabulary and the sound clue triggers one of them. From the point of view of learning to read, however, this sound clue is paired with the letter to which the adult is pointing and at which the child is looking, a situation that surely provides useful information to the child about some of the more abstract (and generalizable) features of the writing system.

Recently, five months into the school year in an urban classroom, an attendance chart of the pocket and plain name card variety replaced the photo and name card type that had been in use since the beginning of the school year. Not surprisingly, children had difficulty the first few weeks picking out their names from among the array that contained the 15 name cards for the class. The most common error involved selecting someone else's name when it began with the same first letter as the child's own name. Clearly, four months of putting names on the attendance chart in this classroom had not helped the children learn to recognize their names. (Names had not been used in other contexts in this classroom either. For example, there were no helpers' charts or labels on coat hooks.) Furthermore, there was a striking change in the number of interactions that occurred between children and teachers or parents at the attendance chart. Except for the first week of school, when the basic procedure for using the photo attendance chart was explained to children when they entered the classroom for the day, virtually no teacher–child interactions had occurred at the attendance chart. Children were able to use it independently. The new attendance chart, however, which could not be used independently, given the absence of external clues to indicate whose name was whose, continued to elicit considerable adult–child interaction even after four weeks of use. Through these interactions, children obtain information about letter names, letter-sound associations, and directionality of print.

Clearly, not all attendance charts are equal with respect to their potential for providing children with literacy information – nor are all helpers' charts or the procedures for using them. In the same urban school where various attendance charts were being experimented with, different procedures for using helpers' charts also have been tried. In some preschool classrooms, jobs were assigned on a weekly basis by posting names on a helpers' chart. In two classrooms, jobs were assigned daily, by posting children's names on the same kind of jobs chart. By the end of the school year, significantly more children in the classrooms with daily posting of jobs recognized names of classmates than was the case in the classrooms where jobs were assigned on a weekly basis.

It would, of course, be overwhelming to children (and a management nightmare for the teacher) to start the school year using print without any contextual clues to its meaning. On the other hand, as the year progresses, it is possible to remove some of the external, physical supports to the meaning of environmental print in classrooms and to provide teacher or parent interaction, for a time, to help children learn to read it.

Research indicates that preschool children do not differ in their ability to read environmental print (Dickinson & Snow, 1987; Harste, Woodward, & Burke, 1981). However, children do differ in the skills they use to read it, with some children remaining tied to the contextual clues to decipher the print and other children able to read the print without its typical physical context. It has been suggested by Dickinson and Snow (1987) that adult–child interactions about environmental print might vary, and that this helps to determine which children remain context-dependent when reading environmental print and which children learn to use graphic clues.

Changes in the design of the charts discussed above are likely to elicit more discussion about print and to make adults help children focus on graphic–phonemic features that generalize across situations.

Variations in the Design of Poem Charts

Teachers often are encouraged to write out songs or poems in chart form, to read some of these during a group story or music time, and to leave the charts where they are accessible to children during free-choice periods of the day. We had done this for several years in the Boston University preschool, and children indeed often learned the poems by heart and often read the poems to each other at various times throughout the day. However, except in relatively few instances when the child was reading conventionally, or was beginning to learn to do so, children typically did not know exactly where various words appeared on the charts, even though they might have been able to recite the entire poem verbatim.

During the past two years, teachers have begun to make some key words of poems removable, by sticking them onto the posterboard with Velcro. The poems are used at group times, in the same way that they were in the past, but during free-choice periods a specific chart of current interest is mounted on the wall and the key words are taken off the chart and placed in a tray on the floor. Children who play with the charts try to place the words in the correct spaces on the chart.

Not surprisingly, this change in design increases teacher–child inter-action. Children often start the interaction when they pick up one of the words from the tray and ask, "What does this word say?" A teacher is likely to say, "Well, let's see; why don't we read the chart from the beginning and see what words are missing." The teacher starts, perhaps point-ing to the words, as he or she reads. When reaching the first blank, the teacher often pauses to let the children, who are familiar with the poem, fill in the missing word. And then the search for the written word is made from among the four or five words on the tray. The teacher gives helpful clues to guide children's selections. Perhaps the teacher pronounces the word again, emphasizing its first phoneme. Then, he or she might say, "We need to look for a word that starts with *P*."

One chart typically stays out for independent use for one week at a time, and, then, the next week, a new chart is put up. It, too, is familiar, having been learned during the previous week or two during a group time. Familiar charts are rotated through again in a few weeks, if teachers think children would enjoy them or if they fit in with what is going on in the classroom.

Children more frequently elicit interactions from teachers when they are using charts designed in this way than when using charts designed in standard fashion (i.e., no words removed from the chart, to be replaced by the children). Preliminary data suggest that children's literacy skills are facilitated more by the second type of chart than by the first type. In classrooms where these materials were used consistently and frequently, more children had high levels of phonemic segmentation ability at the end of the year than in classrooms where these materials were not used.

SUMMARY AND SUGGESTIONS FOR FURTHER RESEARCH

The physical environment sets the stage for early literacy development. Without being surrounded by print, it is doubtful that the very young child would become interested in it. However, it has become more and more apparent over the past few years that being surrounded by a print-rich environment is not enough to support optimal literacy development. For example, research has demonstrated that all children growing up in print-rich environments learn to recognize familiar print *in context*. But not all children learn the more abstract, generalizable information about print that makes possible the transition from the use of emergent to conventional reading strategies (Dickinson & Snow, 1987).

One explanation for these differing levels of development is that adults vary in the way they interact with children in various print settings. Adults are likely to differ not only because of differences in individual style but also because the characteristics of print settings themselves might elicit certain kinds of interactions rather than other kinds. For example, settings in which there are fewer contextual clues to the meaning of the print used in the environment might elicit more graphic–phonemic information from adults than would settings in which there are more contextual clues to meaning. Similarly, the inclusion of books with print-salient illustrations (e.g., *Feathers for Lunch* [Ehlert, 1987], *School Bus* [Crews, 1984]) might elicit more questions from children about words than do books with pictures only in their illustrations. Furthermore, program variations—such as when names are posted on jobs charts on a daily, rather than a weekly, basis, or when teachers model use of literacy props in dramatic play, instead of placing them in the environment without introduction or demonstration — result in differences in the frequency with which children interact with print.

A great deal has been learned during the past 20 years about emergent literacy behavior and about environments that support this area of development. Teachers can use this research to design the physical environments and programs in their preschool and kindergarten classrooms.

Further research needs to continue to look at the effect of variations in classroom design and programming on children's use of literacy materials and on their literacy learning. It might be particularly useful to study the content and style of adult–child interactions in print settings that are varied systematically with respect to design. It would also be useful to study the effect of systematic program and physical design variations on the use of writing areas, in much the same way that Morrow explored the effect of variations on the use of library corners and dramatic play areas. For example, would the inclusion of such things as hole punchers, tape, staplers, and string result in greater use of a writing area than would limiting supplies to a variety of paper and writing tools? Would teacher demonstrations of these tools and materials at a meeting time increase the children's use of them during free play? And would the use of a writing center as a basic supply and support area for other areas of the room, such as for making signs for block buildings, increase the use of the writing area by children for other purposes, compared to classrooms in which sign-making materials are placed in the block area itself? These are the kinds of questions that need to be explored to increase our understanding of how the literacy environment, both physical and social, affects children's literacy development.

REFERENCES

Anbar, A. (1986). Reading acquisition of preschool children without systematic instruction. *Early Childhood Research Quarterly*, *1*, 69–84.

Baghban, M. (1984). *Our daughter learns to read and write*. Newark, DE: International Reading Association.

Bissex, G. (1980). *GYNS at work*. Cambridge, MA: Harvard University Press.

Clarke, M. M. (1976). *Young fluent readers*. London: Heinemann.

Clay, M. (1975). *What did I write?* Portsmouth, NH: Heinemann.

Clay, M. (1987). *Writing begins to home*. Portsmouth, NH: Heinemann.

Crews, D. (1984). *School bus*. New York: Puffin.

Dickinson, D., & Snow, C. (1987). Interrelationships among prereading and oral language skills in kindergarten from two social classes. *Early Childhood Research Quarterly*, *2*, 1–26.

Dunning, D., & Mason, J. (1984, November). *An investigation of kindergarten children's expressions of story characters' intentions*. Paper presented at the annual meeting of the National Reading Conference, St. Petersburg, FL.

Durkin, D. (1966). *Children who read early*. New York: Teachers College Press.

Ehlert, L. (1987). *Feathers for lunch*. New York: Harcourt Brace Jovanovich.

Ferreiro, E., & Teberosky, A. (1982). *Literacy before schooling*. Portsmouth, NH: Heinemann.

Harste, J., Woodward, V., & Burke, C. (1981). *Children, their language and world: Initial encounters with print*. Bloomington: Indiana University.

Heath, S. B. (1983). *Ways with words: Language, life and work in communities and classroom*. Cambridge, England: Cambridge University Press.

Jewell, M. G., & Zintz, M. V. (1986). *Learning to read naturally*. Dubuque, IA: Kendall/Hunt.

Loughlin, C. E., & Martin, M. D. (1987). *Supporting literacy: Developing effective learning environments*. New York: Teachers College Press.

Martinez, M., & Teale, W. H. (1988). Reading in a kindergarten classroom library. *The Reading Teacher, 41*, 568–573.

Mattingly, I. Q. (1979). *Reading, linguistic awareness, and language acquisition*. Paper presented at the Reading Research Seminar on Linguistic Awareness and Learning to Read, Victoria, British Columbia.

Morrow, L. B. (1988). Young children's responses to one-to-one story readings in school settings. *Reading Research Quarterly, 23*, 89–107.

Morrow, L. B., & Rand, M. K. (1991). Promoting literacy during play by designing early childhood classroom environments. *The Reading Teacher, 44*, 396–402.

Morrow, L. B., & Weinstein, C. S. (1982). Increasing children's use of literature through program and physical design changes. *The Elementary School Journal, 83*, 131–137.

Ninio, A. (1980). Picture-book reading in mother–infant dyads belonging to two subgroups in Israel. *Child Development, 51*, 587–590.

Piaget, J. (1952). *The origins of intelligence in children* (M. Cook, Trans.). New York: Norton.

Piaget, J. (1954). *The construction of reality in the child* (M. Cook, Trans.). New York: Ballantine.

Read, C. (1975). *Children's categorization of speech sounds in English*. Urbana, IL: National Council of Teachers of English.

Rossman, F. (1980). *Preschoolers' knowledge of the symbolic function of written language in storybooks*. Unpublished doctoral dissertation, Boston University.

Schickedanz, J. (1990a). *Adam's righting revolutions*. Portsmouth, NH: Heinemann.

Schickedanz, J. (1990b). Developmental spelling: What's the teacher's role? *ORBIT, 21*(4), 10–12.

Schickedanz, J. (1986). *More than the ABCs*. Washington, DC: National Association for the Education of Young Children.

Schickedanz, J., & Sullivan, M. (1984). Mom, what does u-f-f spell? *Language Arts, 61*(1), 7–17.

Schrader, C. T. (1989). Written language use within the context of young children's symbolic play. *Early Childhood Research Quarterly, 4,* 225–244.

Schwartz, J. I. (1988). *Encouraging early literacy: An integrated approach to reading and writing in N–3.* Portsmouth, NH: Heinemann.

Smolkin, L. B., Conlon, A., & Yaden, D. B. (1988). Print-salient illustrations in children's picture books: The emergence of written language awareness. In J. E. Readence & R. S. Baldwin (Eds.), *Dialogues in literacy research. Thirty-seventh yearbook of the National Reading Conference* (pp. 59–68). Chicago: National Reading Conference.

Strickland, D., & Taylor, D. (1989). Family storybook reading: Implications for children, families, and curriculum. In D. Strickland & L. B. Morrow (Eds.), *Emerging literacy: Young children learn to read and write* (pp. 27–34). Newark, DE: International Reading Association.

Sulzby, E. (1985). Children's emergent reading of favorite storybooks: A developmental study. *Reading Research Quarterly, 20,* 458–481.

Torrey, J. W. (1969). Learning to read without a teacher: A case study. *Elementary English, 46,* 550–558.

Vygotsky, L. (1929). The problem of the cultural development of the child. *Journal of Genetic Psychology, 26,* 415–434.

Vygotsky, L. (1978). *Mind and society.* Cambridge, MA: Harvard University Press.

Yaden, D. B. (1988). Understanding stories through repeated read-alouds: How many does it take? *The Reading Teacher, 41,* 556–566.

Yaden, D. B., Smolkin, L. B., & Conlon, A. (1989). Preschoolers' questions about pictures, print conventions, and story text during reading aloud at home. *Reading Research Quarterly, 24,* 188–214.

CHAPTER 9

The Role of Parents in Supporting Literacy Development of Young Children

Elizabeth Sulzby and Patricia A. Edwards

In the past decade, we have seen a pair of related shifts in how we view the literacy development of young children, from infancy through around 6 to 8 years of age, or whenever a child becomes conventionally literate, which in rare cases happens much younger. The first is a shift from a "reading readiness" perspective about young children's literacy development to that of an "emergent literacy" perspective. The second shift is a renewed interest in what parents do and what they can do to support children's literacy development. In this chapter, children's significant others — mothers, fathers, stepparents, grandparents, aunts, uncles, close family friends, and others who have a long-term and intimate familylike relationship with the child that includes literacy involvement — are also included in the term *parent*.

This chapter is divided into three parts. The first part focuses on what we know about children's emergent literacy development, beginning with the basis and importance of the shift away from a reading readiness perspective to emergent literacy. The second section reviews descriptive research on home environments and the things that parents have been observed to do that seem to support or fail to support children's literacy development, with special attention to minority and low-income children. The final part of the chapter highlights the history of programs that have encouraged parents to take part in their children's literacy development. It particularly emphasizes current programs that support the emergent literacy of children prior to the time they become conventionally literate.

CHILDREN'S LITERACY DEVELOPMENT:
THE SHIFT TO AN EMERGENT VIEW

The history of research in literacy development has been traced in detail elsewhere (Mason & Allen, 1986; Teale & Sulzby, 1986), so our treatment here will be brief. During a period beginning in the 1930s and continuing into the 1970s, reading instruction in the United States was governed by a skills approach emphasizing the mastery of discrete skills as a precursor to children's becoming able to comprehend text. Such skills were treated as being "readiness" for the "real thing" — conventional literacy — yet already the foundations were being laid for treating early development as a significant part of literacy itself.

Reading Readiness: Children as Preparing for Literacy

During the 1960s and 1970s, reading instruction for young children was based on at least two ruling ideas. First, while children could not really read until they had mastered lower-level skills such as auditory and visual perception, letter names and sounds, and sequencing, teaching such skills to preschool and kindergarten children could get them "ready" for formal reading instruction. This instruction included learning to recognize words at sight ("sight vocabulary") and to decode words, using knowledge about the sounds that letters represented in words. After children could decode and recognize words, they could begin to comprehend short, often artificially designed texts, then gradually move on to harder and harder texts.

Second, since research in child language acquisition and intellectual development was beginning to have an impact in reading instruction (Teale & Sulzby, 1986; Sulzby, 1991), children were viewed as able to learn more and more at an earlier age. Formalized programs of reading readiness were becoming more common in classrooms for young children, including kindergartens and special classes such as Head Start, and, for older children with low levels of performance, remedial reading classes, and Title I (later renamed Chapter I) programs. The early years were seen as the period during which priceless growth could and should be made, not a period for gradual maturation or unguided exploration.

Federally funded Head Start and Title/Chapter I programs encouraged and, as much as possible, required parental involvement with their children's academic achievement and literacy, but provided little basis about whether or why such involvement would help. During that period, there was very little research on parent–child interactions involving literacy; rather research was concerned with language outcomes.

Most of the child language development literature of the era emphasized the commonalities of child language development: (1) that all children acquire language, seemingly with little input from instruction and much from having adults talk with them; (2) that children abstract rules from the language they hear around them; and (3) that children's speech "errors" reflect intelligent hypotheses about language and often show their linguistic growth. This research treated oral language as primary and disregarded written language, considering it as a secondary coding system requiring direct instruction.

Research in linguistic differences (e.g., Hess & Shipman, 1965) in this era tended not to connect with the literature in child language acquisition and to stigmatize minority groups, but it did point to differences in parent–child language interactions that are now being reexamined. Research on linguistic differences, based on a deficit model of language acquisition for minority and poor children, initially had more impact on recommendations for parental involvement than did the language acquisition research that pointed to the vitality and growth in the language acquisition of all children.

During this period, parents of poor, minority, or low-achieving children were often encouraged or coerced into helping their children inside or outside school, but parents of mainstream or higher-achieving children were often cautioned that "teaching" at home might interfere with the school curriculum. The shift to an emergent literacy interpretation of this age span included a constructivist developmental perspective toward children's written language acquisition and a social construction orientation to parent–child interaction (Teale & Sulzby, 1986).

Emergent Literacy: Children as Actively Acquiring Reading and Writing

Research in emergent literacy (for reviews, see Mason & Allen, 1986; Strickland & Morrow, 1989; Sulzby, 1991; Sulzby & Teale, 1991; Teale, 1986; Teale & Sulzby, 1986) has changed the way many educators look at young children's literacy development and the role that parents play in their development. In short, children's emergent literacy is viewed as a set of behaviors and concepts about literacy that precede and develop into conventional literacy (Sulzby, 1989). So, rather than young children needing to learn prerequisite skills they are treated as readers and writers long before they can read independently from a book that they have never seen or heard read before and before they can write a text that another conventionally literate person can read. Skills are not prerequisites; instead, they are part of literacy development. They may not look like small versions of adult concepts (Ferreiro, 1986; Goodman, 1984; Harste, Woodward, & Burke, 1984). Instead, they may be used in unusual-appearing, child versions that may look like errors when they are actually moves forward (for example, scribbling or writing using repeatedly reordered letters from one's name).

The term *emergent* in describing literacy development (see Clay, 1966; Teale & Sulzby, 1986) connotes both continuity and discontinuity; it draws attention to the *continuity* between early roots of literacy, or what comes before, and conventional literacy, or what comes after, and still affirms that something is *new* in development. Thus the reading and writing of the 2-, 3-, and 4-year-old is treated seriously as literacy, and yet the conventional literacy of the 6-, 7-, or 8-year-old is treated as a significant, new development with ties to the child's earlier, emergent literacy. In the next section, we examine two primary categories of emergent literacy research, storybook reading and writing.

Emergent Storybook Reading. In addition to research on the relationship between parents reading to their preschool children and subsequent reading achievement, research began to look at precocious young readers. Durkin (1966) and Clark (1976) interviewed parents and teachers of young children who came to school already reading conventionally. One of their findings was that these children had been read to by their parents and most had been exploring writing, asking questions about how written language worked. Both studies suggested the need for actually observing preschoolers in their homes.

Doake (1981) and Holdaway (1979) reported a series of observations of children reading with their parents in homes. In these observations, children were seen to gradually take over more and more of the "reading," or reenacting of the stories as their parents read books to them repeatedly. In a series of studies of children's independent reading attempts, Sulzby (1985) found that children who had been read to repeatedly from the same books would respond to the request, "Read me your book," with speech that reflected the text of the book itself. She proposed and tested a developmental scheme showing that younger and less experienced children recited books with wording and intonation appropriate for oral situations. Older and more experienced children used language that was worded increasingly like written language and the book itself, and their intonation sounded like reading even before they began to attend to the text as the source of reading. Finally, children began to attempt to read from the printed text and to become conventional readers.

In a second study of children aged 2 to 5 from varied ethnic backgrounds and income levels in a daycare center (Sulzby, 1985), teachers read books to their children repeatedly, children were videotaped at quarterly intervals, and their parents were interviewed about the children's favorite storybooks. These children were found to use the same emergent reading behaviors as those shown by children from middle- to upper-middle socioeconomic status (MSES) homes. Parents defined a favorite as a book that children asked to have read to them over and over; they often corrected the parents' reading of the book; and most of the children began to "read" the book independently.

Low socioeconomic status (LSES) Anglo American kindergarten children and LSES bilingual preschoolers and kindergartners from Mexican American immigrant families (Sulzby & Teale, 1987) were found to use similar reading behaviors after teachers had read books to them repeatedly. The bilingual children used these behaviors in both Spanish and English emergent storybook readings.

During the early 1990s, it became increasingly common practice for teachers to read books to children repeatedly in literature-based programs of instruction (Hiebert, 1988; Teale, Martinez, & Glass, 1989) and in book-sharing programs based on Holdaway's (1979) recommendations. In these programs, children were encouraged to "read" books, reciting their texts and beginning to track print.

As we will see later, there are varieties of ways that parents read to children and guidelines that can be constructed about how to keep children engaged during story reading. In the studies conducted thus far, children from different socioeconomic and ethnic groups have been found to take part in emergent readings and to show similar emergent reading patterns. Nevertheless, there continue to be group and individual differences that the research has not yet explained fully. One possible explanation is the type of literacy background in the homes of preschoolers.

Emergent Writing. Just as preschoolers "read" books, they also "write," using emergent forms. From infancy forward, children who have access to writing utensils and have writing modeled around them engage in writing attempts (Burns & Casbergue, 1992; Dyson, 1985; Ferreiro & Teberosky, 1982; Goodman, 1984; Harste et al., 1984; Sulzby, 1989). Children write with many forms, such as scribble, drawing-as-writing, letter strings, and invented spelling. Children also use conventionally spelled words long before they hold a conventional concept for them. Finally, they develop toward conventional writing, in which they write readable texts that they themselves can read conventionally and that other conventionally literate people can read (Sulzby, 1989). Dyson (1985, 1988), Harste and colleagues (1984), and Rowe (1986) have provided rich transcripts of children's composing activities, showing how children shift back and forth between marking and use of oral language to explain and comment on their graphic compositions.

Ferreiro (1986; Ferreiro & Teberosky, 1982; see also Tolchinsky Landsmann & Levin, 1987) has used a Piagetian framework to examine how children's writing attempts and explanations reveal the active, constructive nature of their reading and writing. Ferreiro's tasks involve asking children to write monosyllabic or multisyllabic words or sentences dictated by an adult and then to answer questions concerning what has been written. She showed that younger children do not necessarily think that all spoken words need to be written and that they use a variety of child-invented ways to encode language in graphics. She says that younger children only gradually realize that writing is alphabetic rather than standing for some features of the physical referent (an example would be needing many marks for *train* because a locomotive and its attached cars make up a physically long object). Other hypotheses that children generate include the idea that words need a minimum number of letters (usually three or four) or that particular letters "belong" to a person whose name begins with that letter (Ferreiro, 1986). In a programmatic line of research across nations and languages, she has shown that children construct many common ideas about writing, ideas that are not taught by adults—and, indeed, that most adults find surprising.

With writing even more than storybook reading, researchers (Dyson, 1985, 1988; Gundlach, McLane, Stott, & McNamee, 1985; Rowe, 1986) have pointed to the social nature of children's engagements with literacy. As children write, they talk about their writing and weave their talking into the writing itself. After writing, they reread and discuss their reading, often making revisions even in products such as scribble (Sulzby, 1989). Nevertheless, there has yet been little in-depth, detailed research on the ways that parents support children's writing development, with the exception of Burns and Casbergue (1992). As we will show in the next section, the portraits of children's home writing interactions are few and lack the kinds of details about parental scaffolding that have been presented about storybook reading.

THE ROLE OF HOME ENVIRONMENTS AND PARENTS

Research in emergent literacy has made strides beyond the well-documented finding that there is an association between socioeconomic status (SES) and literacy achievement and that children from poor and minority families tend to lag far behind children from mainstream families (Teale, 1986). It should be noted, however, that there remains a paucity of research on middle- and upper-middle SES minority families; most of the research has been with white middle- to upper-middle SES families or with LSES families. Research concerning what happens in the home can be divided into two types: research on the general literacy environment in homes and research in parent–child interaction, particularly with story-book reading.

The So-Called Literacy-Rich Home

Retrospective research on children who enter school advanced in reading (Clark, 1976; Durkin, 1966) led to the conclusion that the key was in the interaction between the parents and children in home settings. Some children, relatively independent of such factors as measured IQ, seemed to be particularly curious about literacy, to have personalities that engaged parents, and to concentrate in literacy activities for periods of time. The parents seemed to support their children's efforts and to find the children interesting to spend time with. All of these reports were indirect and led to attempts to uncover what made particular home set-tings literacy-rich or literacy-impoverished for children. This required lon-gitudinal, descriptive research in the homes of families.

Taylor (1983) used ethnographic techniques to study six families in which there was a successful reader. She found that the homes were "rich" in having literacy materials available; additionally, the children were ac-tively engaged in literacy events with their parents. Some of these events were extended in time and intensity, but many others were brief and transient. The picture that Taylor created was one of homes in which parents had much interest in their children and the time and resources to support their children's total lives, including literacy.

Heath (1982, 1983) painted a similar picture in the homes of main-stream families in the Piedmont Carolinas. Mainstream parents were found to support their children by asking questions about past events, asking for "why" explanations of events, and relating stories of events. They engaged in conversations in situations such as car rides, in which children were expected to talk about events. Bedtime stories were typical events for these children; "literacy events" were woven into their everyday life and matched the expectations of the schools they attended.

The stereotype is that there are literacy-rich homes in which there are multiple literacy materials and many literacy events (events involving literacy either directly or indirectly, in which children are observers or active participants), and where parents are physically and emotionally available to interact directly to encourage children with activities that closely match those found in school environments. Such an environment would support children's active explorations in literacy. Actual observations point to greater variety and complexity than the stereotype.

For example, Heath's (1982) research pointed to much variation even in the familiar activity of bedtime reading across ethnic and socioeconomic groups. As we will see below, research in parent–child interaction provides a way of depicting interaction that moves beyond stereotypes of physical environments to specific social environments in literacy.

In discussing how to study the literacy environments of families, Leichter (1984) suggested that the physical environment, interpersonal interactions, and emotional and motivational climates all merit consideration. Understanding the foundations families provide is complex. Research uncovering the literacy experiences of nonmainstream families does not yield a uniform picture. Differences exist, but these cannot be traced necessarily on the basis of cultural background, social class, or ethnicity. Leichter cautioned against using group membership as a yardstick to measure what children know about written language on entering school. She also challenged narrow conceptions about what constitutes a rich literacy environment and which parents are able to support their children's development in reading and writing.

Homes of poor and minority children often have been depicted as lacking in literacy, yet further research supports the claim that such generalizations by income or ethnic groups are too broad to be useful at the level of the child. Anderson and Stokes (1984) and Teale (1986) conducted ethnographic observations in the homes of 24 LSES Hispanic, African American, and Anglo American families. One goal of the research was to uncover "hidden" literacy in the everyday lives of families and their children, literacy events that might or might not match school expectations.

Anderson and Stokes (1984) contended that many of the literacy experiences that occur in the homes of poor families were easy to underestimate because mainstream educators tend to look for activities such as reading storybooks to children and helping children with homework and overlook a range of reading and writing experiences that these young children participated in or witnessed. Sources of experiences in literacy, in addition to typical school or "literacy-for-literacy's-sake" activities, included literacy events for daily living needs (e.g., paying bills, obtaining welfare assistance), entertainment (e.g., solving a crossword puzzle, reading a television guide), and religion (e.g., Bible-reading sessions with children). Teale (1986) added that while there were substantial differences in the number and types of literacy experiences in the homes, some of these children were "well on their way" to becoming readers and writers (p. 192). Furthermore, all of the preschoolers observed lived in homes that had some writing materials, and children were seen showing intentions to write. However, in some homes the writing materials were not close at hand and children in these homes often did not actually write (Anderson & Stokes, 1984; Teale, 1986).

Taylor and Dorsey-Gaines (1988) further challenged some preconceived notions of what it means to be a poor preschooler. They provided a complex picture of the families and lives of black, urban 6-year-olds who were successful in learning to read and write. In spite of overwhelming personal and economic hardships, including homelessness, these families provided a rich literate environment. Tanya, for instance, had been a mother of two children since the end of eleventh grade and lived in an abandoned apartment building; yet Tanya considered reading aloud to her children an important means to helping them learn how to read and write. In fact, Taylor and Dorsey-Gaines found that the literacy experiences in these homes were more akin to rather than different from those of black and white mainstream families described by Heath (1983).

Schieffelin and Cochran-Smith (1984) revealed still another path to literacy through sharing the experiences of a Sino-Vietnamese family, where the son had entered school in Philadelphia in second grade and was successful in learning to read and write at 9 years of age. A prominent feature of this home was its lack of reading materials or an abundance of print. Parents neither read to their children nor provided children materials to read on their own. However, literacy was functional, meaningful, and relevant in the lives of this family and other Asian refugees studied. In addition to being part of the long Chinese tradition of literacy, this family and others placed a high value on becoming literate in English. Furthermore, although book reading was not a prominent feature of the home, literacy played an important role in maintaining relationships with others. Exchanging letters with relatives occurred often. Also, children frequently helped parents complete forms and correspond with others in the community because the children had stronger skills in written English.

Clay (1976) suggested that the way children view the significance and functions of written language may provide a basis for interest and success in reading and writing. Clay studied Pakeha (English-speaking), Maori, and Samoan children in New Zealand and found that while the Samoan children had the poorest average scores on oral English tests at every age, the Maoris had the poorest reading averages. Clay noted that the Maoris had little contact with printed materials prior to entering school and had few opportunities to learn concepts about print. The Samoan children did not have homes filled with books, but oral Bible reading in the home was part of their culture and writing letters to friends and relatives back home was routine.

Edwards's (1989) study of five low-SES households revealed that four of the five mothers did not share books successfully with their children. That is, they did not engage their children in the reading events. Additionally, they needed assistance with their own personal literacy skills. This study suggested an urgent need for ongoing intervention in low-SES homes and continued, expanded literacy training for parents, both for themselves personally and their interactions with their children.

As we have moved into these descriptions of the varieties of literacy experiences of young children, we have moved closer and closer to the questions: Just what is it that parents do? What is the role of teaching in children's homes? What guidance can be provided for parents, if any, in helping their children become more confident readers and writers?

Parent–Child Interactions: Scaffolding Engagement

The phenomenon of scaffolding has been evoked as a key explanation of how parents interact with their children in storybook reading. This phenomenon is similar to expansion in oral language development, except that the documentation of the efficacy of scaffolding in storybook reading seems clearer than in oral language development in general. This may be due to the fact that storybook reading appears to be a particular kind of routinized speech event (Snow, Dubber, & Blauw, 1982) that is widely known in mainstream U.S. culture. That is, parents who were read to as children know how parents are "supposed to" read to their children; the speech that they use is similar to the speech used by their own parents. While they may not choose the same books, the act of choosing will seem familiar. Some parents who have not had the experience of reading with their own parents may nevertheless be familiar with the routine from being around other parents and children sharing reading. For parents with little or no experience in storybook reading, the greatest difficulty may not be the words to be read but creation of a total social routine.

But what is the storybook routine? Ninio and Bruner (1978; Ninio, 1980; see also DeLoache & DeMendoza, 1987; Snow & Ninio, 1986) observed that parents begin in infancy acting as if the infant is "reading" along with them by asking the child to respond to labeling questions, such as "What's that?" Parents then act as if the child is taking part in a two-part dialogue: "That's right, horsie!" The child's earliest response may be as subtle as a glance, but as soon as the child begins responding at a given level, the adult raises the expectation by asking for more, accepting a grunt or /sE/ for "horsie." This idea — that the adult acts as if the child is taking part in a well-ordered routine and gradually shifts more and more of the responsibility to the child as the child develops — is a powerful one taken from Vygotsky's (1978) theory of the development of higher psychological processes through an internalization from interpersonal exchanges to intrapersonal processes.

Internalization, however, does not appear to be all that is going on in emergent literacy for the young child. Constructivist ideas from Piagetian psychology appear to provide another part of the picture. Constructivists emphasize the child's active exploration and engagement with the world, including literacy. Ferreiro (1986) studied young children who were trying to write their names and found that children only incorporated part of what parents and other intimate adults tried to "teach" them. They appeared to take in what they were ready for and assimilate it to their previously developed schemata.

Sulzby and Teale (1987) used a sample of parents who agreed to read to their preschoolers (beginning when the children were 18 months to 3 years old) and audiotape in-home reading sessions over an 18-month period. The eight families were divided into four groups: LSES and MSES Hispanic families and LSES and MSES Anglo families. During the time the families participated in the study, all the focal children began to do independent emergent readings with books their parents had read to them. Additionally, parents used scaffolding behaviors; that is, they encouraged children's verbalization and adjusted their speech to children's gradually increasing levels of involvement. As children became more familiar with books and written language, they began to request that longer and longer stretches of the book be read to them without interruption. Their own reenactments became fuller versions of the books while looking at pictures, although they were not rote or verbatim recitations (Sulzby, 1985). Advanced "readings" included overgeneralizations of written language patterns not taught in the interaction. Other patterns not taught by the parents but seemingly constructed by the child occurred as the children began to try to read from print (e.g., sounding out to nonsense words; reciting lists of known words out of story sequence, etc.).

What may be happening in these interactions is that, as the child becomes more independent in attempting to read, the "attuned" adult steps back and lets the child try his or her wings creatively with the text. Yaden, Smolkin, and Coulon (1989) studied the questions that children ask when their parents read to them repeatedly and found that, as children became older and more proficient, their range of questions became wider and parents supported these shifts.

But what about interactions that do not go well or do not seem conducive to positive literacy development? A picture is beginning to form that focuses on interactions rather than group membership, although the negative behaviors are more frequently found with LSES, minority, and infrequently-read-to children. The interaction of interest that we have been calling *scaffolding* appears to be one of *mutual engagement*, in which the more mature member, the parent, holds an internal model of the child's level of development to guide his or her own role.

When parents have been asked to read to their children in settings without interventions, some behaviors have been observed that do not seem conducive to mutual engagement. Parents may read without engaging the child's interest (Edwards, 1989; Heath with Thomas, 1984). Parents who have been asked to read to children who have not been read to regularly often spend a greater amount of time on disciplinary or controlling interactions (Bus & IJzendoorn, 1988) than do parents of children who had been read to. These controlling interactions decreased as children became more familiar with being read to and as the children themselves became more active in the interactions.

Pellegrini, Brody, and Sigel (1985) tracked the ways in which parents of normally developing children attuned themselves to the child's levels of engagement. Other researchers have found these behaviors to be associated with SES (e.g., Ninio, 1980), but SES was often confounded with language and/or ethnicity.

Some researchers (Pappas, 1987; Pappas & Brown, 1988; Pellegrini, Perlmutter, Galda, & Brody, 1990) have indicated that the emphasis on storybook reading has led us to overlook parental involvement with other text types. Pellegrini and colleagues (1990) found that African American Head Start mothers with moderate levels of literacy had different ways of interacting with two levels of narrative and two levels of nonnarrative texts. Teale and Sulzby (1987) reported different patterns of interaction with alphabet and other nonfiction books than with storybooks.

Little research has been done on how parents interact with their children in writing. Burns and Casbergue (Morrison, Casbergue, & Rice, 1992) asked LSES and MSES white and African American parents to write a letter with their 3- to 5-year-old children. They found that the children of parents who exhibited more controlling behavior and allowed their children less room to take initiative performed at a more mechanical level (less input and verbalization) than did children of less controlling parents. The children of controlling parents produced written products that looked more conventional but were often written by or "hand-over-hand" with the adult, while the children of less controlling parents produced more "emergent-looking" products (scribbling, letter strings). These children took more initiative and gave a greater emphasis to meaning. An important feature of this study was that both sets of parents were judged to be warm and positive with their children, yet their models of and expectations about writing as literacy were quite different.

A number of intervention studies (Edwards, 1989; Whitehurst et al.,

1988) have begun to show that parents can be taught to model the behaviors of parents who are successful in engaging their children about literacy. In addition to laboratory-designed research, intervention programs are being designed for practical settings, such as Even Start (Nickse, 1989, 1992; Popp, 1991) and other intergenerational literacy projects.

In the next section, we examine a group of studies, not limited to the emergent literacy level entirely, in which parents have been taught to engage their children around literacy activities. These studies, as a group, illustrate the growing interest in and partial success in working with parents. The final studies focus on how to use knowledge about children's emergent literacy to help parents maintain mutual engagement with their children.

PROGRAMS DESIGNED TO SUPPORT LITERACY DEVELOPMENT

The following studies and reports demonstrate the range of parent–child interactions that have been recommended to further a child's development as a reader and writer and are illustrative of some of the ways parents have been encouraged to participate in their children's learning. The goal of most of the programs is to teach parents to engage their children through specific types of activities. The expectation is that this involvement will give parents additional ways to influence, assess, and take responsibility for fostering their children's learning. Only a few of these programs appear to be built closely on detailed information about children's literacy development.

Helping Parents Develop Instructional Games

Cassidy and Vukelich (1978) developed a program that focused specifically on parents' construction of games to reinforce what were considered to be survival reading skills. An unusual feature was an informal pretest, sent to parents before each workshop, in which the parents assessed their children's knowledge of the skill to be stressed so that they would know how difficult to make the game. Vukelich (1978) designed PROP (Preschool Readiness Outreach Program) to help parents enhance their children's beginning reading skills. For 26 weeks, parents constructed games and activities to use with their children to develop oral language, visual discrimination, auditory discrimination, and listening. While organized around more traditional "skills," the program design encouraged the parent to plan the games and activities with their child's levels of functioning in mind.

Clegg (1973) provided low-income black parents with individually planned learning games in order to help them increase the reading achievement of their second-grade children. Raim (1980) developed a reading club for low-income Hispanic parents. The purpose of the reading club was to show parents how to construct instructional devices appropriate for their children and to rehearse how to use these devices before using them with their children. Burgess (1982) provided eight two-hour workshops for parents in which the educator presented some information about reading and the parents prepared a game to take home to use with their preschoolers. The following session the parents first shared their experiences with the previous week's game and then were presented more information, with which they designed a new game. These programs all suggested close communication with parents concerning their children's reading progress.

Developing Reading Activities for Parents to Help Their Children at Home

Sittig (1982) provided parents with packets of ideas for sharing reading activities at home. Families were asked to complete a minimum of eight activities over a two-week period. The project was designed as a parent involvement program that would be noncompetitive, open to all grade levels, and focus on children's experience of success in reading as an enjoyable pastime. Lengyel and Baghban (1980) developed a family reading program and a Sustained Silent Reading (SSR) program. The major objective of the program was to encourage parents to read to their children for 15 minutes a day, seven days a week, for a period of nine weeks. Siders and Sledjeski (1978) provided parents with activities in the form of a calendar with a home activity given for each day of seven months.

Involving Parents as Tutors of Their Children

Criscuolo (1974) suggested that parents could learn a great deal about reading by observing in the classroom. Crosset (1972) involved low-income black parents in a PPR (Parent Participation in Reading) program. Parents observed their child at school in a reading group and then received personal instruction and materials for home study with the child from a teacher at a "family learning center."

McWilliams and Cunningham (1976) designed Project PEP (Parents Encourage Pupils) to teach parents in the community how to help their school-age children benefit from reading instructions in the schools and how to provide a home environment that would help their preschoolers develop those readiness skills expected of a beginning reader. Shuck, Ulsh, and Platt (1983) encourage low-income parents to tutor their children using PEP calendar books and individualized homework activities.

More recent projects of this sort can be found in intergenerational literacy programs such as Even Start. Nickse (1992) and St. Pierre (1992) provide a picture of families that is important for the 1990s. Even Start projects are supposed to focus on the literacy growth of both parents and their preschool children, as well as on parenting skills. Providers of services are faced with a dilemma in that participants are supposed to participate in all parts of the program. Yet some parents were reported to be under such stress that it took a long time before they were able to become full participants. Under those circumstances, the parents and children make much slower progress and actually fall outside of the guidelines for services. Early results indicate that, when all parts of the projects are functioning, Even Start is helping to support parenting around literacy and children's literacy development, including literacy with computers (Popp, 1991).

Aiding Parents in Sharing Books with Their Children

The notion that parents could profit from receiving assistance in book reading has been suggested by a number of researchers. Spewock (1988) proposed that parents who have poor attitudes toward school because of their own negative experiences as students could profit from being trained to teach their preschoolers through children's literature. Pflaum (1986) suggested that "children with little experience in one-to-one verbal interaction with their parents may profit from instruction that provides such interactive focus. Parents may be able to supplement their interactions through training" (p. 89).

Several researchers have developed successful book-reading models. For example, Arrastia (1989) developed the Mothers' Reading Program, which taught adults to read through group creation of literature. Participants in this program would "read" the world, through dialogue about issues in the community—such as reading and not reading, education, parenting, and the myriad issues that affect mothers in present-day New York City. The dialogue was then transformed into written texts. This community literature became the core reading material and was used to build language skills. Gaj (1989) designed the MOTHERREAD program for mothers separated from their children by imprisonment. The program focused on creating connections between parents and children around books, capitalizing on the shared history, intimacy, and motivation that make the parent unique as teacher.

One program in particular was based on emergent literacy principles.

Edwards (1991) developed a book-reading program for low literate parents. The program, which operated from October 1987 to May 1988 in a rural Louisiana community, consisted of 23 two-hour sessions divided into three phases: coaching, peer modeling, and parent–child interactions. Each phase lasted for approximately six to seven weeks.

During the first phase, coaching, Edwards met with the mothers as a group. She modeled effective book-reading behaviors and introduced a variety of teacher videotapes, which highlighted specific book-reading techniques. The tapes often began with the teacher providing a rationale for why a book was appropriate for accomplishing a particular objective. The objective could include such activities as pointing to pictures, labeling and describing pictures, and making connections between the events in the book to one's own life experiences and vice versa. The teacher, working with a child, would then model book reading, highlighting the particular objective they had selected. After parents viewed the teacher tape, Edwards involved them in a guided discussion of the applications of the strategy modeled by the teacher. The parents could stay on after the sessions to review tapes and interact with her.

During the peer-modeling phase, Edwards helped the parents to manage the book-reading sessions and strategies. This phase was based on Vygotsky's (1978; see also Edwards & Garcia, in press) work, which states that "the zone of proximal development defines those functions that have not yet matured but are in the process of maturation" (p. 86). She assisted the parents by (1) guiding their participation in book-reading interactions with one another, (2) finding connections between what they already knew and what they needed to know, (3) modeling effective book-reading behaviors when such assistance was needed, and (4) providing praise and support for their attempts.

During the last phase, parent–child interactions, Edwards ceded total control to the parents and functioned primarily as a supportive and sympathetic audience. In this final phase, the mothers shared books with their own children and implemented book-reading strategies they had learned in the previous two phases (coaching and peer modeling). From these interactions, the mothers learned the importance of involving their children in a book-reading interaction. This program appears to model kinds of interaction with parents that are similar to the ones used to engage children in reading.

In general, programs suggesting ways in which parents may help their children appear to be increasing in number but not necessarily in quality. Our review was more extensive than the entries shown here, but few articles merited in-depth examination.

FURTHER CONSIDERATIONS

In the body of research that treats children's literacy development as being emergent, children have been viewed as active constructors of concepts that are different but move toward adult, or conventional, concepts; as we observe parent–child interaction, we see that children are dependent on input from parents and other caretakers in developing these concepts. Although we have begun to learn about how parent–child interactions foster children's literacy growth, we still have much more to learn. Also, as we turn our attention increasingly toward parental input, we must not neglect the child's constructions and input. Hence, we continue to need to focus on the interaction of the participants in the physical and social environments they inhabit.

We also need much research focused on kinds of literacy other than storybook reading. Examples of topics that would be fruitful include writing, reading from nonstorybook texts, reading and writing for daily life tasks, and the use of computers as literacy tools.

As more attention is being paid to interventions, the theoretical underpinnings of these interventions need to be examined. Intergenerational literacy studies (e.g., Nickse, 1992; St. Pierre, 1992) bring us once again to the realization that we need to take a life-span perspective on emergent literacy (Sulzby, 1991), but we need to apply it now to parents as well as today's children.

This review leads us to emphasize the importance of further investigation of the idea of mutual engagement in literacy, with a particular focus on understanding the similarities and differences in families from differing backgrounds. While this idea is important in parent–child interaction, it also appears to have much promise for examining how teachers can make their interactions with children more fruitful.

REFERENCES

Anderson, A. B., & Stokes, S. J. (1984). Social and institutional influences on the development and practice of literacy. In H. Goelman, A. Oberg, & F. Smith (Eds.), *Awakening to literacy* (pp. 24–37). Portsmouth, NH: Heinemann.

Arrastia, M. (1989). Mothers' reading program. In *First teachers: A family literacy handbook for parents, policy-makers and literacy providers* (pp. 31–34). Washington, DC: Barbara Bush Foundation for Family Literacy.

Burgess, J. (1982). The effect of a training program for parents of preschoolers on the children's school readiness. *Reading Improvement, 19,* 313–316.

Burns, M. S., & Casbergue, R. (1992). Parent–child interaction in a writing context. *Journal of Reading Behavior*, *24*, 289–312.

Bus, A. G., & van IJzendoorn, M. H. (1988). Mother–child interactions, attachment, and emergent literacy: A cross-sectional study. *Child Development*, *59*(5), 1262–1272.

Cassidy, J., & Vukelich, C. (1978). Survival reading for parents and kids: A parent education program. *The Reading Teacher*, *31*, 638–641.

Clark, M. M. (1976). *Young fluent readers: What can they teach us?* London: Heinemann.

Clay, M. M. (1966). *Emergent reading behaviour*. Unpublished doctoral dissertation, University of Auckland, New Zealand.

Clay, M. M. (1976). Early childhood and cultural diversity in New Zealand. *The Reading Teacher*, *29*, 333–342.

Clegg, B. E. (1973, April). *The effectiveness of learning games used by economically disadvantaged parents to increase the reading achievement of their children*. Paper presented at the annual meeting of the American Educational Research Association, San Francisco.

Criscuolo, N. (1974). Parents: Active partners in the reading program. *Elementary English*, *51*, 883–884.

Crosset, R. J., Jr. (1972). *The extent and effect of parents' participating in their children's beginning reading program: An inner-city project*. (ERIC Document Reproduction Service No. ED 076 946)

DeLoache, J. S., & DeMendoza, O. A. P. (1987). Joint picturebook interactions of mothers and 1-year-old children. *British Journal of Developmental Psychology*, *5*, 111–123.

Doake, D. B. (1981). *Book experience and emergent reading behaviour in preschool children*. Unpublished doctoral dissertation, University of Alberta, Edmonton.

Durkin, D. (1966). *Children who read early: Two longitudinal studies*. New York: Teachers College Press.

Dyson, A. H. (1985). Individual differences in emergent writing. In M. Farr (Ed.), *Advances in writing research: Vol. 1. Children's early writing development* (pp. 59–126). Norwood, NJ: Ablex.

Dyson, A. H. (1988). Negotiating among multiple worlds: The space/time dimensions of young children's composing. *Research in the Teaching of English*, *22*(4), 355–390.

Edwards, P. A. (1989). Supporting lower SES mothers' attempts to provide scaffolding for bookreading. In J. Allen & J. Mason (Eds.), *Risk makers, risk takers, risk breakers: Reducing the risks for young literacy learners* (pp. 222–250). Portsmouth, NH: Heinemann.

Edwards, P. A. (1991). Fostering early literacy through parent coaching. In E. Hiebert (Ed.), *Literacy for a diverse society: Perspectives, programs, and policies* (pp. 199–213). New York: Teachers College Press.

Edwards, P. A., & Garcia, G. E. (in press). The implications of Vygotskian theory for the development of home–school programs: A focus on storybook reading.

In V. John-Steiner, C. Panofsky, & L. Smith (Eds.), *Interactionist approaches to language and literacy*. Cambridge, England: Cambridge University Press.

Ferreiro, E. (1986). The interplay between information and assimilation in beginning literacy. In W. H. Teale & E. Sulzby (Eds.), *Emergent literacy: Writing and reading* (pp. 15–49). Norwood, NJ: Ablex.

Ferreiro, E., & Teberosky, A. (1982). *Literacy before schooling*. Exeter, NH: Heinemann.

Gaj, N. (1989). MOTHERREAD, Inc. In *First teachers: A family literacy handbook for parents, policy-makers and literacy providers* (pp. 27–30). Washington, DC: Barbara Bush Foundation for Family Literacy.

Goodman, Y. (1984). The development of initial literacy. In H. Goelman, A. Oberg, & F. Smith (Eds.), *Awakening to literacy* (pp. 102–109). Exeter, NH: Heinemann.

Gundlach, R., McLane, J. B., Stott, F. M., & McNamee, G. D. (1985). The social foundations of children's early writing development. In M. Farr (Ed.), *Advances in writing research: Vol. 1. Children's writing development* (pp. 1–58). Norwood, NJ: Ablex.

Harste, J. E., Woodward, V. A., & Burke, C. L. (1984). *Language stories and literacy lessons*. Portsmouth, NH: Heinemann.

Heath, S. B. (1982). What no bedtime story means: Narrative skills at home and school. *Language in Society, 11*, 49–76.

Heath, S. (1983). *Ways with words: Language, life, and work in communities and classrooms*. Cambridge, England: Cambridge University Press.

Heath, S. B., with Thomas, C. (1984). The achievement of preschool literacy for mother and child. In H. Goelman, A. Oberg, & F. Smith (Eds.), *Awakening to literacy* (pp. 51–72). Portsmouth, NH: Heinemann.

Hess, R., & Shipman, V. (1965). Early experiences and socialization of cognitive models in children. *Child Development, 34*, 869–886.

Hiebert, E. H. (1988). The role of literacy experiences in early childhood programs. *The Elementary School Journal, 89*, 161–171.

Holdaway, D. (1979). *The foundations of literacy*. Sydney, Australia: Ashton Scholastic.

Leichter, H. J. (1984). Families as environments for literacy. In H. Goelman, A. Oberg, & F. Smith (Eds.), *Awakening to literacy* (pp. 38–50). Portsmouth, NH: Heinemann.

Lengyel, J., & Baghban, M. (1980). *The effect of a family reading program and SSR on reading achievement and attitudes*. (ERIC Document Reproduction Service No. ED 211-925)

Mason, J., & Allen, J. B. (1986). A review of emergent literacy with implications for research and practice in reading. In E. Z. Rothkopf (Ed.), *Review of research in education 13* (pp. 3–47). Washington, DC: American Educational Research Association.

McWilliams, D. R., & Cunningham, P. M. (1976). Project PEP. *The Reading Teacher, 29*, 635–655.

Morrison, L., Casbergue, R. M., & Rice, J. (1992). *Socioeconomic status and cultural differences in parent–child interactions in the context of writing.* Unpublished manuscript, Tulane University, New Orleans.

Nickse, R. S. (1989). *The noises of literacy: An overview of intergenerational and family literacy programs.* Washington, DC: Office of Educational Research and Improvement.

Nickse, R. S. (1992, April). *Early findings from the national evaluation of the Even Start Family Literacy Program: In-depth studies.* Paper presented at the First National Conference on Family Literacy: Reaching America's Educational Goals Through Family Literacy, Chapel Hill, NC.

Ninio, A. (1980). Picture-book reading in mother–infant dyads belonging to two subgroups in Israel. *Child Development, 51,* 587–590.

Ninio, A., & Bruner, J. (1978). The achievement and antecedents of labelling. *Journal of Child Language, 5,* 1–15.

Pappas, C. C. (1987). Exploring the textual properties of "protoreading." In R. Steele & T. Threadgold (Eds.), *Language topics: Essays in honour of Michael Halliday* (Vol. 1) (pp. 137–162). Amsterdam, The Netherlands: John Benjamins.

Pappas, C. C., & Brown, E. (1988). The development of children's sense of the written story language register: An analysis of the texture of "pretend reading." *Linguistics and Education, 1,* 45–79.

Pellegrini, A. D., Brody, G. H., & Sigel, I. E. (1985). Parents' book-reading habits with their children. *Journal of Educational Psychology, 77,* 332–340.

Pellegrini, A. D., Perlmutter, J. C., Galda, L., & Brody, G. H. (1990). Joint book reading between Black Head Start children and their mothers. *Child Development, 61,* 443–453.

Pflaum, S. W. (1986). *The development of language and literacy in young children* (3rd ed.). Columbus, OH: Merrill.

Popp, R. J. (1991). *Summary of research for the Kenan Trust family literacy programs.* Louisville, KY: National Center for Family Literacy.

Raim, J. (1980). Who learns when parents teach their children? *The Reading Teacher, 34,* 152–155.

Rowe, D. W. (1986). *Preschoolers as authors: Literacy learning in the social world of the classroom.* Unpublished doctoral dissertation, Indiana University, Bloomington.

Schieffelin, B. B., & Cochran-Smith, M. (1984). Learning to read culturally: Literacy before schooling. In H. Goelman, A. Oberg, & F. Smith (Eds.), *Awakening to literacy* (pp. 3–23). Portsmouth, NH: Heinemann.

Shuck, A., Ulsh, F., & Platt, J. S. (1983). Parents encourage pupils (PEP): An inner-city parent involvement reading project. *The Reading Teacher, 36,* 524–529.

Siders, M., & Sledjeski, S. (1978). *How to grow a happy reader: Report on a study of parental involvement as it relates to a child's reading skills* (Research monograph No. 27). Gainesville: University of Florida.

Sittig, L. H. (1982). Involving parents and children in reading for fun. *The Reading Teacher, 36,* 166–168.

Snow, C. E., Dubber, C., & Blauw, A. D. (1982). Routines in mother–child interaction. In L. Feagans & D. C. Farran (Eds.), *The language of children reared in poverty* (pp. 53–72). New York: Academic Press.

Snow, C. E., & Ninio, A. (1986). The contracts of literacy: What children learn from learning to read books. In W. H. Teale & E. Sulzby (Eds.), *Emergent literacy: Writing and reading* (pp. 116–138). Norwood, NJ: Ablex.

Spewock, T. S. (1988). Training parents to teach their preschoolers through literature. *The Reading Teacher, 41*, 648–652.

St. Pierre, R. G. (1992, April). *Early findings from the national evaluation of the Even Start Family Literacy Program*. Paper presented at the First National Conference on Family Literacy: Reaching America's Educational Goals Through Family Literacy, Chapel Hill, NC.

Strickland, D. S., & Morrow, L. M. (Eds.). (1989). *Emerging literacy: Young children learn to read and write*. Newark, DE: International Reading Association.

Sulzby, E. (1985). Children's emergent reading of favorite storybooks: A developmental study. *Reading Research Quarterly, 20*(4), 458–481.

Sulzby, E. (1989). Assessment of writing and of children's language while writing. In L. Morrow & J. Smith (Eds.), *The role of assessment and measurement in early literacy instruction* (pp. 83–109). Englewood Cliffs, NJ: Prentice Hall.

Sulzby, E. (1991). The development of prekindergarten children and the emergence of literacy. In J. Flood, J. Jensen, D. Lapp, & J. R. Squire (Eds.), *The handbook of research in the teaching of the English language arts* (pp. 273–285). New York: Macmillan.

Sulzby, E., & Teale, W. H. (1987, November). *Young children's storybook reading: Longitudinal study of parent–child interaction and children's independent functioning*. Ann Arbor: University of Michigan.

Sulzby, E., & Teale, W. H. (1991). Emergent literacy. In R. Barr, M. L. Kamil, P. Mosenthal, & P. D. Pearson (Eds.), *Handbook of reading research* (Vol. 2, pp. 727–757). New York: Longman.

Taylor, D. (1983). *Family literacy: Young children learning to read and write*. Exeter, NH: Heinemann.

Taylor, D., & Dorsey-Gaines, C. (1988). *Growing up literate: Learning from inner-city families*. Portsmouth, NH: Heinemann.

Teale, W. H. (1986). Home background and young children's literacy development. In W. H. Teale & E. Sulzby (Eds.), *Emergent literacy: Writing and reading* (pp. 173–206). Norwood, NJ: Ablex.

Teale, W. H., Martinez, M. G., & Glass, W. L. (1989). Describing classroom storybook reading. In D. Bloome (Ed.), *Classrooms and literacy* (pp. 158–188). Norwood, NJ: Ablex.

Teale, W. H., & Sulzby, E. (1986). Emergent literacy: A perspective for examining how young children become writers and readers. In W. H. Teale & E. Sulzby (Eds.), *Emergent literacy: Writing and reading* (pp. iv–xxv). Norwood, NJ: Ablex.

Teale, W. H., & Sulzby, E. (1987). Literacy acquisition in early childhood: The roles of access and mediation in storybook reading. In D. Wagner (Ed.), *The future of literacy in a changing world* (pp. 111–130). New York: Pergamon.

Tolchinsky Landsmann, L., & Levin, I. (1987). Writing in four- to six-year-olds: Representation of semantic and phonetic similarities and differences. *Journal of Child Language, 14*, 127–144.

Vukelich, C. (1978). Parents are teachers: A beginning reading program. *The Reading Teacher, 31*, 524–527.

Vygotsky, L. S. (1978). *Mind in society: The development of higher psychological processes* (M. Cole, V. John-Steiner, S. Scribner, & E. Souberman, Eds.). Cambridge, MA: Harvard University Press.

Whitehurst, G. J., Falco, F. L., Lonigan, C. J., Fischel, J. E., DeBaryshe, B. D., Valdez-Menchaca, M. C., & Caulfield, M. (1988). Accelerating language development through picture book reading. *Developmental Psychology, 24*(4), 552–559.

Yaden, D. B., Smolkin, L. B., & Coulon, A. (1989). Preschoolers' questions about pictures, print conventions, and story text during reading aloud at home. *Reading Research Quarterly, 24*, 188–214.

CHAPTER 10

Preparing Teachers to Support the Literacy Development of Young Children

Lesley Mandel Morrow and Muriel K. Rand

Five-year-old Brian proudly handed a folded paper stuffed in an envelope to his teacher. "I wrote you a letter. Read it, please!"

Mrs. Green unfolded the paper, finding rows of wavy lines across the page. "Oh, Brian! You wrote such a long letter, would you like to tell me about it?"

Brian was excited and eager to share the contents of his writing. "It says, 'My grandma is coming to visit me tonight.'"

For the next few minutes, Brian told his teacher all about his grandma's visit. His teacher listened attentively and encouraged him to write again when he felt like it. Before skipping over to the writing center, Brian said, "I'm going to write a letter to my grandma now and when I'm done, maybe I'll write a letter to you!"

Mrs. Green's response to Brian's writing reflects her understanding and acceptance of how literacy develops in young children. She supports his early attempts at writing, although the writing is not yet conventional, and she offers oral language interaction and positive reinforcement. She has designed a classroom environment with appropriate centers and materials, and she regularly plans activities that provide for literacy learning in a meaningful and functional social setting. Mrs. Green's preparation as a teacher has included not only educational principles, but also studies of child development and, more particularly, of literacy development in early childhood.

This chapter focuses on how we can prepare teachers to support the literacy development of young children. Various professional organizations, such as the International Reading Association (IRA), the Association of Teacher Educators (ATE), and the National Association for the Education of Young Children (NAEYC), have developed position statements on the preparation of reading professionals and early childhood educators. The IRA (in press) statement notes that views of reading instruction that served well in the past may not be sufficient in preparing students of the future. It suggests that knowledge we have gained in the past should be integrated with current research to produce newer guidelines for teacher preparation. Finally, it outlines professional components that reading educators should master, including:

1. *Philosophies and theories* of reading instruction
2. *Knowledge* about language development, cognition and learning, and the reading process
3. *Teacher activities* that involve creating a literate environment, organizing and planning effective instruction, demonstrating knowledge of instructional strategies, and applying assessment principles and techniques.

Understanding the unique developmental characteristics of young children leads teachers to interact with them in ways that promote growth in a more effective manner (Ruopp, Travers, Coelen, & Glantz, 1979; Weickart, 1989). The joint position statement of the ATE and NAEYC (1991) addresses early childhood teacher certification standards, emphasizing a specialized knowledge base for early childhood educators. It lists five elements that should be included in teacher preparation programs:

1. *Liberal arts knowledge* in a variety of disciplines plus pedagogical knowledge and teaching strategies
2. *Theories of child development* and implications for classroom practice
3. *Awareness of the significance of play* in educational development and strategies for facilitating and enriching play
4. *Understanding of families* as the primary context for learning, and subsequent acquisition of skills for interacting with parents while respecting diversity in family backgrounds
5. *Opportunities to learn supervision and coordination* of teaching with others through shared decision making, especially to reflect on one's own professional development

This chapter has two major purposes: (1) to outline the knowledge base needed by teachers of early literacy and (2) to suggest experiences that provide effective preparation for preservice and inservice teachers.

These goals, of course, seek to support the language and literacy development of young children and will be discussed here in the context of suggestions from both reading and early childhood education professionals.

KNOWLEDGE BASE IN LITERACY DEVELOPMENT FOR EARLY CHILDHOOD TEACHERS

As noted in the IRA position statement, the field of literacy development has undergone a paradigm shift. It has moved away from a model of learning in which students passively receive knowledge transmitted from a teacher, to a model in which knowledge is gained through an interactive process (Harste, 1985). The application of this more recent model is valuable at all levels of learning and is useful as a theoretical base from which to examine the knowledge teachers need in preparing to support early literacy development. The basic premises of the Whole Language philosophy of how children learn can also be applied to how teachers learn (Short & Burke, 1989). Modeling the training of teachers to include experiences basically similar in nature to those we advocate for children fosters an interactive learning process. If we summarize the current knowledge of children's early language and literacy development, then identify a framework for that knowledge base, we can explore how to impart that knowledge to preservice and inservice teachers during their professional development.

Emergent Literacy

As explained in the Introduction to this volume, a growing and changing body of research has led to a reconceptualization of children's early reading and writing development. The term *emergent literacy*, coined by Marie Clay (1966), is currently used to emphasize the continuous nature and development of literacy that begins to "emerge" from birth onward. Even very young children possess certain elements or precursors of literacy, although their skills are not fully developed and do not match our conceptions of mature reading and writing (Teale, 1986). The concept of emergent literacy also encompasses the interrelatedness and concurrent development of reading, writing, and oral language. Finally, literacy development occurs in the daily contexts of home, school, and community, and in social, collaborative atmospheres.

In a classroom designed and guided from the perspective of emergent literacy, meaning and function for literacy behaviors is provided by the extensive use of children's literature and in environmental print as called for and encouraged by children's intrinsic interests, their real-life experiences, and the integration of literacy experiences into all content areas.

Experiences for learning are created with deep respect for the social, emotional, physical, and intellectual development of the child.

Before the definition and widespread acceptance of an emergent literacy perspective on instruction, maturation was considered an essential factor, if not *the* essential factor, in learning to read, and formal instruction was postponed until the child was considered "developmentally ready." An influential study by Morphett and Washburne (1931), for instance, set the age of "readiness to read" at 6 years, 6 months. A model of reading readiness developed in which, instead of seeking appropriate times for formal instruction, educators provided experiences that were believed to help the child achieve "readiness." A narrow focus developed on a set of perceived prerequisite skills that were subsequently taught to all children with no consideration of any nascent or active elements of literacy they might have acquired beforehand.

How Children Learn

More recent research into literacy development has led to instructional strategies based more appropriately on principles of child development. Piaget's influence has focused educators on the interaction between children's thoughts and actions and their social and physical environment. Children, it is now generally believed, must participate actively in the learning process through exploration, experimentation, problem solving, and social negotiation, especially in projects involving literacy activities (Piaget & Inhelder, 1969).

Vygotsky (1978) suggests that children learn by internalizing the social interactions of their world. An adult or more competent peer helps the child by "scaffolding" literacy learning, for example, by providing an exemplary model of reading aloud. The child is supported in his or her own reading at whatever level of development such support is needed. Support becomes less necessary and less frequent as the child is able to function independently.

Botel, Botel-Sheppard, and Renninger (in press) have adapted such theoretical constructs into a framework applicable to preservice and inservice teacher preparation. It focuses on four precepts: that literacy learning occurs

1. In meaningful and functional contexts
2. Through social interaction in varied contexts
3. Through active involvement with literacy experiences and materials
4. Through the integration of reading, writing, speaking, and listening in all content areas

These four precepts outline a knowledge base that informs language and literacy development. They also imply or suggest certain classroom practices. Both knowledge base and classroom practices are explored in the sections that follow.

Meaningful, Functional Contexts. Studies indicate that early readers tend to come from homes where language is stimulated, encouraged, and used as a component of everyday living to accomplish tasks and communicate in a meaningful way (Snow & Perlmann, 1985). Such use of language enhances literacy development by providing not only for social collaboration and the communication of ideas, but also by providing a conduit to familiarity with the foundation of language structures. K. S. Goodman (1967), for example, views reading as the reconstruction of an author's message rather than simply as decoding. The sequences and patterns of written symbols, he maintains, represent the sequences of oral language. Our experiences with the structures of language structure help us anticipate and verify written words as we encounter them in text.

Halliday (1975) also emphasizes the importance of a functional context for children's language development. According to his theory, children acquire language by learning its functions, that is, how language can serve their needs. Children's first words are meaningful because they usually help them acquire something they need. The child's need to interact in social situations provides the impetus for language.

The child's life experiences provide a context for the acquisition of reading skills as well (Y. Goodman, 1986; Mason & McCormick, 1981). Experiences such as reading a road sign to help find a destination, selecting food from a menu in a restaurant, and helping pick out groceries from a prepared list in the supermarket are meaningful, functional literacy events that promote reading development by helping children derive meaning from print.

Likewise, children emerge as writers from having experienced written messages embedded in familiar, real-life situations (Gundlach, McLane, Scott, & McNamee, 1985). Such experiences usually begin in the home with family members leaving notes for one another, making grocery lists, or writing thank-you notes. The functions of writing are learned from the real purposes children experience for communicating through writing.

Social Interaction. So, too, is social interaction a real-life, meaningful experience critical in learning to read (Clark, 1976; Smith, 1983). Children learn when they are involved in literacy activities that are scaffolded or supported by adults or other children who are capable of more sophisticated abilities in reading and writing (Teale, 1982). Holdaway

(1979) identified four processes related to social interaction that facilitate the acquisition of reading and writing. Children, he wrote, need to *observe* adults or peers involved in their own literacy activities. They need to *collaborate* with others in a socially interactive manner, then *practice* literacy behaviors with others or alone. Finally, literacy needs to be shared through *performance*, such as in reading a story that one has written to classmates or a friend.

Effective social collaboration becomes instrumental in the classroom, even in the development of comprehension, through such strategies as small-group and one-to-one story readings. Such formats make interactive readings possible, encouraging responses, participation, and elaboration that cannot realistically occur during whole-group reading (Morrow, 1988). Shared book experiences help children recreate the meaning of the story through their collaborative participation (Holdaway, 1979).

When children are provided blocks of time for socially collaborative literacy projects, they increase, develop, and enhance such skills as oral reading, comprehension, and writing. They learn by explaining material to one another and by listening to one another's viewpoints (Sharkey, 1992).

Active Involvement with Literacy Experiences and Materials. In the 1960s and 1970s, studies of how children acquire language indicated that although maturation and imitation play a large part, children also actively construct language (Cazden, 1981; Halliday, 1975). According to the constructivist theory, children actively participate in their own language development by generating their own language forms as they test out and discover rules governing the language they hear. Language errors are an essential part of this experimental learning process (Harris & Smith, 1980). Constructivists see language development as a continuous social process, taking place in settings in which children interact with one another and play with language by making up words, trying out new words, and engaging in monologues.

Becoming a competent reader requires not only active involvement, but practice and motivation as well (Anderson, Hiebert, Scott, & Wilkinson, 1985). Studies reveal a positive correlation between the amount of time children spend reading and high levels of reading achievement. Daily story reading and storytelling with felt boards, puppets, and props can attract young children to books and provide active involvement for different learning styles (Morrow, 1989). Time for independent reading and writing, during which children choose the literacy activities in which they want to participate, also promotes achievement in reading — activities such as looking at books, listening to taped stories, dramatizing stories, or reconstructing texts with literature manipulatives (Morrow, 1992).

Active involvement is crucial to writing development. The forms of writing are learned through experimentation in which structures and arrangements of language are invented and reinvented (Bissex, 1980). Children need plenty of time for such exploration, which is even more effective when self-initiated (Teale, 1986).

Integration of Literacy Experiences. From the perspective of emergent literacy theory, reading and writing are linked within a unified system of communication. As children experiment with writing, they construct and refine their knowledge of written language, a process that, in turn, helps to make reading possible. When children write, they benefit from the opportunity to integrate their knowledge of reading into writing.

The importance of collaboration and integrating literacy into content areas is typically promoted through group projects. Classrooms based on a philosophy of curricular integration are carefully designed to include learning centers so that children can choose activities freely and collaborate with others. The daily schedule in a classroom based on emergent literacy constructs also reflects the integration of content areas. Large blocks of time are included for thematic group projects that integrate literacy into all activities.

APPROACHES TO TEACHER PREPARATION

A classroom teacher's professional training typically begins in a college classroom. Because the subject knowledge within a given field is constantly changing, however, teacher education should become a career project of continuous preparation (Meyers, 1991). Both preservice and inservice teachers benefit by learning the knowledge and action base for early literacy development in ways that are meaningful, integrated, and part of a supportive, interactive social context.

Alvermann (1990) reviewed teacher-education programs in reading and delineated three contrasting approaches to teacher preparation. First, she found the "traditional craft" approach in which reading teacher education is an apprenticeship of refining the craft of teaching through observing model teachers at work. Second, she identified a "competency-based" approach in which learners demonstrate skills from a list of competencies in effective teaching. Finally, she described "inquiry-oriented" education in which teachers reflect on their knowledge, making implicit theories explicit and considering alternatives in teaching practice. This inquiry-oriented approach parallels the learning experiences presented above as providing meaningful, functional contexts, social collaboration, holistic integration of subjects, and active involvement in literacy development itself.

Other reports on teacher preparation recommend an inquiry-oriented approach. Bondy (1990), for example, suggests components of teacher preparation based on implications from a study of children's definitions of reading. Children observed in the study based their definitions on their individual views of reading as either an externally imposed task or a personally meaningful activity, either of which was derived in part from the type of learning experiences provided by their teachers. Bondy then suggests that teacher educators need to help inservice and preservice teachers to identify their own assumptions about teaching and learning in order to develop professional knowledge about reading, to learn diagnostic observation skills, and to recognize and develop educationally sound reading practices.

The following section integrates some of the ideas presented by these several authors into our framework of categories for organizing teacher preparation that will support language and literacy development in early childhood — a framework that

1. Incorporates meaningful, functional experiences, social collaboration, opportunities for active learning through participation and reflection, and integration of literacy learning into content area teaching
2. Is governed by an interactive view of learning in which participants initiate learning through personal questions, determine agendas, and connect new knowledge to past understandings and future needs

An attempt is made to demonstrate how teachers can be taught in a way that models the kinds of experiences that we advocate for children, those embodied in an interactive learning process. If they learn by example, both future and inservice teachers are more likely to be able to practice what they learn, since they will have a model before them for what they are to teach.

Continuous Professional Growth

The backbone in preparing teachers who will most appropriately support literacy development in young children is the knowledge base of theory and practice presented briefly in the first part of this chapter. The subject matter concerning literacy instruction will not remain the same throughout a teacher's career. Rather, it will need to be analyzed and understood in the light not only of past knowledge but also of continual updating (Meyers, 1991). The major challenge for teacher educators is to make theory and knowledge accessible to teachers so that both are meaningful and readily applied to classroom practice. Such accessibility can be facilitated through discussions about reading material centered around identifying problems, needs, and concerns. The range of professional reading can include textbooks, teacher handbooks, research reports, journal articles, teachers' magazines, and newsletters from professional organizations. Inservice and preservice programs must provide updated reference lists and identify where resources can be obtained. Professional materials must be accessible in college and university libraries and in sections of school libraries set aside for the professional development of teachers.

An important component of professional preparation and continued development is an introduction to professional organizations such as the IRA in Newark, Delaware; the NAEYC in Washington, D.C.; and the Association for Childhood Education International (ACEI) in Wheaton, Maryland. Such associations are a rich resource for keeping up with the state of the art in what we know of early literacy. They also develop a sense of belonging to a professional community.

Collaboration with Colleagues

Teachers also need to learn, adapt, and develop practical classroom strategies in setting and carrying out goals, in planning, and in evaluating. Included in such a corpus of information and skill are strategies and techniques of instruction that Saracho and Spodek (1983) have categorized into six roles that teachers play in the classroom:

1. *Decision maker* — choosing content, methods, and materials for instruction
2. *Curriculum designer* — organizing experiences that promote learning
3. *Instructional organizer* — incorporating grouping and placement, and arranging schedules, classroom materials, and equipment
4. *Diagnostician* — assessing children's capabilities through child-study techniques
5. *Learning manager* — creating the environment, and planning and developing activities, routines, and transitions to meet individual needs
6. *Counselor/advisor* — providing for emotional needs and establishing positive self-images as motivation to learn

Collaboration with colleagues provides a context for learning such pedagogy, and case studies provide a mechanism for practicing and examining the strategies and techniques for instruction that are involved. Through case studies, both preservice and inservice teachers can collaborate to solve the problems they themselves have posed through brainstorming. In the process, as many ideas as possible are gathered and evaluated, based on the theoretical and research background they represent (Merseth, 1991). Case studies have long been written by teacher-education faculty; however, collections are now appearing in full-fledged professional volumes—for example, *Case Studies for Teacher Decision Making* (Greenwood & Parkay, 1989) and *Case Studies for Teacher Problem Solving* (Silverman, Welty, & Lyon, 1992). The following sample lets the preservice and inservice teacher play the roles of decision maker, curriculum designer, instructional organizer, diagnostician, learning manager, and counselor/advisor. Support materials for the exercise should be made available when and where necessary.

A case dealing with diversity in the classroom. This year, unlike other years, you have many children in your classroom with special needs. Others have been identified as "at risk" because of poor test scores, but still others have been classified as gifted.

How will you handle the needs of these different children within your literacy program? How will you measure their progress? Be sure to describe parental involvement since, in many cases, without the support of the home or instruction for the parents, you cannot be successful at school.

Teachers can take responsibility for professional development themselves by preparing workshops for other teachers. Each participating teacher, inservice or preservice, can identify concerns of the group or areas of their own particular interest and prepare presentations to share. Teaching others requires synthesizing the information in a way that leads to a greater understanding than is possible as a passive observer.

Schools may choose to set aside regular time for professional development or collaboration each week. The school setting can become an ideal place for collaborative experiences in continuing education. Regular planned meeting times for teacher support groups allow teachers to pursue in depth the types of activities suggested here (Watson & Stevenson, 1989). Such planning allows administrators to demonstrate support for professional staff development.

Movies and videotapes can be incorporated into such programs to demonstrate and analyze effective teaching strategies and to set up scenarios for further analysis. They can be produced locally to share exemplary programs or they can be used as diagnostic tools with which individual teachers can refine their observation skills and offer suggestions for improvement. One's own teaching can be analyzed by videotape during actual instruction. Professionally produced videos are already available to help bring theoretical positions and research programs to life.

Field Experiences: Preparing and Practicing
Current Classroom Strategies

Hollingsworth (1988) emphasizes the need to link schools and universities so that preservice teachers can more appropriately and realistically integrate pedagogy and content and reflect on their teaching. Teachers need the inquiry skills that will prepare them to go beyond the practicing models they see in their fieldwork. Hollingsworth also points out that student teaching is reported as the most valuable experience in preservice training. It is essential, therefore, to provide quality experiences in student teaching that include two important components. First, student teachers need to experience a model of effective teaching that corresponds to the theoretical and research perspectives they are learning. Second, student teachers need opportunities to participate actively in the classroom. Planning and carrying out activities, collecting assessment information, and meeting with parents and other teachers are all necessary experiences for the student teacher's growth.

For inservice teachers the school setting is already in place and the classroom becomes a learning laboratory for new ideas. Following are just a few strategies that either inservice or preservice teachers can try. All reflect current theory about promoting language and literacy in young children.

- *Storytelling.* After a literacy skill has been identified, teachers select a piece of children's literature, then choose a creative storytelling technique, such as using a felt board or puppets, to develop the identified skill. Presentations can be carried out in a classroom with children or during a professional development session with peers. The learning experience is evaluated, and ideas for further extension or improvements are shared. Videotaping a presentation allows self-evaluation or further group evaluation and sharing.
- *Interdisciplinary Thematic Literacy Units.* Inservice and preservice teachers can prepare and carry out interdisciplinary curriculum units.

Objectives are specified for all curriculum areas, but literacy development is included as a component in all activities. Unit plans should include daily activity suggestions, characteristics of specific learning centers, assessment procedures, children's literature to be used, and other pertinent teacher resources. Once implemented, units can be critiqued and shared with colleagues.

- *Journals.* Both preservice and inservice teachers can benefit from regular journal writing as a way of recording and reflecting on their own growth. Students can evaluate their observations of other teachers or reflect on lessons they themselves have carried out. Critical analyses of professional material are a valuable experience as well. When teachers keep journals, they gain firsthand knowledge of the journal-writing process, an experience they will probably want to provide for the children they teach.

- *Preparing the Environment.* The use of learning centers is a strategy that strongly supports early literacy development. Creating a literacy center in a classroom, including a library corner and "student author's" spot, can also be a project toward which teachers, students, parents, and community representatives all work together. Activities within an early childhood classroom can emanate from and around that literacy center — such activities as developing assessment portfolios, creating a family literacy program that includes newsletter articles for parents, and establishing reading and writing periods that provide for social collaborative experiences or the opportunity to work alone, with such decisions left to each individual child.

Teacher as Researcher

Keeping abreast of new information about early literacy can be viewed as a research process for teachers. Being a teacher/researcher entails formulating questions about such topics as teaching strategies, classroom environments, and children with special needs (Copper, 1991). Daily experiences become the generating force behind research questions. When teachers reflect on their own teaching, they identify their own strengths and weaknesses, clarify issues, and generate new ideas.

Once a teacher decides on an area of inquiry, a method for data collection is developed. Data can be collected by observing and recording anecdotes; videotaping children engaged in literacy behaviors; collecting samples of children's work; interviewing children, teachers, and parents; and both informal and formal testing. Data provide the teacher with an objective basis for interpreting and resolving research questions. Collaboration on projects with other teachers helps refine the methodology and interpretation of research findings (Nixon, 1987). Among ideas for class-room research are:

1. Trying different storybook reading strategies to improve the experience
2. Observing social behaviors during independent reading and writing periods to determine how children support one another in literacy development
3. Creating a parent component of the literacy program to determine its effect on attitudes and literacy development

The teacher/researcher participates in both the art and the science of teaching. The science of teaching involves the process of inquiry through reading, observing, and collecting data. The reflection on and interpretation of those findings and suggestions for change involve the art of teaching.

Opportunities for classroom research are not limited to inservice teachers. Preservice teachers can also benefit greatly from posing questions about classroom practice, then becoming involved in collecting and interpreting data. Students involved in such research during their teacher preparation have described their learning in the following ways:

The hands-on experiences of being in a real-life situation taught me more than any book or lecture could.

During my research experience I designed literacy centers for classrooms. This is something I will never forget and will include in my own classroom.

The research activities provided me the opportunity to solve problems; they were a creative way to learn.

Change needs to come from teachers rather than being mandated by administrators or recommended by authorities outside the school district. Taking this responsibility empowers teachers and allows them to be decision makers and catalysts for change. Teacher research requires support groups, discussions about projects, and regular collaboration with colleagues (Pinnell & Matlin, 1989).

Professional Development Programs Related to Reading

A collection of rather recent professional development programs in reading instruction has been reviewed by Alvermann (1990) in a chapter in the *Handbook of Research on Teacher Education*. Among them, they reflect the three conceptions of reading teacher education described earlier: traditional craft, competency-based, and inquiry-oriented. One of these programs, Reading Recovery, is described in Chapter 6. Descriptions of some other programs follow. They can be used as a reference point for discussion and reflection.

Collaboration for School Improvement (Ogle, 1986) involved faculty from the National College of Education and was carried out in multiple sites in Illinois. The principals and teachers in each school were introduced to theories of reading and writing strategies to develop a shared knowledge base. These theories were translated into practice and demonstrated by master teachers. Other teachers then adapted these strategies to their own programs, were observed monthly, and were given feedback. The program began with a view of teacher education close to the traditional craft model. After assessment and evaluation, new applications of the program have moved toward inquiry-oriented professional development.

The Kamehameha Early Education Program (KEEP) was developed with a competency-based conception of teacher education, although it shared features of an inquiry-oriented and traditional craft view as well (Au et al., 1986). The program was carried out in a laboratory school that served low-achieving students in Hawaii. The goal was to implement an instructional leadership model so that teachers could develop their own language arts program.

The year-long training program included seminars, practical experiences, and on-site training. Teachers were given time and opportunities to reflect on their current practices and how those practices had changed, if at all. Consultants modeled instructional techniques and worked with individual teachers to develop instructional goals and classroom management techniques.

Evaluation of the KEEP program has come from experimentation, program evaluation, and qualitative studies. Periodic observations of teachers assure that research findings are translated into practice within the program.

The Metcalf Project (Tierney, Tucker, Gallagher, Crismore, & Pearson, 1988) resulted from a long-term collaboration of teachers, administrators, teacher educators, and researchers to develop an inquiry-oriented staff development program. Teaching was viewed as a continuing experiment, with reading and writing viewed as a problem-solving experience. The final goal was for teachers to become self-initiators and be able to carry on their professional development independently.

The Benchmark School (Gaskins, 1988) developed an inquiry-based teacher education program in a private, ungraded school for intellectually bright children with reading problems. The program focused on four features:

1. The climate of the school was one of trust in which administrators were responsive to staff needs.
2. Teachers were involved in identifying instructional problems, field testing alternative practices, and making decisions about what practices to implement.
3. Teachers were given the role of decision maker to enhance their feelings of ownership of the program.
4. The knowledge base in literacy education was enhanced with weekly research seminars, a professional library, and monthly in-service programs with researchers.

These model professional development programs provide further insight into the possibilities for preparing teachers to support the language and literacy development of young children.

CONCLUSIONS

The framework presented in this chapter offers a view of teacher education as an interactive process best supported through meaningful, functional activities and active involvement of practitioners in determining and implementing teaching strategies — a process that allows ample opportunity for collaboration and reflection. Ideally, the participants in such a program do what we want them to encourage children to do in their own classrooms: They are speaking and listening, reading and writing. They are actively involved in making instructional decisions. They collaborate with colleagues by sharing and supporting one another and by developing cooperative activities. As participants, they feel investment and ownership in what they do, and they see themselves as part of a professional community of learners.

REFERENCES

Alvermann, D. E. (1990). Reading teacher education. In W. R. Houston, M. Haberman, & J. Siknula (Eds.), *Handbook of research on teacher education* (pp. 687–704). New York: Macmillan.

Anderson, R. C., Hiebert, E. H., Scott, J. A., & Wilkinson, I. (1985). *Becoming a nation of readers*. Washington, DC: National Institute of Education.

Association of Teacher Educators and the National Association for the Education of Young Children. (1991). Early childhood teacher certification. *Young Children, 47*(1), 16–21.

Au, K. H., Crowell, D. C., Jordan, C., Sloat, K. C. M., Speidel, G. E., Klein, T. W., & Tharp, R. G. (1986). Development and implementation of the KEEP Reading Program. In J. Orasanu (Ed.), *Reading comprehension: From research to practice* (pp. 235–252). Hillsdale, NJ: Erlbaum.

Bissex, G. (1980). *GNYS at work: A child learns to write and read.* Cambridge, MA: Harvard University Press.

Bondy, E. (1990). Seeing it their way: What children's definitions of reading tell us about improving teacher education. *Journal of Teacher Education, 41*, 33–45.

Botel, M., Botel-Sheppard, B., & Renninger, A. (in press). Integrated language arts: Facilitating change in school programs. In L. Morrow, L. C. Wilkinson, & J. K. Smith (Eds.), *Integrated language arts: Controversy to consensus.* Boston: Allyn & Bacon.

Cazden, C. (Ed.). (1981). *Language in early childhood education.* Washington, DC: National Association for the Education of Young Children.

Clark, M. M. (1976). *Young fluent readers.* London: Heinemann.

Clay, M. M. (1966). *Emergent reading behavior.* Unpublished doctoral dissertation, University of Auckland, New Zealand.

Copper, L. R. (1991, Summer). Teachers as researchers. *The Kappa Delta Pi Record,* pp. 115–117.

Gaskins, I. W. (1988). Helping teachers adapt to the needs of students with learning problems. In S. J. Samuels & P. D. Pearson (Eds.), *Changing school reading programs* (pp. 143–159). Newark, DE: International Reading Association.

Goodman, K. S. (1967). Reading: A psycholinguistic guessing game. *Journal of the Reading Specialist, 4*, 126–135.

Goodman, Y. (1986). Children coming to know literacy. In W. H. Teale & E. Sulzby (Eds.), *Emergent literacy: Writing and reading* (pp. 1–14). Norwood, NJ: Ablex.

Greenwood, G., & Parkay, I. (1989). *Case studies for teacher decision making.* New York: Random House.

Gundlach, R., McLane, J., Scott, F., & McNamee, G. (1985). The social foundations of early writing development. In M. Farr (Ed.), *Advances in writing research: Vol. 1. Children's early writing development* (pp. 1–58). Norwood, NJ: Ablex.

Halliday, M. A. K. (1975). *Learning how to mean: Exploration in the development of language.* London: Edward Arnold.

Harris, L., & Smith, L. (1980). *Reading instruction and diagnostic teaching in the classroom* (3rd ed.). New York: Holt, Rinehart & Winston.

Harste, J. (1985). Portrait of a new paradigm. In A. Crismore (Ed.), *Landscapes: A state-of-the-art assessment of reading comprehension research, 1974–1984* (pp. 1–24). Bloomington: Indiana University Press.

Holdaway, D. (1979). *The foundations of literacy.* Sydney, Australia: Ashton Scholastic.

Hollingsworth, S. (1988). Making field-based programs work: A three-level approach to reading education. *Journal of Teacher Education, 39,* 28–36.

International Reading Association. (in press). *Standards for reading professionals.* Newark, DE: Author.

Mason, J., & McCormick, C. (1981). *An investigation of prereading instruction: A developmental perspective* (Technical Report No. 126). Urbana: University of Illinois, Center for the Study of Reading.

Merseth, K. K. (1991). The early history of case-based instruction: Insights for teacher education today. *Journal of Teacher Education, 42,* 243–249.

Meyers, M. (1991). Issues in the restructuring of teacher preparation. In J. Flood, J. M. Jensen, D. Lapp, & J. R. Squire (Eds.), *Handbook of research on teaching the English language arts* (pp. 394–404). New York: Macmillan.

Morphett, M.V., & Washburne, C. (1931). When should children begin to read? *Elementary School Journal, 31,* 496–508.

Morrow, L. M. (1988). Young children's responses to one-to-one story reading in school settings. *Reading Research Quarterly, 23,* 189–207.

Morrow, L. M. (1989). *Literacy development in the early years: Helping children read and write.* Englewood Cliffs, NJ: Prentice-Hall.

Morrow, L. M. (1992). The impact of a literature-based program on literacy achievement, use of literature, and attitudes of children from minority backgrounds. *Reading Research Quarterly, 27,* 250–275.

Nixon, J. (1987). The teacher as researcher: Contradictions and continuities. *Peabody Journal of Education, 64*(2), 20–32.

Ogle, D. (1986). Collaboration for school improvement: A case study of a school district and a college. In J. Orasanu (Ed.), *Reading comprehension: From research to practice* (pp. 287–301). Hillsdale, NJ: Erlbaum.

Piaget, J., & Inhelder, B. (1969). *The psychology of the child.* New York: Basic Books.

Pinnell, G. S., & Matlin, M. L. (Eds.). (1989). *Teachers and research.* Newark, DE: International Reading Association.

Ruopp, R., Travers, J., Coelen, C., & Glantz, F. (1979). *Children at the center: Final report of the Nation Day Care Study* (Vol. 1). Cambridge, MA: Abt Books.

Saracho, O. N., & Spodek, B. (1983). Preparing teachers for bilingual/multicultural classrooms. In O. N. Saracho & B. Spodek (Eds.), *Understanding multicultural experience in early childhood education.* Washington, DC: National Association for the Education of Young Children.

Sharkey, E. (1992). *The literacy behaviors and social interactions of children during an independent reading and writing period: An ethnographic study.* Unpublished doctoral dissertation, Rutgers University, New Brunswick, NJ.

Short, K. G., & Burke, C. L. (1989). New potentials for teacher education: Teaching and learning as inquiry. *The Elementary School Journal, 90*(2), 193–206.

Silverman, R., Welty, W., & Lyon, S. (1992). *Case studies for teacher problem solving.* New York: McGraw-Hill.

Smith, F. (1983). A metaphor for literacy: Creating words or shunting information? In F. Smith (Ed.), *Essays into literacy* (pp. 117–134). Exeter, NH: Heinemann.

Snow, C., & Perlmann, R. (1985). Assessing children's knowledge about book-reading. In L. Galda & A. Pellegrini (Eds.), *Play, language, and stories* (pp. 167–181). Norwood, NJ: Ablex.

Teale, W. (1982). Toward a theory of how children learn to read and write naturally. *Language Arts, 59,* 555–570.

Teale, W. (1986). The beginning of reading and writing: Written language development during the preschool and kindergarten years. In M. Sampson (Ed.), *The pursuit of literacy: Early reading and writing* (pp. 1–29). Dubuque, IA: Kendall/Hunt.

Tierney, R. J., Tucker, D. L., Gallagher, M. C., Crismore, A., & Pearson, P. D. (1988). The Metcalf Project: A teacher-researcher collaboration. In S. J. Samuels & P. D. Pearson (Eds.), *Changing school reading programs* (pp. 207–226). Newark, DE: International Reading Association.

Vygotsky, L. S. (1978). *Mind in society: The development of psychological processes.* Cambridge, MA: Harvard University Press.

Watson, D. J., & Stevenson, M. T. (1989). Teacher support groups: Why and how. In G. S. Pinnell & M. L. Matlin (Eds.), *Teachers and research* (pp. 118–129). Newark, DE: International Reading Association.

Weikart, D. (1989). *Quality preschool programs: A long-term social investment* (Occasional Paper No. 5, Ford Foundation Project of Social Welfare). New York: Ford Foundation.

CHAPTER 11

Language and Literacy Programs in Early Childhood Education: A Look to the Future

Bernard Spodek and Olivia N. Saracho

As noted in the Introduction, the contents of this book reflect a major change in the views of early childhood educators regarding language and literacy programs. Recent studies of language development and the application of Vygotskian theory to language and literacy education, especially in the early childhood period, have led to a major change in our understanding of how language and literacy develop in young children. These, in turn, have led to the development of new approaches to teaching language and literacy that have significant implications for early childhood education. The concept of emergent literacy and the Whole Language approach need to be understood by teachers and reflected in the programs they provide.

Thomas Kuhn, in his book *The Structure of Scientific Revolutions* (1970), discusses how, in science, different paradigms evolve as theories are challenged or modified. These paradigms determine how scientists view theories and drive different forms of research. As implied throughout the chapters in this volume, we are seeing the development of a new paradigm, emergent literacy, in the area of language and literacy education. This new paradigm is currently competing with the older paradigm of reading readiness. Each paradigm represents a view of what it takes to become competent in learning to read.

Reading-readiness programs clearly dominate the concerns of kindergarten educators and even many early childhood educators concerned with prekindergarten education. In many kindergartens reading and mathematics readiness programs represent a major portion of the curriculum, with a concern for academic and program readiness or learning academics the primary focus of those classes (Karweit, 1993). Reading-readiness programs fit these concerns very well. Many publishers of reading series provide sets of kindergarten materials that develop what are considered readiness skills and prepare children for first-grade instruction within the series. There is a sort of face validity to these programs in that the tasks required of children in the readiness programs are similar to those required of children in the reading instructional programs. Since these skills are introduced to children prior to formal reading instruction and a great deal of practice is provided in workbooks, teachers assume that work with these materials provides good preparation for reading.

This view of preparation for formal reading instruction is challenged by the emergent literacy paradigm that underlies the discussions in the chapters in this volume. This new paradigm of language and literacy education should not be difficult for early childhood teachers to accept. Early childhood teachers have always seen children's learning as resulting from their direct, firsthand experience with the physical and social world. Children were seen as constructing knowledge as a result of these experiences, and the early childhood years were viewed as a period of rapid intellectual development.

We are now coming to see that this early childhood period is also one of rapid language development. As the contributors to this volume have pointed out, children become meaning makers and symbol makers early in their lives. It is in the context of creating symbols and comprehending symbols that language and literacy learning takes place.

IMPLICATIONS FOR TEACHERS

The change in the way language and literacy programs are conceived necessitates major changes in how teachers view themselves and how they function in the classroom. We would like to list just a few of them:

1. *Early childhood teachers will have to give up the false dichotomy that had been created by the concept of reading readiness.* It is inappropriate for early childhood teachers to sit back passively and wait for children to become "ready to read." Because we now see reading as a competency that begins to emerge as children develop oral language, even teachers of 2- and 3-year-olds need to consider themselves reading teachers. This does not mean that they will provide reading primers and workbooks to preschool children. It does mean that they need to provide each child with emergent literacy experiences that are consistent with his or her level of development — providing challenging activities that will move that child's development forward.
2. *Primary teachers will have to understand that reading is more than*

sounding out letters and that reading programs require more than primers and workbooks. There will need to be a change in the way reading instruction is conceived and in the perceived relationship between reading and other subject areas. The Whole Language approach seems logically related to a view of emergent literacy. Even as this view considers reading, writing, listening, and speaking to be interrelated, it also views language and literacy activities as interrelated with all educational activities in the classroom. The use of units, projects, or thematic teaching—whereby the curriculum is developed around a particular topic and all subject areas are addressed in relation to that topic—also seems appropriate to this view of language and literacy education.

3. *Early childhood teachers will have to provide a literacy-rich environment in their classes.* Teachers need to assess the materials provided and the activities offered to children in terms of the consequences of their use for children's developing language and literacy. Book corners need to be accessible and inviting to children. They need to be stocked with books that serve children well and that are read and reread to and by the children. Dramatic play areas need to be designed so that they nurture language learning. Group time, when group discussions take place, needs to be designed to ensure that each child is helped to develop expressive and receptive language skills. The arts program needs to be evaluated to determine whether it helps children create meanings from their experiences and helps them symbolize those meanings. Exploratory experiences with a range of media is not enough.

4. *Early childhood teachers need to become aware of the consequences of their actions for language learning.* Teachers in kindergarten and prekindergarten classes engage in a variety of language and literacy activities, often without being aware of it. The way group time or discussions are held in a class, the way books are presented and read to children, as noted above, are obvious language activities. But there are other activities in the early childhood programs that serve a variety of different purposes. Preprimary teachers seldom consider the consequences for literacy learning of dramatic play, art, and music activities, yet these also contribute to language and literacy learning. Teachers need to be aware of children's attempts to create meanings from their experiences and to symbolize those meanings in a variety of ways.

5. *Early childhood teachers need to work collaboratively with parents in support of language and literacy programs.* The development of language and literacy competence in young children is a complex affair. While the school context contributes to the development of this competence, the family context also makes a significant contribution. In fact, the quality of language experiences that young children have

at home may make a major contribution to their language and literacy competence. Some families provide considerable support for the development of these competences; unfortunately, however, not all families do.

FACILITATING CHANGE

In the previous section we have set a heavy agenda for teachers. Yet, even if teachers do all these things, it would still be difficult for changes to take place in our schools' language and literacy programs. We have learned over the years that schools as institutions are particularly resistant to change (Sarason, 1982). Teachers who try to implement change toward more child-responsive education in their classrooms, even though they are not trying to influence school policy, find themselves confronted with resistance from both their teaching colleagues and administrators (Halliwell, 1992). In addition to the schools themselves, there are a number of strong vested interests concerned with maintaining current language and literacy programs in our schools. These include publishers of reading programs and test developers.

If we are to see changes toward this new paradigm of language and literacy in early childhood education, a number of things must happen. Teachers willing to provide a child-responsive language and literacy program must be provided with supports from a number of sources. Classroom materials including Big Books, a range of children's books, and simple word-processing programs for children need to be made available. These materials will need to compete with formal reading-readiness and beginning reading programs that are currently published.

In addition, informational services need to be available to teachers. College and universities will have to provide workshops and courses in newer ways of providing language and literacy education for both preservice and inservice teachers. Teacher organizations also need to provide such assistance through journal articles, separate publications, and conference program sessions. Teachers will need to provide their own supports as well. Grass-roots networks of teachers, such as the Whole Language network for primary teachers, will need to be established.

Teachers will also need to develop skills in using informal means of evaluating children's language learning, as opposed to standardized tests. Current language and literacy programs linked with programs' standardized tests create a serious block to the use of alternative educational programs. Too often the school curriculum is test-driven (Shepard, 1991). Alternative ways of evaluating children's language learning will need to be provided, and their use must become widely accepted.

CONCLUSION

The area of language and literacy education is undergoing major changes today. Many of these changes suggest the importance of the early childhood years for children in becoming competent in language and successful readers. These changes affect our understanding of bilingual as well as monolingual children as they develop competence in language and literacy.

These changes in views of language and literacy have significant implications for how we function in early childhood classes. Teachers need to reassess how they design their program and how they support children's learning. They also need to reassess how they evaluate language learning in young children.

If the changes we suggest are accomplished, a new relationship will be established between primary education and preprimary education. Developmentally appropriate programs will be created that are closely related at all levels, providing for better vertical integration. Preparation for reading will be reconceptualized. A broad range of educational experiences will be seen as the proper preparation for learning to read.

Programs will also have better horizontal integration. Integrated approaches to education and the use of units, projects, or topics as the focus on instruction will help children make better sense of the world and help them to become symbol makers as well. All of this presents a challenge to early childhood educators at all levels, working with the broad range of children currently served in our many early childhood programs.

REFERENCES

Halliwell, G. L. (1992). *Dilemmas and images: Gaining acceptance for child-responsive classroom practices*. Unpublished doctoral dissertation, University of Queensland, Brisbane, Australia.

Karweit, N. (1993). Effective preschool and kindergarten programs for students at risk. In B. Spodek (Ed.), *Handbook of research on the education of young children* (pp. 385–411). New York: Macmillan.

Kuhn, T. S. (1970). *The structure of scientific revolutions*. Chicago: University of Chicago Press.

Sarason, S. B. (1982). *The culture of the school and the problem of change*. Boston: Allyn & Bacon.

Shepard, L. A. (1991). The influence of standardized tests on the early childhood curriculum, teachers, and children. In B. Spodek and O. N. Saracho (Eds.), *Issues in early childhood curriculum: Yearbook in early childhood education* (Vol. 2, pp. 166–189). New York: Teachers College Press.

About the Editors and Contributors

Anne Haas Dyson is Professor of Education at the University of California, Berkeley. A former classroom teacher, she studies children's oral and written language in classroom settings. Among her publications are *Multiple Worlds of Child Writers: Friends Learning to Write* and the forthcoming *The Social Work of Child Composing: Learning to Write in an Urban Primary School* (both from Teachers College Press).

Patricia A. Edwards is Associate Professor of Reading and a Senior Researcher on Teacher Learning at Michigan State University. She is also the author of two nationally acclaimed family literacy programs: *Parents as Partners in Reading: A Family Literacy Training Program* and *Talking Your Way to Literacy: A Program to Help Nonreading Parents Prepare Their Children for Reading*. Her research interests include topics in family/intergenerational literacy and emergent literacy, with a special focus on semiliterate and illiterate parents and children. Recent publications include a chapter, "Fostering Early Literacy Through Parent Coaching," in E. Heibert (Ed.), *Literacy for a Diverse Society: Perspectives, Practices, and Policies* (Teachers College Press) and an article, "Involving Parents in Building Reading Instruction for African-American Children," in *Theory into Practice*.

Celia Genishi, a former preschool and secondary Spanish teacher, is a faculty member of the Department of Curriculum and Teaching, Teachers College, Columbia University. She has also taught at the Ohio State University and at the University of Texas at Austin. She is the author of *Ways of Studying Children* (with Millie Almy; Teachers College Press), and *Language Assessment in the Early Years* (with Anne Haas Dyson; Ablex) and editor of *Ways of Assessing Children and Curriculum: Stories of Early Childhood Practice* (Teachers College Press). Her interests include children's language use in multicultural classrooms, bilingualism, and collaborative research on teacher-based assessment.

Kris D. Gutierrez is Assistant Professor in Curriculum in the Graduate School of Education at the University of California, Los Angeles. Her research interests include a study of the sociocultural contexts of literacy development, particularly the study of the acquisition of academic literacy for language-minority students. She teaches courses in literacy and curriculum.

Violet Harris received her A.B. in history from Oberlin College, her M.A. in Reading Education from Atlanta University, and her Ph.D. in Reading Education from the University of Georgia. She is an Associate Professor in the Department of Curriculum and Instruction at the University of Illinois at Urbana-Champaign, where she teaches courses in children's literature. Her research interests include children's literature, historic literacy materials for African American children, and multicultural children's literature. She is the editor of *Teaching Multicultural Literature in Grades K–8* (Christopher Gordon) and has authored articles and book chapters on children's literature. She is on the editorial boards of *The Reading Teacher, Language Arts,* and the *Reading Research Quarterly.*

Lesley Mandel Morrow is Professor and Chair of the Graduate School of Education at Rutgers University. She has published numerous research articles dealing with early childhood literacy development in journals such as the *Reading Research Quarterly* and the *Early Childhood Research Quarterly.* She is the author of several books; her most recent is the second edition of *Literacy Development in the Early Years: Helping Children Read and Write* (Allyn & Bacon). She is co-editor of the *Journal of Reading Behavior* and a Principal Research Investigator for the National Reading Research Center.

Gay Su Pinnell is Professor of Theory and Practice at the Ohio State University, where she teaches on language development, literacy, and children's literature. She is formerly a primary school teacher and now teaches children daily as part of the Reading Recovery Program. Her books include *Teaching Reading Comprehension, Discovering Language with Children,* and *Teachers and Research: Language Learning in the Classroom.* She has also authored numerous articles on language and literacy learning. With her colleagues at the Ohio State University she has been responsible for implementing Reading Recovery and conducting a research program, which resulted in the recent book, *Bridges to Literacy: Learning from Reading Recovery.* She is principal investigator for the Early Literacy Research Project, sponsored by the John D. and Catherine T. MacArthur Foundation.

Muriel K. Rand is co-adjunct faculty member and research consultant at Rutgers Graduate School of Education. For the last six years she has taught early childhood curriculum courses and early literacy courses to undergraduate and graduate students. Before coming to Rutgers, she was the head teacher at a preschool in Somerset, New Jersey, for five years. She has also taught in gifted-and-talented programs for inner-city kindergartners in Newark and is currently the head teacher for a preschool class at the laboratory preschool at Cook College. She received her masters and doctorate in Education from Rutgers and has recently become involved in the professional development of inservice teachers. She has published several book chapters and journal articles on promoting literacy through play and using thematic instruction in integrated language arts programs.

Olivia N. Saracho (editor) is Professor of Education in the Department of Curriculum and Instruction at the University of Maryland. She completed her Ph.D. in early childhood education at the University of Illinois in 1978. Prior to that, she taught Head Start, preschool, kindergarten, and elementary classes in Brownsville, Texas, and was Director of the Child Development Associate Program at Pan American University. Her current research and writing are in the areas of cognitive style, academic learning, and teacher education in relation to early childhood education. Her most recent books are *Professionalism and the Early Childhood Practitioner*, edited with Bernard Spodek and Donald J. Peters (Teachers College Press, 1988), and *Foundations of Early Childhood Education*, with Bernard Spodek and Michael J. Davis (Prentice-Hall, 1987, 1991). Dr. Saracho is co-editor of the Teachers College Press YEARBOOK IN EARLY CHILDHOOD EDUCATION series and of the three previous volumes of that series, *Early Childhood Teacher Education; Issues in Early Childhood Curriculum*; and *Issues of Child Care*. She is also editor, with Roy Evans, of *Early Childhood Teacher Education: An International Perspective* (Gordon & Breach).

Judith A. Schickedanz is Professor of Early Childhood Education at Boston University. She has authored two books on emergent literacy, *More Than the ABCs* (NAEYC), and *Adam's Righting Revolution* (Heinemann). She is director of the Early Childhood Laboratory Preschool at Boston University, where she pioneered strategies to support emergent literacy development in preschool children. Since 1990, she has served as the early childhood consultant to the Chelsea (Massachusetts) Public Schools, under the Boston University/Chelsea Partnership, and works with teachers to develop rich language and literacy experiences for a diverse population of children.

Catherine E. Snow is Professor of Education and Academic Dean of the Harvard Graduate School of Education. She holds a B.A. from Oberlin University and a Ph.D. in psychology from McGill University. She has carried out extensive research in the areas of parent–child interaction, first- and second-language acquisition, the development of conversational and literacy skills in first and second languages, and the role of children's out-of-school experiences in contributing to their school achievement. She is Principal Co-Investigator of the Home-School Study of Language and Literacy Development.

Bernard Spodek (editor) is Professor of Early Childhood Education at the University of Illinois, where he has taught since 1965. He received his doctorate in early childhood education from Teachers College, Columbia University, then joined the faculty of the University of Wisconsin–Milwaukee. He has also taught nursery, kindergarten, and elementary classes in New York City. His research and scholarly interests are in the areas of curriculum, teaching, and teacher education in early childhood education.

He has lectured extensively in the United States, Australia, Canada, China, England, Greece, Israel, Japan, Korea, Mexico, and Taiwan. From 1976 to 1978 he was president of the National Association for the Education of Young Children, and from 1981 through 1983 he chaired the Early Education and Child Development Special Interest Group of the American Educational Research Association. He is widely published in the field of early childhood education.

His most recent books are *Professionalism and the Early Childhood Practitioner*, edited with Olivia N. Saracho and Donald J. Peters (Teachers College Press, 1988); *Foundations of Early Childhood Education*, with Olivia N. Saracho and Michael J. Davis (Prentice-Hall, 1987, 1991); and *Today's Kindergarten: Exploring its Knowledge Base, Expanding Its Curriculum* (Teachers College Press, 1986). He is co-editor of the Teachers College Press YEARBOOK IN EARLY CHILDHOOD EDUCATION series and of the three previous volumes of that series, *Early Childhood Teacher Education, Issues in Early Childhood Curriculum*, and *Issues of Child Care*. He is also editor of the *Handbook of Research on the Education of Young Children* (Macmillan).

Elizabeth Sulzby is Professor of Education at the University of Michigan, where she is on the faculties of the programs in Reading and Literacy, Early Childhood Education, Instructional Technology, Linguistics, and the Combined Program in Education and Psychology. Her research area is emergent literacy. She particularly studies low-income and minority children and their teachers. In addition to studies of emergent storybook reading and emergent writing, she is now investigating children's use of the computer as an emergent literacy tool. She received her Ph.D. from the University of Virginia, her M.Ed. from the College of William and Mary, and did graduate work in philosophy at Harvard Divinity School. Her undergraduate work in philosophy and in English was done at Birmingham-Southern College.

Patton O. Tabors is a Research Associate at the Harvard Graduate School of Education and Project Director of the Home–School Study of Language and Literacy Development. She holds a B.A. from Smith College, an M.A. from Syracuse University, and an Ed.D. from Harvard Graduate School of Education. Her research has included an investigation of the naturalistic acquisition of a second language by preschoolers; her present research centers on the connections between early language and later literacy development of low-income children.

Index

SUBJECTS

African Americans, 123–24, 127, 129, 130–32, 169

Asian Americans, 132–33, 164

Assessment: alternative, 66–78; and anecdotal records, 67–68, 74, 78; and audio/videotapes, 71–72, 77; and checklists, 68–69, 74; and the curriculum, 64, 77, 199; and developmental theory, 96; of disorders, 65–66; and emergent literacy, 66; and the future of language and literacy programs, 199, 200; and play, 73–74; and portfolios, 72–77, 78; program, 50–54, 56; purpose of, 77–78; and reading readiness, 62, 64–65; and Reading Recovery, 108, 110–11, 113; and the selection of tests, 63–66; self-, 55, 72–73, 113, 188; and special needs children, 61–62; and storytelling, 73–74; of students, 54–56, 60–78, 108, 199, 200; and teachers' roles, 67–78, 199, 200; types of, 60–61. *See also* Observation; Standardized tests

At-risk children, ix, 84–85, 104–6. *See also* Reading Recovery

Biculturalism, ix–x

Bilingualism, x, 34, 83, 84–94, 160

Biliteracy, x, 83, 84–97

Books: children's questions about, 147–48, 152; children's selection of, 146–47; illustrations in, 147–48, 152; in library corners, 144–45

Children: learning by, 181–84; nature of, 62; questions asked by, 147–48, 152, 166; selection of books by, 146–47; teachers/adults' interactions with, 142, 147, 149–51, 152, 165–72. *See also* At-risk children; Students

Children's literature, 123–37

Classrooms: and at-risk children, 105; design of, 141–53; and emergent literacy, 141–53, 180, 183, 184; and the future of language and literacy programs, 198; influences on use of materials in, 144–46; as laboratories, 188–89; and language-minority children, 85, 86, 92, 95–97; and language skills related to literacy development, 1, 14–16; physical/social arrangements of, xi, 143–44; and reading instruc-

tion, xi; research in, 190; teachers' roles in the, 186, 198; and the Whole Language approach, 45–50

Culture, ix–x, 91–92, 95, 97, 123–37

Curriculum, 37–38, 47, 64, 66, 77, 83, 106, 199

Developmental theory, vii–ix, 67, 87–88, 96, 181, 197

Dramatic play. *See* Play

Drawing. *See* Graphic symbolism

Emergent literacy: and assessment, 64–65, 66; and bilingualism, 160; and the classroom, 141–53, 180, 184; contexts of, 180, 181, 182; definition of, x, 141, 159, 180; and developmental theory, 197; and ethnicity, 159–60, 163; and the future of language and literacy programs, 196–97, 198; and the home environment, 161–68, 182; and income, 159–60, 161–62, 163, 164–65, 166–67, 169; and minorities, 161–62; parental/adult role in, 142, 147, 152, 165–72; and play, 145–46, 152–53; and readiness, 141, 156, 157–61, 181, 196–97; and social class, 159–60, 161–62, 163, 164–65, 166–67; support programs for, 168–71, 172; and teachers, 180–81, 197; and the Whole Language approach, 198. *See also* Reading; Writing development

Ethnicity, ix–x, 159–60, 163

Evaluation. *See* Assessment; Standardized tests

Graphic symbolism, 23–36, 37

Hispanics, 90–91, 133–34, 169

Home, 89–91, 161–68, 182, 198–99

Instruction, x, 44, 48–49, 86–87, 96–97, 197

Labels/names, 27–30, 105, 106

Language: commonalities in development of, 158; discourse rules of, 5–6; disorders, 65–66; future of programs concerning, 196–200; nature/function of, 2–6, 62–63, 182; pragmatics of, 5–6. *See also* Oral language; Writing development

205

NAMES